THE BOOK OF HOCKEY

The Book of Hockey

A Miscellany of Hockey writings

Compiled by
David Wiggins, Patrick Rowley
and
Brian Lewis

Edited by
Patrick Rowley
Hockey Correspondent, Exchange Telegraph News Agency

MACDONALD : LONDON

First published in 1964 by
Macdonald & Co. (Publishers), Ltd.
Gulf House, 2 Portman Street, London, W.1.

Made and printed in Great Britain by
Waterlow & Sons Limited
London . Dunstable . Hyde

ACKNOWLEDGMENTS

Acknowledgments and very grateful thanks are due to the following:
Mr David Morgan, for his assistance in countless ways;
Mr C. E. Rowley, for checking the manuscript and proofs;
Mrs F. E. Grinham, for acting as "Hon. Secretary";
Mr David Belchamber, for many translations;
and also to
W. Comben-Longstaff ("Hockey Association"); M. G. Cowlishaw; Rene Frank (Hon. Sec. Federation Internationale de Hockey); Tony Hallas (Photographer); K. Howells; S. E. Jones; Charles Newham; Ernest Wall (Scottish H.A.); John Wood; various members of the International Federation of Women's Hockey Associations, and members of Richmond Hockey Club.

The Editor is also grateful for assistance received from the following people in different countries around the world:
Argentine—Jorge Parsons (President, A.A.A.).
Australia—Hec Cormie (Editor, "Hockey Circle").
Austria—Emil Hierhold (Sec. O-H-V.).
Belgium—Jean Noel.
British Guiana—H. A. Shepherd (Hon. Sec. B.G.M.H.B.C.).
Canada—Tony Boyd. (Former Sec. C.H.A.).
Ceylon—Jair Virasinghe.
Czechoslovakia—J. Vanek.
Denmark—H. A. Bierrum, Allan Jahnsen (Hon. Sec. D.H.U.)
Finland—V. Jerkku (Sec. S.M.)
France—A. Danet (President, F.F.H.); Etienne Glichitch.
Germany—(east) Gerhard Schulze, Zweck (Sec. D.H-S.); (west) M. Suhl (Vice. Pres. D.H-B.).
Ghana—Ohene Djan (Dir. of Sports).
Hong Kong—David Metcalf (Hon. Treas. H.K.H.A.).
India—A. Kumar (Pres. I.H.F.), R. Sriman, S. K. Gurunathan.
Italy—E. Quaranta (Hon. Sec. F.I.H.P.).
Jamaica—Miss H. Samuel (Hon. Sec. J.W.H.A.).
Kenya—Jasmer Singh, P. de Souza.

Malaya—Dr. A. Durairatnam (Vice Pres. M.H.F.).
Morocco—M. Caparros (Vice Pres. F.R.M.H.).
Netherlands—Van den Heide (Hon. Sec. K.N.H.B.), P. J. Bromberg.
Netherlands Antilles—A. J. P. Kusters (Chairman N.A.H.A.).
New Zealand—W. Havilah Down (Life Member, N.Z.H.A.).
Nigeria—Jack Farnsworth.
Pakistan—Sultan F. Husain (Editor, "Sportimes").
Poland—Z. Kurowski (Pres. P.Z.H.T.), Jerzy Makow.
Rhodesia—B. Napier, B. Puttergill.
Singapore—Norman Buck.
South Africa—Stuart McIldowie (Former Sec. S.A.H.U.), Bill Malherbe.
Spain—Miguel Rinon ("Stick"), Clemente Vidal.
Switzerland—Jacob Schenkmann (Former Tres. S.L-V.).
Tanganyika—Hon. Sec. T.H.A.
Trinidad and Tobago—Mrs. Irma de Lima (Hon. Sec. T.T.W.H.A.).
U.A.R.—M. Rafaat (Hon. Gen. Sec. A.H.F.), Aziz Iskander.
Yugoslavia—Ivo Zlatar.

and from the following in Britain :
Alex Bannister; Brig. A. E. Belchamber; C. Bell; Charles Bisset; Frank Brewin; Alec Burt (1908 Olympics); Maj. C. E. Calderari; T. S. C. Dagg; K. S. Duncan (British Olympic Assoc.); Geoffrey Eames; Tony Ewing-Gay; John Falconer; Eric Green; John Harvey-Samuel; Miss Melvyn Hickey; R. L. Hollands (Editor, "Hockey News"); Kenneth Ingledew (Welsh H.A.); H. M. Lindley-Jones; Mrs M. Macdonald (Sec. A.E.W.H.A.); M. Pearce; T. Podesta; Dr N. L. Stevenson (1908 Olympics); H. Stolz; R. Tattersall (Hon. Sec. British Hockey Board); P. McWeeney; C. T. A. Wilkinson (1920 Olympics), and countless others.

CONTENTS

LIST OF PLATES

I

HOCKEY 4,000 YEARS OLD

DAVID MORGAN

B.B.C. Midlands Hockey Correspondent

It isn't really surprising that Victorian England popularised sport. Adventure stirred in every walk of life: new industry, great wealth, social progress, the telegraph, the telephone, newspapers, growth in population, and railways linking the new large cities and towns. Small wonder the nation needed relaxation.

The mill-hands, the miners, the workers, took readily to football. It was easy to learn and could be played almost anywhere there was a space—in factory yards, on vacant lots, behind slag heaps; and when professionalism arrived, busy people began to watch instead of play.

The employers, the scholars, the clergy, the upper-middle classes also needed relaxation, but they did it without the clamour of soccer—almost shyly, shunning publicity, avoiding the jeers of the mob. The game was the thing, the result barely worth noting. So they played cricket, golf and tennis in the summer and anything but soccer in the winter. Rugby football and hockey were thus born amateur, played for their own sake and for the fine company after the match—in the true Olympic spirit. Rugby eventually lost a section to professionalism, and hockey was left as one of the few truly amateur games played to be enjoyed; enjoyed so that the trials of the work-a-day week can be endured until the next match.

The history of hockey is fascinating, though somewhat sketchy—for the very nature of the game has precluded minute recording of details.

There is strong evidence that some form of hockey was played as long ago as 2,000 B.C., for about that time Tomb No. 16 was built at Beni Hasan in the Nile Valley near Minia and on a wall of the tomb is a clear drawing which appears to picture two people "bullying" (see illustration).

There are pictures on the walls of all the Tombs at Beni Hasan and this is one of a series of six showing different kinds of Egyptian games.

Tomb at Beni Hassan

The pictures are not to scale and the sticks are very thin with the sharp hook at the end of each being almost at 90 degrees.

An authority on Beni Hasan, now deceased, believed the players had their sticks locked in a hoop but it could well be they are playing with a ball for the artist who painted the illustration would have had great difficulty in making the picture clear if he had depicted the ball black like the figures and sticks.

Balls in that age often had leather covers and were filled with scraps of leather and cloth but even if the ball was, in fact, a hoop, the illustration is certainly a clear record that a stick game was popular 4,000 years ago.

Prior to the discovery of this picture the home of hockey was thought to be Persia, where polo was played about 500 B.C. Polo was thought to be the most ancient game to be played with stick and ball, but it now seems more likely that, for the comfort and convenience of the nobility, the crude form of hockey originally played on foot for a great many years, was adapted to allow it to be played on horseback—and not *vice versa*.

Certainly not very much later in history, the Japanese had a game called kachi or dakyu, which was played on foot, while the Aztec

Indians of South America played cheuca, and Red Indian tribes swung deer legs decorated with emblems of speed at wooden balls. The pipe of peace would often have proved a blessing, for the game must have been pretty rough stuff.

There is a charming story that the object representing Zeus on the altar during the Dionysian Festivals at Atticus was the ball which Aphrodite gave her son Eros, to cast at his victims instead of arrows. Dionysus, of course, is inseparably connected with the winepress, and it may be this is the reason all true ball players enjoy a noggin after the match. It can be reasonably assumed that Eros once missed his target and so mere mortals found themselves with the world's first ball. Was it stone, wood, hair, cork, rubber, string, feathers, cloth or a combination? Certainly it must have been a far cry from the white-painted cricket ball that was finally adopted for hockey.

Watch your two-year-old son playing with a ball. First he will pick it up and throw it to you. Then he becomes brave and kicks it. Finally, he will pick up a piece of wood to strike the ball, and all his primitive instincts will produce something akin to the first form of hockey. If it is third nature to hit a ball with a piece of wood, the inhabitants of most countries must have spent some of their leisure time playing a form of hockey.

There can be little doubt that hurling, as played in Ireland, has had the greatest influence in the development of hockey. It was first mentioned in connection with the battle of Magh Tuireadh, fought close to Cong, in County Mayo, as long ago as 1272 B.C. While the adversaries prepared for the battle, twenty-seven men from each side engaged in a hurling match to help pass the time. It was played until all one side were "defeated and slain".

It was the Greeks who gave us the second picture of hockey. In 1922 a masterpiece of Greek art was found built into the Athens city wall in a small yard behind a hat factory. The owner of the ground, while clearing the earth near the wall, discovered two blocks of marble. They were the bases of statues, decorated on three sides in low relief. The earlier, from the 6th century B.C., showed men playing ball, wrestling, and a dog straining on a leash at a cat. The second base is remarkable and unique. A group of six men is depicted, two of whom are engaged in a bully with the sticks upside down, and between the sticks is a ball. There is no other known example in Greek art, either in sculpture or vase painting, of such a scene, and had it not been found in the Wall of Themistocles there might have been great controversy as to its authenticity. It belongs to the ten years preceding the battle of Marathon, about 490 B.C., when war was in the air and the Persians were about to encroach on the Greek cities of Asia Minor. The wall at the Piraic

Gate, near where the Elgin Marbles were found, is within a stone's throw of the Cerameikos—the great cemetery of Athens—and it is probable that Themistocles ruthlessly pillaged this cemetery to build the wall and save his beloved city from the Persians. There was no false sentiment about the Greeks—their masterpieces were used as the foundations of the new city that startled the world with its science, philosophy, art and sport. Obviously Hockey was important enough to deserve a statue base.

It is surprising that the next known picture of a bent stick game does not appear until about A.D. 1200. In the north choir aisle of Canterbury Cathedral, a series of stained glass windows depict the "Six Ages of Man", Pueritia, or Boyhood, being a standing boy, a curved stick by his right side, holding in his left hand, near his shoulder, a small ball with a hole through it. As the great English cathedrals were also schools the game must have had some importance.

This may be confirmed by the noble east window of Gloucester Cathedral, the largest in England and said to be the largest in the world. It is a war memorial, commemorating the deeds of the local barons and knights at the battle of Crecy (1346) and the siege of Calais (1347). Erected in 1350 by Sir Thomas Bradstone, all 2,736 square feet of it have twice been removed for safety. The only sporting feature is a headless figure striking at a ball with a crooked stick. It is underneath the shield of an earl, though it is not thought to be in its original position. Golf historians claim this as the world's first golfer, and the cathedral guide tells everyone this is so. It is difficult to believe, however, that a game that supposedly originated in Scotland in the fifteenth century was given the honour of a stained glass window in Gloucester in 1350! It was far more likely to be a hockey player who was thus depicted.

From Greece, the Romans apparently developed Paganica, a bent stick and ball game, played with a leather ball filled with feathers, and it is probable that this game was passed on to the conquered European nations by the legions. The German game of kolbe, and the Dutch game of het kolven, played on ice and the forerunner of ice hockey, may have been direct descendants of the Roman game. The French had several forms of hockey under different names.

But the most interesting historical reference to continental hockey is an altar cruet now in the Copenhagen Museum, which depicts two players in an orthodox bully. On the base is a Paris hallmark—a lily—and on the rim of the paten are the date letters of 1333. A cruet being a "vas non sacrum", scenes of the parable of the Prodigal Son appear side by side with amusing little representations of the games and grotesque beasts. All that is known for certain is that a Lübeck merchant, one Heyne Boltzen (died *c.* 1473), had the cruet in his possession for a while, possibly as pawn. The inscription on the paten mentions the pious donor, Brother Petrus Regneri. There was in 1320 a monk called Petrus Rogneri in Sorö monastery, and if the donor were this same monk, perhaps this superb example of the Parisian enameller's art once belonged to the monastery, thus again linking hockey with the Church. So this may have been the game learned in France by the English knights and depicted in Gloucester Cathedral.

About the same time, from a tapestry now in the British Museum, there appears a picture almost identical with the Greek bas relief. This can be seen in Strutt's "Sports and pastimes of the people of England", while in the "Book of Games" (1810) there is an engraving showing four boys striking at a round bung with knobbly sticks.

Alexander the First of Scotland (died 1124) took an interest in shinty, the Scottish equivalent of hurling. It was derived from a game played by the heroes of the Celtic legends and sagas, tribe against tribe, clan against clan, over large tracts of heather. It was often known as shinny, the cry being "Shin ye!" as players advanced to the attack. The players were inspired by the bagpipes, and the prize, often shared, was a keg of whisky.

Bandy was another stick game that became popular in England and possibly gave us Shakespeare's only reference to a form of hockey. He says in "Romeo and Juliet", written in 1591, "The prince expressly hath forbidden bandying in Verona streetes". Bandy-on-the-ice was played extensively when the weather allowed and the *Manx Sun* of October 23, 1835, says, "We request the police to put a stop to the dangerous game called bandy which the boys are playing on the quay, the pier and in various parts of the town. Several gentlemen have had severe raps on the legs and no person is free from danger."

The most popular and widespread form of hockey was known as Commock or comocke, obviously derived from "caman" the Gaelic for "bent stick." References stretch from 1425 to 1821 and the word "hockey" could well be an abbreviation of "comocke". However, some historians suggest that hockey is derived from hocquet (Old French—shepherd's staff or crook), while the Anglo-Saxon for hook was hoc, another possibility. The harvest celebrations in some eastern counties of England were known as the hockey, hawkey, hooky or horky, and "the man who went foremost through the harvest with a scythe or sickle was honoured with the title of lord, and at the horkey collected what he could". The comparison with that fifth team full back tracking down his opponents is obvious.

Although there is an isolated reference to "hockie" in the Galway Statutes of 1527, the first clear mention of hawkey as a game comes from West Sussex in 1838, from "Holloway": "The object is to strike the ball to the further end to touch the fence of the opposite part, thus scoring one. Supposing nine to be the game, the party scoring that number first, wins." But in 1853, Lord Lytton wrote: "On the common were some young men playing at hockey. That old-fashioned game, now very uncommon in England, except at schools, was still preserved in the primitive vicinity of Rood by the young men and the farmers." So the game was already "old-fashioned" by 1853.

At Magdalen College School, Oxford, the original "Wall Game", played nine-a-side in the playground, existed from time immemorial, and Westminster School played an informal sort of hockey in the eighteenth and nineteenth centuries. It seems probable that as far back as 1800 the boys of Tonbridge School cut their own sticks from near-by woods and after steaming and bending them to the required shape, dried them in a huge school chimney. There was no limit to the number of players, and few rules. Types of hockey were played at several of the English public schools, though football in various forms was a bigger attraction.

Soccer in the 1860s became almost a purely upper-class game like polo or squash, and the first attempt, in October 1863, to form a football association was resisted by the public schools. Inevitably, however, football was transferred to the towns and mining villages in the Midlands and the North, and it is not surprising to find that the emergence of hockey as a club game coincided, in 1871, with the formation of the Rugby Union and the start of the Football Association Cup Competition, closely followed in 1872 by the County Cricket Championship. So the old game of hockey was revived by the muscular, mustachioed Victorian gentlemen, who wanted exercise but without competition.

The first hockey club was undoubtedly Blackheath (London). A society of golfers had been formed on Blackheath Common in 1608, the oldest golf club in the world, and the hockey club must have been a natural evolution. The Blackheathens are believed to have met as early as 1840, when members of the Blackheath Proprietary School carried their school sporting activities on to the heath; but the earliest Blackheath Hockey Club minute book dates from 1861. The first page is headed quite distinctly, "1861—Blackheath Football and Hockey Club".

Players would arrive at the Princess of Wales Hotel and would choose either a red or blue hat from a sack, to distinguish which team they were to play for. Red and blue are still the Blackheath club colours. Originally both sides of the stick were used, but eventually sticks were made of oak bent by steam with a flat back, possibly for a foot assist. The Blackheath game was robust, but rules with a modern flavour were soon introduced. The ball was a solid cube of pure rubber, with rounded corners, as supplied by Mr. Irish, saddler; the ground was at least two hundred yards long and sixty yards wide. Blackheath needed plenty of space and this was the greatest disadvantage in the development of its game.

In the autumn of 1871, Mr. John Barton and several former footballing members of another London club, the Teddington Cricket Club, tired of irregularities in soccer, borrowed the outfield, made wide ash sticks, painted some cricket balls white, donned their yellow shirts and white flannel trousers, and founded Teddington Hockey Club. Thus began the more sophisticated form of hockey that has been modernised and refined into the game we know today. Cricket grounds were ready made for hockey—adapt the game to fit the ground.

Teddington, whose ground was cropped close by sheep and the Royal deer, found that hockey was ideal training for their cricket; it was played in the same spirit. At first the captains acted as appeal judges, but umpires were soon recruited, and by 1874 their minutes refer to a sticks rule, a ten-yard hit-out and a throw-in from the side lines. At first Teddington played in shy seclusion, having little desire to play other clubs, but when, in 1874, several London cricket clubs started to play hockey, Teddington relented and along with Surbiton, Richmond, Sutton, East Surrey and the Strollers, introduced a new game to the Victorian world—a skilful contrast to Association and Rugby Football. The date of the first inter-club match is obscure, but a Teddington team to meet Richmond late in 1874 is quoted in their minutes without a note of whether the match was ever played.

On Wednesday, February 3, 1875, Teddington and Surbiton met in Bushey Park. The Surbiton minute book records that Surbiton won 2—1, "Bulmer Howell taking the first and Cyril Holmes the second. The goal Teddington obtained was by a sudden run away, our (Surbiton) men being all up and our goalkeeper being unable to prevent it single-handed".

Surbiton, formed in the autumn of 1874 with twenty-six members, were undefeated for their first three seasons. Instead of counting wins and losses, the criterion was the balance of goals scored over those forfeited.

There were many variations in the rules, and it was the East Surrey Club that took the initiative in trying to standardise them. They decreed that (Rule 2) "A cricket ball must be used"; (Rule 7) "The stick must not be raised above the shoulder"; and (Rule 9) "That no goal be allowed if the ball be hit from a distance of more than 15 yards from the nearest post".

It was the old Richmond Club that realised the need to put the game on a proper footing, and once the East Surrey playing rules had been standardised, Mr. C. J. P. Lawrell, the Richmond secretary, made the first attempt to form an association of clubs. A Hockey Conference was convened on April 16, 1875, at the Cannon Street Hotel, London, and officials attended from Richmond, Teddington, Surbiton, Sutton, East Surrey, Upper Tooting and the Strollers. Rossall School, owing to the distance from London, were unable to be represented but their written views almost exactly coincided with general opinion. So the "1875 Association" was optimistically founded.

Sadly, the Blackheath representative, Mr. T. S. Haynes, said it would be useless for him to remain to give an opinion of the rules of the new Association as "the Blackheath game" was so totally different from the game to be played by the other clubs. So Blackheath found themselves in a difficult position, for as the Association game took root, they ran out of opposition in London. With Marlborough School influencing hockey near Bristol, playing with a rubber ball, Blackheath naturally turned to the expanses of the West Country, and there began a series of matches with Bristol that were played annually from 1875 to 1893. Unfortunately for them, Marlborough decided to conform with the new Association rules, and the Blackheath influence began to wane.

In the Association, the Strollers proceeded to invite players to form the teams for the first county match. It was played on Thursday, January 27, 1876, at the Kennington Oval, and Surrey beat Middlesex 5—0, while a novel fixture was played a few weeks later between teams representing the Stock Exchange and Lloyds. It was in this year, too, when Mr. Edgell Westmacott, in Teddington's game with Surbiton in Bushey Park on December 9th, first marked out a fifteen-yard circle, to ease the lot of the umpires.

Despite the spread of the game, particularly in the Army, the attraction of soccer and rugby proved too great and the first association disbanded in 1882. The chief difficulty was lack of regular opponents, and certain clubs tended to discourage "outside fixtures", preferring to play amongst themselves. So if some clubs did not actually disintegrate, hockey declined sadly.

In 1883 Blackburn Olympic took the Football Association Cup north for the first time and it left the amateur footballers forever. It was at that time common knowledge that some northern players were paid for playing football, despite an F.A. rule forbidding it. So when, in July, 1885, professionalism in soccer was eventually legalised, a mass exodus of amateur footballers gave hockey a new status. One by one, the gentlemen who played once a week found themselves outclassed and they deserted football, leaving the way clear for the professionals. They are even reported to have found veiled professionalism, "Shamateurism", in Rugby, so they turned to hockey.

This second revival had, in fact, been anticipated in 1883 by Teddy Brookes, who left Surbiton to form a new club at Wimbledon. Several Surbiton men joined him in an exhibition match, and using a heavier stick and the cricket ball, they recruited several former members of the defunct East Surrey Club to lead a revival that led to the present organisation of the game throughout the world to-day.

Further clubs were coaxed into being at Cambridge University Colleges, Molesey and Ealing; and Teddington and Surbiton sprang back to life with great enthusiasm.

The honour of calling the meeting which founded the present Hockey Association in England fell to Mr. A. L. Agar of Wimbledon, and on Monday, January 18, 1886, in the Holborn Restaurant in London's Strand, the meeting attracted representatives from Wimbledon; Molesey; Blackheath; Teddington; Surbiton; Ealing; Trinity College, Cambridge, and Eliot Place School, Blackheath. The proposal to form an association was accepted unanimously, and Mr. Frank G. Howell became the first secretary and treasurer.

After coming down from Trinity, Cambridge, the Duke of Clarence showed his continued interest in the game by accepting the Presidency of the Hockey Association at its formation. With such distinguished patronage, hockey was at last socially acceptable, and a stained glass window was erected in St. Cuthbert's Church, Philbeach Gardens, London, in thanksgiving.

When the playing rules of the Hockey Association were decided upon, the Blackheath Club had second thoughts and again withdrew their support. Accordingly, Blackheath and Bristol decided to form a rival National Hockey Union, under the presidency of the Duke of Beaufort. Fortunately for the peace of hockey, the Association game gained favour, especially among former footballers in the midlands and the north, and the West Country clubs fell by the wayside. When the London County Council deprived Blackheath of their ground in 1894, the Blackheath form of the game came to an end.

So that was how it all began. There was a long way to go before county, divisional and international matches became properly organised, but grow it did.

The ladies took kindly to the game at Oxford University in 1887 among the undergraduates of Lady Margaret Hall, playing with plain ash sticks and a string-covered ball. The first ladies club was formed at East Molesey, followed quickly by Ealing and Wimbledon. The first Oxford v. Cambridge University men's match took place in March 1890, and the first men's international between Wales and Ireland in

January 1895. From these beginnings hockey has spread, not only through the length and breadth of Britain, played by both men and women, but throughout the world.

2

IN PRAISE OF HOCKEY

JEREMY POTTER

Hampstead H.C., London

Hockey is a life sentence. Already, at forty-two, my kind of retirement is well behind me: from inside left to left back twelve years ago. My playing career to date extends across a third of a century, and I expect to keep going in a mild sort of way for another eighteen years, sliding gracefully down the elevens and employing less and less mobility and more and more guile.

How the rules, like us players, have changed for the worse! One of the happiest memories of my childhood is of hooking sticks. You flicked up your opponent's stick ever so delicately from behind, converting his epic swipe into a humiliating airshot, and then you stole the ball away while he was angrily unwinding. In those days, too, you stopped the ball with your feet proudly, without a twinge of conscience or peals of horror from the chap with the whistle. I can re-live a couple of dozen enthralling penalty bullies, mostly as a forward, gaining in tempo on the goal-keeper at every tap, some as a back putting on a sly rallentando performance. No ichabod; the penalty bully has departed, replaced by a soccerish importation.

I have played hockey on grass and gravel, mud and sand, concrete and wood—even on that fiendish pitch at Dean Close, where wooden parapets prevent the ball from ever going out of play and you'll be lucky if you're allowed a half-time. For me there are no pitches like Indian pitches. There the ball travels fast and true, the tactics are a matter of the instant calculation of angles, and the Sikhs' feet are temptingly bare. There the game is played in the right temperature and at the right time of day—when the sun is nearly down, the tropical heat dying a slow death, and the second half cooler than the first. If only cricket's stranglehold on the grounds could be broken and we could have full seasons of summer hockey in England! Hockey in gym shoes in the sunshine; hockey on hard, dry pitches instead of in rain and slush and frost and fog.

Even as things are, no other activity has given me so much pleasure over quite so long a period as playing hockey. It attracts because it is a team game for individualists, and not a long-drawn-out one like cricket, or one steeped in professionalism, like soccer. Not for us hockey players the unbearable egocentricity of the lawn tennis addicts. Not for us, either, the bovine anonymity of second-row rugger forwards. We gather the ball, we bring it under control, we preen ourselves with a modest display of stickwork while finding an opening, and then—we pass. There is scope for the opportunism of a dashing wing or a weaving inside; a half may have a private duel marking his man out of the game; but when the crunch comes it is the forward line as a whole which scores, and a dovetailing defence which keeps the ball out of the net.

Thus the successful club is the one which turns out the same team week after week, not the one with the stars who twinkle in and out of the side. In one three-year stretch with the Hampstead Club, I didn't miss a single game, and the rest of the defence was almost as regular. Our combined endeavours became infinitely better than the sum of our individual merits, and in two of those three years I believe we were the only London club unbeaten by those thoroughly professional-thinking amateurs at Hounslow. We all went through our favourite private antics, but as an instinctive part of an intricate pattern which I find satisfying even in retrospect. In every emergency everyone sensed where everyone should be, and there, by a series of stunning coincidences, everyone usually was. Doubtless we would have been all the better for some hard work with a blackboard off-field, but the joy of acting on individual impulse would have gone. As the enemy swept down the field we would somehow form and re-form in depth with (almost) military precision, but undrilled and uncommanded.

Hockey has its perils as well as pleasures. I am scarred on the cheek for life by a blow from the stick of a centre-forward from the other side of London (we dropped the fixture the next season, naturally). Usually, though, it is the centre forward who suffers. There was one I used to play inside who was an Anglo-Indian—a mixture of bloods which for some reason produces the best hockey players in the world. He rarely scored fewer than four goals a match, and each one with an effortless diffidence which made it all the more galling to those at the receiving end. One day the opposing goalkeeper became so infuriated as number six went in that he abandoned the ball for good and set about the man with his stick—not a smart tap on the ankle such as even respectable defenders unleash from time to time, but full-scale belabouring round the shoulders. That was an Army game, and it ended months after the final whistle in courts-martial and dishonour.

On quite another occasion my own goalkeeper, finding the opposing centre-forward providentially at his feet, proceeded to kick him gravely and systematically out of the circle. That was in Germany, and there was already some tension in the air owing to what the papers would call "amazing allegations" of body-checking against myself and our centre-half, a player of unblemished character from the stockbroker belt in Surrey. (The point at issue was who is fouling whom when blond fliers from Hamburg tap the ball ahead and try to run through you and you simply stand.) The goalkeeper incident came as a climax, therefore, and the umpire's whistle sounded like a signal for World War 3. Our goalie stood impassively to attention while being harangued in broken English, and at the end remained silent and unapologetic, leaving it to us to explain that the team's only goalkeeper was at our hotel sweating out a fever under one of those huge feather mattresses, and this was an obliging fellow from Munich (where Hamburgers were unpopular?) who didn't speak a word of English.

Now let me dogmatize and, breaking the golden rule for backs, commit myself. At the age of nine I was told that I would never be able to play hockey properly because I was left-handed. But as the seasons passed I discovered this to be what is politely known as the reverse of the truth. The greatest natural advantage in playing hockey is to be left-handed. On the reverse side this should be obvious, yet it's astonishing how few opponents realise that one is left-handed, let alone the implications. At left back, for instance, I positively encourage inside rights to try to take the ball round my reverse side, and they never tag on.

But left-handedness goes further. If you are a left-handed cricketer, bowl left-handed by all means, throw in left-handed (though not at first from cover-point—keep it for the quick single to your left-hand side), but don't bat left-handed. Leave that to right-handers who have enough sense. For if you play a two-handed shot from the right-hand side of your body at cricket or hockey or any other game, the right hand merely guides. What counts is the left wrist, and if you use your left hand for all the manual chores of life yours will be stronger and suppler than any right-hander's.

The effect of left-handedness is one pecularity of hockey; another is the variety of its manifestations. Because of differing atmospheres and attitudes, Saturday and Sunday hockey in Britain are virtually different games: staid Bromley men break out the very next day as Bandits; and Syphons and Tankards and Heathens, too, are specially reserved for the sabbath. Women's hockey, again, is a world apart, and according to my observation one Saturday at Wembley (in the company of 60,000 schoolgirls) a far, far cleaner one than men's. Mixed hockey, on the other hand, occupies a dangerous half-world of its own: an unholy blend of extramural and intramural sports.

But, so far as memories are concerned, the heights of hockey are achieved in yet another manifestation: the festival. Here, Pink Elephants and Hairy Goats abound. Here, spectators actually appear on the touchlines. Festivals have taken me to The Hague, where I found that Holland wasn't a flat country after all; to Guernsey, where I was expected to share a bed with a large centre-half; to Folkestone and Bournemouth and that unlucky venue the National Physical Laboratory; but above all to Le Touquet, the quintessence of festivals. Au Touquet, as they say, one unlimbers in the scramble for free champagne at the Mayor's reception, then follow the fierce encounters on the field with long-legged Dutchmen and short-legged Belgians, and afterwards there are nocturnal junketings at the Café des Sports and dark rumours of other encounters in the tents among the pine-trees. One year, such is the fervour of festival hockey, we even transported our right-half across the Channel and safely back again without benefit of transport!

Hockey is not for watching (except by small boys who can fetch the balls). Hockey is not for making money out of. Nor is it really for writing about. Hockey is for playing.

3
LESSONS IN INDIA

JOHN WOODCOCK
Oxford University and Travellers

On January 5, 1964, soon after 3 p.m., the British hockey side, travelling by motor-coach, approached the stadium at Lucknow where they were to play the fifth of the seven international matches which they undertook on their tour of India. The sight that greeted them was unforgettable. With only twenty minutes to go before the start of the game, there were perhaps 20,000 people storming the ground in an effort to break in. The only way of entry was by two small and closely-guarded gates. Here were two prevailing features of the Indian scene: a wonderful enthusiasm for hockey and a cheerful lack of public order.

This match, like the others, reflected many of the differences between the game in India and in Britain. These differences are due partly to ethnology and partly to the conditions of play. The British can learn a great deal from the Indians, as indeed they did on this tour; but they can never hope to master, to such an extent, the art of stickwork. For one thing, they lack the same suppleness of wrist and quickness and certainty of eye. For another, they play their hockey on grounds that are often heavy with grass and mud. The Indians have every chance to develop ball control; without it they would never be considered for the top-ranking sides. In Britain, on the other hand, there is a future for the lusty, hard-hitting defender or the tear-away forward; in India, there is none. Conversely, the Indian sorcerer in an English quagmire can be totally ineffective.

There is one other marked difference between East and West, or at any rate between British and Indian sides. This is in outlook. Great Britain take their hockey seriously these days compared with time past. They subject themselves to training week-ends. In an Olympic year they have a long programme of preparation. Now, in the search for improvement, they have sent a side to India. Someone like Howard Davis or John Neill or, for that matter, any of the leading British players, must expect to give up much and to devote most of his annual holiday to hockey. It is right that he should when so much money and effort and hope are being offered. Yet compared with the Indians, the Pakistanis, or even the Japanese, we in Britain still only dabble at the game.

Before an Olympic Games an Indian side will train and travel and practise together for months on end. When the British team was in India, the Indians had two elevens, plus a few reserves who were more or less full-time players. Hockey in India is a highly competitive sport, just as football is in England. Thus it causes no particular surprise if the greatest of their players is enticed from one side of the country to the other for the club season. The clubs in Calcutta, for instance, tend to provide richer "perks" than those in Bombay. This, of course, is a matter for the Indian Hockey Federation and I, for one, would be reluctant to deny the Indian with a flair for the game the chance to better his lot. It seems to me that nowadays the distinction between the amateur and the professional over most of the world is too spurious to be retained.

But to return to Lucknow! Great Britain played India's "B" team that day, having lost to the "A" team in Jullundur, some 500 miles distant, the day before. Between "A" and "B" there was virtually nothing to choose. The pitch was like lightning and the excitement at fever pitch, many years having passed since Lucknow had seen an International side. That same day, after an early lunch, Babu, a legendary figure among Indian inside forwards, had talked to the British players on stickwork and tactics. He could still practise what he preached when it came to juggling with the ball. It was a revelation. And soon afterwards, India, with seven Sikhs in their side, were making Great Britain do the running, their supremacy based on ball control.

Great Britain lost the match by one goal to five. Their only goal came from a penalty flick; their only other real chance came at a penalty corner. Chances in the ordinary run of play were few and far between. This was the pattern of the tour. For a fortnight the British defence stood up gallantly to a heavy bombardment. With each match they learnt a little more about the tricks of the Indian trade and how to counter them; they grew gradually wiser as to the way an Indian likes to beat his man; they began, as it were, to read the Oriental mind. Yet there was never a game when the British goalkeeper was not in the hottest place. If he had an off-day, as George Black did in Calcutta, Great Britain were trounced. If he was in brilliant form, as Harry Cahill generally was, and Black was in Gwalior, the score was kept reasonably in check. At Lucknow it was the sheer wizardry of some of the ball play rather than the combination and team-work of the Indians that created the openings and had the British defenders running hither and thither. Give them a stick and a ball, and Joginder Singh or Harbinder Singh or Inam-Ur-Raman will perform like members of the Magic Circle.

Simply as defenders the British, I think, were the equal of the Indians. India had no centre-half the superior of Davis, nor a better back than Neill; and wherever he played, Cahill, a prodigious kicker, was acclaimed for his goalkeeping. Yet in their forward play Great Britain for a long time could make no impression. No one seemed to have the subtlety to find a gap. They were too easily dispossessed. They seemed like lightweights trying to knock down a heavyweight; and some of these Sikhs are indeed heavy, robust and strong. When, occasionally, Great Britain maintained an attack the Indians looked, if not vulnerable, at least not infallible. Too many of the British forwards were too inexperienced or too lacking in dexterity to make a mark. As we saw in Lucknow, the ball was being constantly fired back towards the English "25" and, after a while, the pressure told. High-class forward play must be based on intelligence, intuition and stickwork. In Britain we seldom see it.

After Lucknow the side went to Calcutta. By then they had lost the international matches 0–7, 0–3, 1–5, 1–3 and 1–5, and the three British goals had all come direct from the penalty spot. The tour had been too intensive. Too much had been asked of the side in too short a time. They played eleven matches in fourteen days. And yet they showed in their last two matches that, by playing so often against such strong opposition, their own standards had improved. Although they lost 2–8 in Calcutta, on the most perfect of pitches and in face of the most masterly play, they managed to create more chances than before. They could very well have scored four goals, which was decidedly encouraging. And then in Madras, in the last of the seven internationals, against a mixture of the two Indian teams, they forced a draw which was as welcome as many a victory on the European front. As everywhere else, except in Bombay, they played before a full house. In Madras thousands were turned away and Great Britain had their full share of an eventful game.

What then was the extent of Britain's improvement between the time of their first crushing defeat in Bombay and the relative triumph of their final draw? It was, I think, appreciable, and it lay basically in their adjustment to an environment. Although physically tired, they were playing much faster by the end of the tour because they *had* to. Their stickwork and tactics were more attuned to Indian conditions. Thinking together for a fortnight and talking over their problems among themselves, as well as with the Indian players, had helped considerably. From watching, they had learnt. And by always striving to play attacking hockey they had endeared themselves to the Indians. By crowding their circle they could have lessened the margin of defeat, but only at the expense of their ideals.

When the next British side tours India I shall expect them to be overwhelmed in the same way by the heat and brilliance that await them. This is hockey played at a faster pace and in a higher temperature than anything they are accustomed to. Without wishing to seem fatalistic about it, I believe Great Britain will almost inevitably meet their match against the Indians in India, though not necessarily in England. So long, however, as they show the same spirit and determination as Davis's pioneers, the advantages of such a tour will be unquestionable, both to the game as a whole and the individuals who take part. This first side returned, as any side must do, with a host of happy memories. They were indebted to the Indians for their opportunity, and to them they were duly grateful.

4

THE FEDERATION INTERNATIONALE DE HOCKEY

L. J. QUARLES VAN UFFORD

President of the F.I.H. since 1946

In 1924 the International Olympic Committee decided to exclude hockey from the Olympic Games that were to be held in Paris that year. This decision was not received too kindly by leading hockey officials and it was a Frenchman, Paul Leautey, who realised the game needed a special international organisation to promote its interests throughout the world, and to make sure hockey was included in the programme for the next Olympiad at Amsterdam in 1928. The representatives of seven countries (Austria, Belgium, Czechoslovakia, France, Hungary, Spain and Switzerland) met in Paris on January 7, 1924, and decided to found the Fédération Internationale de Hockey sur Gazon (F.I.H.), and Leautey became the first president.

There were many other sports with international federations incorporating many countries at the time, but the F.I.H. soon grew. In 1925 Denmark joined, followed in 1926 by Holland and in 1928, prior to the Amsterdam Olympic Games, by Germany and India. Later that year Poland and Portugal affiliated.

Since 1928 the F.I.H. has been exclusively responsible for the technical arrangements and control of the Olympic hockey tournaments, and hockey has always been included in the Olympic programme. This has proved an important stimulus to countries to become members of the F.I.H. and to-day, forty years after the founding of the F.I.H., there are fifty member countries representing hundreds of thousands of hockey players.

The African Hockey Council, the Asian Hockey Federation, and the Pan-American Field Hockey Federation are, moreover, members, as recognised continental groupings.

Great Britain, though it took part in the 1908 Olympic Tournament in London with a team from each of the three home countries (England, Scotland and Wales) and an Irish team, and took part in the 1920 Olympic hockey tournament at Antwerp with an English team only—had to become affiliated to the F.I.H. in 1947 in order to be able to participate in the 1948 Olympic hockey tournament in London.

Since then close and loyal co-operation has marked relations between the F.I.H. and Great Britain. This was evidenced by the appointment of three F.I.H. representatives on the International Hockey Board, the only organisation empowered to lay down and amend rules. In 1957 the number of F.I.H. representatives was increased to four and in 1964 the voting strength of the F.I.H. on the Board became even greater.

The first meeting in 1924 was followed by an F.I.H. congress in Amsterdam in 1928, and by another congress in Paris in 1932. Ever since, congresses have been held once every two years.

There have been five presidents in the forty-year history of the F.I.H. A well-known French sports editor, Frantz Reichel, who died suddenly in 1932, succeeded Paul Leautey; another Frenchman, M. Bellin du Coteau held the office from 1932–1936; Georg Evers (Germany) from 1936–1945; and the writer, Jhr. L. J. Quarles van Ufford (Netherlands), has been President since 1946.

Robert Liegeois (Belgium), who was appointed a vice-president when the F.I.H. was founded in 1924, assumed the interim presidency from 1945 to 1946.

Only three persons have carried out the important duties of secretary-general—Francisco Botella of Spain, from 1924–1929, Albert Demaurex

(Switzerland), from 1929–1950, and Rene G. Frank (Belgium) who has since filled this arduous post. The F.I.H. has had only two treasurers, the Frenchman Jehan Daubresse, from 1924 to 1958, and Albert Demaurex (Switzerland) who still fills this responsible post.

A technical committee was created in 1928, composed of members of the F.I.H. Its first president, Robert Liegeois, remained in office until 1946, when he had to give up membership of the committee because he wished to retire from the F.I.H. He was succeeded as president by Jhr. L. J. Quarles van Ufford, who had been a member of the Technical Committee since 1932. The committee plays a very important role in international hockey, dealing with all the technical matters regarding the rules of the game, international games, tournaments, umpiring and, last but not least, the Olympic hockey tournament. Initially it was five strong, but gradually it proved necessary to expand it, and the technical committee now has fifteen members.

Since 1952, the F.I.H. have controlled indoor hockey, which is to-day played in several countries during the winter. The first president of the Indoor Hockey Committee was Henning Holst of Denmark and he is still in office.

A women's committee, which looks after the interests of female players of the member-countries, was founded in 1930 under the presidency of Mrs. M. Galvao-Rieck (Germany). She was succeeded in 1946 by Miss E. de Josselin de Jong (Holland) who still holds this office.

During its forty years' existence, the F.I.H. has done much in the interests of hockey all over the world, always taking the strictly non-professional nature of hockey into account. Thanks to this principle, hockey is still one of the very few games in the world which is played by amateurs only.

Hockey demands the utmost physical fitness of its players, and it is important that very great care be given to the proper physical development of young players. The F.I.H. must pursue the aim of preserving hockey as a game for amateurs as a source of enjoyment, and thus make a valuable contribution to the physical education of young people all over the world.

5

I REMEMBER

MARJORIE POLLARD

Editor *Hockey Field*

Looking back over some sixty years of hockey playing, with nearly fifty of them very active, is rather an alarming experience. Somehow the events and incidents of the long ago are now so much more clear and seem so much more important than anything that happened last week. Obviously memory plays strange tricks and as I have kept no personal records I am going to defend none of the dates I mention, nor perhaps the actual chronological sequence of the events that come to mind.

There is another thing about memory: I know I am apt to remember only what I want to remember. That means, of course, that the pleasing incidents and the personal successes will, by now, have overlain and smothered the many disappointments and embarrassments. So anyone who has read as far as this has been warned. This is no authenticated, biographical exercise; it is reminiscence.

It is a fact that I can never remember when a ball game, hockey or cricket, was not being played in the yard or front hall at home. Having a brother and sister, both older but both keen and good games players, a father who was an enthusiast and a mother who looked the other way, there was always opportunity and someone willing to play something. Even now I can remember, while at infant school, that I used to hit a ball at a wall with a large hockey stick, stop it on the rebound, and whack it back again.

So when at the age of eleven I got a scholarship (to the surprise of all) to the Peterborough Secondary School, where my sister was then head girl and games captain, I could really hit a ball and run after it. When I was asked later in life, in august and serious company, what my theory of ball games was, I said with truth, "When I see the ball I give it a good clout and run after it." It hasn't altered at all.

The second day I was at school (and this I can remember with crystal clarity) I played my first real game of hockey. The place was the Show Ground at Peterborough, the teacher a Miss Andreae. The grass was long, there were no lines marked, but there were goalposts. We had no instruction as to how to hit the ball, but the twenty or thirty of us were divided into two lots and let loose. I enjoyed myself thoroughly and was admonished time and time again for trying to do it all myself. That characteristic and the admonitions followed me for a long time.

At school, to contemplate hockey once a week, was to cause me to quiver with excitement. I have seldom experienced anything like it since; it was the jewel of the week. I became form captain when in the lowly 2B class and, to my amazement, was chosen to play goal for the school. Now, in 1911, hockey for girls was pretty rudimentary and at times forthright, if not rough. Goalkeepers—with no special protective equipment—were hard to come by. Virtually they were asked to stand in a place of danger, expecting miracles. I learned afterwards that no one else's mother would let her play in goal, and mine did not know. We played March High School at March, lost 0–17, and I never played goal again, which wasn't surprising!

School hockey to me, even though it took place through the war years 1914–1917, was absolutely delightful. I was so keen, so eager, so high-spirited that I often got into trouble at school, and then my punishment was no hockey for a fortnight. The more appropriate thing would have been to let me play three or four times a week to get rid of my energy and high spirits. I never quite forgave the members of staff who kept me away from the games field. The remembrance of what I did, the angry feelings I had, and what trouble I caused in the detention room when others were out playing hockey, has helped me considerably in my attitude towards young people now that I am a Justice of the Peace. To confine energy is to ask for rebellion.

I became school captain, and though our fixture list was curtailed because of the war, we did enjoy our matches. We cut, rolled, and marked out the pitch, and being by that time a forward I always saw to it that both circles were well rolled. We were a good united school team, most ably and sensibly coached by our games mistress, for whom we would all have rolled every pitch in sight, and even now, some fifty years later, there are those of us who meet occasionally and say, "Do you remember . . .?"

The last match at school I recall was when we beat March High School 6–4, to win the Fenland Public Schools League Cup. I have never felt so proud or so important since. School hockey is the nursery, and now when I see some 50,000 schoolgirls watching a match at Wembley Stadium, I rejoice and feel that the future is in good hands. Whether school hockey is any better than it was is not the point. What is important is that far, far more girls play to a reasonable standard, and they have the opportunity of seeing the game played to a high standard.

Leaving school in 1918 with a wearying war (and a hungry one) just ended, left people, especially girls of my age, high and dry. There were no training schemes, no opportunities. I played hockey with the Peterborough Club, which was mixed in a way, though both men and women had their separate matches at times. I never liked mixed hockey: I still think it is a mule of a game, producing nothing. I found it somehow engendered aggression and exhibitionism in the males, and a kind of silly I'm-as-good-as-you-at-this-kind-of-thing in the females. The sexes cannot play team games in opposition; individual games, maybe, where handicapping is possible, but the style of games as played by men and women is different.

By 1920 things were settling down a bit and I had learnt that there was a Northamptonshire Women's Hockey Association in being. I had ambitions. The men in the club, and they, of course, held the offices which mattered, said it was useless to affiliate and, anyway, it would cost a guinea. I paid the affiliation fee, played for Northamptonshire, Midlands and England that same season, and that guinea, more than my week's salary, was the finest investment I ever made.

Club hockey—and I formed the North Northants Club—I thoroughly enjoyed, but county hockey, with its higher standard, its more serious side, and its way to further promotion always fascinated me. So the twenty years I played for Northamptonshire will always remain the real satisfying highlight of a long career. Territorial hockey is different. It is hard, tough, demanding. It is hockey to the highest standard. It is the next step on the promotion ladder and, as such, is watched by the All-England Women's Hockey Association Selectors. Territorial loyalty is very strong indeed: the results matter, and so there is little light-heartedness about the matches. Life becomes very real and very earnest.

By comparison international matches, between 1920 and 1940, were not all that exacting. England during those years reigned supreme—except once, in 1933, when Scotland turned the tables on us, and rightly so.

In 1926 I had my first taste of hockey on the Continent and liked it very much indeed. The English team went to Germany and played four matches. We scored twenty-seven goals with nil against. In Hamburg we saw an England men's team captained by Mr. Lampard Vachell. We watched, enthralled and appalled, as they played Vienna or somebody, and a rougher, more acrobatic, less rule-conscious game I had never seen before. When we started on the same pitch we were all apprehensive but we need not have worried. The German women played their clever, straightforward, hard-hitting game, and though conditions were strange and the ground bumpy, we thoroughly enjoyed ourselves and won comfortably.

It was after that visit that I took teams to Belgium, Switzerland, France, Denmark, Holland or Germany every Easter. We played on the dunes in Dunkirk, round a lovely tree and in wonderful scenery in Switzerland, on a hard court in Magdeburg, and on some fine pitches in Amsterdam, Copenhagen, Leipzig, Hanover and Cologne. Those unofficial tours were sheer joy, and we saw the standard of the game improve tremendously, especially in Holland and Germany. The last time I played for England in Germany was, I think, in 1937, and after a real battle of a match (amid many waving swastikas) we managed to win by 6–4. That was a far cry from the day when we could win, as we did in 1926, by eight goals to nil.

The question is often asked—what is the peak period in the life of a games player? Mine was obviously 1926—28, and as my age goes with the years the arithmetic is simple. Being a forward it is possible to assess success by goals scored; indeed that is how it should be. In those years I scored all eight against Germany, all five against Scotland, seven out of eight against Ireland and thirteen out of twenty against Wales. Looking back now I realise that while the England team of that time was very strong and full of personalities, other countries were only still building

BRITAIN IN THE OLYMPICS. G.B. v. INDIA. Semi-Final. Olympic Games. Rome 1960.
Britain's centre-half, Howard Davis, opens the way for brilliant G.B. goalkeeper, Harry Cahill, to kick clear. India won 1–0.
L–to–R: Joginder Singh, Cahill, Davis, Umpire, V. J. Peter, Udham Singh (10) and J. Bell.

(Photo. Associated Press)

BRITAIN IN THE OLYMPICS. GREAT BRITAIN v. BELGIUM.
Rome Olympics. 1960. Under the burning Italian sun at the marvellous Marmor Stadium, John Neill (2) robs the Belgian forward, Huyghens in the British circle.
L–to–R: Croft, Huyghens, F. Rens, A. Muschs (background), Neill (2), Carnill, and G. Debbaudt

up. Defence play had not developed; it was not organised anything like it is today and so goal scoring, if one had speed, ideas, skills and real determination, was only a matter of time. For an inside-forward to come off a field not having scored (after all there are seventy minutes in which to do so) was considered a personal disgrace.

There is no doubt about it—the years between the war were a heyday for English hockey. Nations came to play and were beaten. Touring teams went to Australia, South Africa, U.S.A., and New Zealand and returned having totted up goals galore. The International Federation of Women's Hockey Associations, an English idea and ideal, was born; three instructional films were made and were seen by thousands of players, and by 1939 the number of affiliated clubs and schools was at its highest peak ever—over 3,000.

It was impossible to be part of all this—and by then I was an official, a selector, a writer, as well as a player—without feeling the tremendous upsurge of enthusiasm: it was a vast tidal wave.

In 1939 England was to be the centre of the hockey world; eighteen nations were to be with us for a tournament—but then came the war.

Starting again was a wonderful experience. There was such energy, such joy, such high hopes; but by then many of us were five years older and a new generation, not quite knowing the old ropes, was with us. I played my last "club" match at Witney when I was fifty—and enjoyed it thoroughly. The spirit was very willing, but the flesh was getting slow and so that was that.

The last fifteen years have seen the rising of the standard of play throughout the world, and England can no longer be certain of success. There need be no real sadness about this; it means that other countries are in the ascendant. At the moment Wales, small in numbers with but relatively few grounds, is riding high. I remember Wales scoring their first goal against England in 1927, and saw them first beat England in 1963, having waited since 1902 to do it. I remember England beating South Africa in 1953 at Folkestone—a game of magnificence and power. Remembering now is international in its widest sense, because within the International Federation of Women's Hockey Associations are twenty-eight nations, and all this had sprung from that fertile period between 1920–1940.

Looking right back to 1911 when I played in goal for my school, I realise my life has gone full cycle. That year I ordered from a stationer's shop in Peterborough a copy of the weekly magazine, *The Hockey Field.* It cost twopence and I saw my name in print for the first time as one of a hockey team. That I have never forgotten, but little did I think, as I stood on the pavement outside the shop with the magic little magazine in my hands, that one day I should be its editor. Since 1946 it has been my property and so, after being schoolgirl, club, county, territorial and international player, selector and president, hockey is still part of my life. I have enjoyed it all and there is still more to come.

6

A NEW APPROACH TO TEAM PREPARATION

HUGO BUDINGER

Rot-Weiss (Köln), and Germany

At the conclusion of my international playing career in 1961, I was selected by the Federal Committee of the German Hockey Association to be its supervising director. At the same time, my future tasks for German hockey were clearly defined, namely, in addition to organising work, to introduce special measures for building up our national team.

The 1960 Olympic Games in Rome were not a success for the German team, as was shown very clearly by its being ranked seventh. The team which had found its touch and won the bronze medal in Melbourne in 1956 continued, without doubt, to show first-class ability until 1959 but often its performances were erratic. In May 1960, during the Olympic qualifying matches against the zonal contenders (East Germany), the efforts of certain of the older and more experienced players were seen to be particularly weak, and it was decided, at short notice, to choose several young players who had shown great promise. Unfortunately, this measure proved unsuccessful in Rome. The hard and tough pace of international competition under unusual climatic conditions—temperatures were near 100 degrees fahrenheit during some matches—exposed quite clearly limitations in performance, particularly among the newly introduced players. Technical skill was not enough; players had to be almost as physically fit as the athletes. This was a concept I had already grasped in Helsinki in 1952 and which had influenced my training and that of my team-mates before the 1956 Games.

Since, in 1961, Germany had an abundance of young talent and the retirement of the older players had been completed, I drew up a special training programme for the candidates for our 1964 Olympic side. In West, North and South Germany and Berlin, I formed four training clubs, each with twelve players, all of whom came under my general direction but were looked after in the various districts by my colleagues on the sports committee.

In 1962, out of a total of fifty players in the training clubs, thirty were engaged in the numerous German provincial matches. In August of the same year I took the best players to the Sports Academy in Cologne, where I am also active professionally, in order to carry out a special performance test, using the most modern medical findings as applied to sport. Under the direction of the lecturer, Dr. Hollmann, tests were carried out, the main object of which was to provide information on the performance of the players at that time. The standard test methods of

Hugo Budinger

Hollmann-Venrath were employed to establish the limits of maximum and continuous effort. Those persons undergoing the tests were connected to the apparatus by a mask allowing full vision. First of all pulse-rate, blood-pressure, oxygen consumption, as well as the depth and frequency of respiration, were ascertained when the subject was relaxed. Then the actual tests were started under a stress of three milli-kilogram/second. The above-mentioned values were again recorded every three working minutes, when the stress was increased by four milli-kilogram/second.

Since the hockey players were graded as occupational sportsmen, we only stopped the tests subject to the point of exhaustion or a pulse-rate of 180 beats per minute being reached. From the general results of the test we were interested in (*a*) the optimum capacity for work by the player, and (*b*) his limit of endurance.

The maximum oxygen assimilation and the maximum oxygen pulse were considered as the criteria for the optimum ability to perform work. The higher the value of the maximum oxygen intake, the greater is the capacity for sustained maximum effort, i.e., an effort which lasts for more than three minutes. The same applies to the oxygen pulse, in that the economy and capacity for work of the cardio-circulatory system are always better, the higher the oxygen pulse for a given degree of stress.

If we estimate that in the case of a normal male who indulges in sport the average oxygen intake is 3,200 milli-litre/minute with an oxygen pulse of 16.5 milli-litre/minute, then with our specially-trained national players, these values will amount eventually to 4,540 milli-litre/minute maximum oxygen intake, with a corresponding oxygen pulse of 20 milli-litre/minute. On this scale of performance, top-class sportsmen can be graded with long-distance runners and swimmers. This result must be considered as most noteworthy if one has followed the views which have been expressed in medical literature hitherto. After the tests the players were accorded individual training tasks in addition to their normal training assignments.

In 1963 special emphasis was laid on conditioning work for the circle of twenty-four players in regular training sessions as well as improving their technique. Most important, the method of training was laid down which would lead to increased skill, endurance, speed, sustained speed, and suppleness. The scope, nature and duration of the thrice-weekly training sessions were put in writing and explained to the players on the courses.

In 1963, for the first time, the summer vacation of the national players took an active form in that they were required to pursue their physical training programme regularly. This meant that although there were no matches there was no break in training.

In July I had the players tested again at the Sports Academy in Cologne, to get an idea how much the break in competitive match-play had affected their condition. The results also formed the basis for the preparatory programme for the international tournament which was due to take place in Lyon three months later. Whilst the Cologne training course had mainly served to provide tuition in playing tactics, the training assignments in the months of August and September were entirely directed towards technical and physical improvement.

The eighteen players which I selected for Lyon were in the finest physical condition for this tournament. The over-all results,* were satisfactory to us and showed very clearly how the work of building-up should be planned for the future.

The excellent performance of the German hockey team in 1963 resulted in its being chosen by the Press as the Team of the Year.

In order to intensify the training of the individual players in the localities where they live, in January 1964, nine months before the Tokyo Games, I engaged eight trainers who had been taught by myself at the Cologne Sports Academy on the lines laid down by the German Hockey Association to look after the players in groups of two to four every Wednesday. The main task was to maintain the physical condition of the players and to try to improve it.†

7
BUTTERCUP

GEOFFREY EAMES, *Bromley H.C., London*

(Author of *A History of Bromley Hockey Club* 1963)

The members of one of the lower elevens, seasoned warriors all, arrive at the ground sporadically but unfailingly. There is never any sense of mission—that is, until their captain, a vast, shambling Fred Emney of a man with fair hair and heavy jowls steps through the pavilion door. He is an institution. Looking grouchy and fit only for a siesta, he settles himself on a changing-room bench. If he recognises any of his players he betrays little sign of it.

Troublesome administrative matters such as umpires, oranges, and hockey balls are left comfortably in abeyance until he is eventually tracked down by the opposing skipper, whom he invariably greets with hurried charm.

When he finally emerges from the pavilion ready for play it is an education to behold the impact on the other side. This heavyweight can't *seriously* be proposing to play! The "old hands" alert themselves to the scurrilous tricks they must surely expect from this monster;

* *Editor's Note: Germany was unbeaten and defeated the Olympic Gold medallists, Pakistan.*

† *Editor's Note: Germany are allowed to send only one team to the Olympic Games and it is therefore necessary for teams representing East and West Germany to play-off for the Tokyo place. In the play-off games West Germany were narrowly beaten by an equally thoroughly-prepared East German team.*

young inside-forwards go noticeably pale, having correctly judged that he plays full-back; and the one man in the side whose humour has not entirely deserted him, sums him up—"either a beast or a god!"

The joke, of course, is that they are all so wrong. Foul play and violence play no part in the big man's technique; he can manage perfectly well without. In less obese days did he not figure at right-wing for his county? He is a stylist and is naturally quick on his feet—just as ex-King Farouk was surprisingly nimble on the tennis court. His stick-work is still impeccable. He is the very antithesis of the flamboyant or the grotesque, and once he deliberately missed a penalty corner which he did not believe in.

He marshals his team with the invariable "Shall we foregather?" and the game commences. As a captain he is a model of rectitude, leading yet not driving, unobtrusive save for an occasional laconic directive such as "Fight!", "Move it!" and "Too square!". His aim is to lead an integrated side with a sense of positional play. Nothing would so appal him as the spectacle of a team running flat out for seventy minutes devoid of all feeling for tactics.

It is at half-time that the skipper reveals that perceptiveness and insight into the game which secure him unchallenged command. Briskly he indicates the wrong and the remedy. He urges but never rants. "Please don't call for passes, Smith. The other side can hear you as well." "Halves—keep out of the far circle. It is a reproach to the forwards if you score." "We must watch that inside-left." It is all sound practical stuff, fully in accord with common sense.

Much of the second half may slip by with the team still a goal down, and the big man blandly surveying operations from full-back. At last an intense face can bear it no longer. "Do you realise time is getting on, we're a goal down, and we haven't lost this season?" Panic measures have never commended themselves to the skipper. Hurt that his rule should be questioned, he gives just the right reply, faintly biblical in its moral. In the end, of course, the two goals are scored—not perhaps quite out of the text book but good enough for present needs.

The game is won, and if on the return journey to the pavilion the visiting skipper looks disconsolate at the travesty of justice, Big Brother shows little sign of discomfort. He has always been able to turn a brave face to the misfortunes of other people!

Tea is a necessary but somewhat lugubrious interval between two pleasures. The skipper is unconversational, prefers not to eat, and snuffles uncertainly at a cup. But the click of an opening hatch is the signal for his countenance to radiate. Rising imperially, he offers a gracious invitation to his opposite number: "Will you take wine with us?" The visiting captain accepts, fairly glowing at this kind thought.

As host the big man dispenses the liquor, with old-world generosity and a homely phrase or two. Now he holds forth on many subjects, for after sundown conversation and controversy are meat and drink to him, and it was once well remarked: "If he were not Alexander, he would be Diogenes." Spaniel-eyed, both teams surround him, marvelling at the sensible things he is saying; at intervals, his speedwell blue eyes fill with concern for the one man who drinks lemonade and he mutters: "You pain me, sir!"

At the height of the discourse the big man lights up a cigar, and judging himself properly fortified for the journey, makes off for some distant hostelry. He takes his leave with portentous grace, and a final roguish dig at his team: "Who gave you blokes permission to break training?"

Now mellowed with a mixture of envy and admiration, the visiting skipper contemplates the retreating form of the colossus. "You have a splendid leader there. But *however* does he do it?" The home side smile mutely. It's not just that they can't reveal trade secrets. Sentiment does play a small part in hockey, and they are wistfully thinking that there'll never be another.

8

HOCKEY, THE LAST SURVIVING GAME

E. M. WELLINGS

Evening News, London

During the past thirty-five years, my period of acquaintance with first-class sport, every game inevitably has changed. With one exception the change has been for the worse; of that I have no doubt at all. It is not a question of playing skill. None can estimate whether Pele is as good as or better than Alex James was on the soccer field in the thirties. None can accurately compare the quality of the fast bowling of Lindwall with that of Larwood more than thirty years ago. To-day's giants may play better than the giants of thirty-five years back—though the "modern" is such a lazy bloke at practice that I doubt it. Actual quality of play does not, for me, decide whether the changes have been for the better or for the worse. The decisive factor is the *manner* in which a game is played, and here the "moderns" fail lamentably. They have gone far towards destroying their sports, by depriving them of their essential quality as games to be enjoyed.

Soccer may be good business to-day, but it is no longer a game. The result has come to mean too much to players and administrators alike. In the most nauseating fashion, players hug and embrace each other when a money-spinning goal is scored. Their fanatical example spreads to crowds, and turns them into vicious partisans, ready to hurl not only abuse but also missiles at opponents and unpopular referees. Too much money is to be had from success in football.

The same is true of cricket. Players do not enjoy their games in the same way as their grandfathers did; they enjoy rather what they can get out of playing cricket well and successfully. The old-timer kept playing the game he loved as long as possible; he retired only when he could no longer hold his own with younger rivals. Players such as Hobbs, Rhodes, Woolley and George Gunn continued in first-class company into their fifties. To-day the star thinks about retiring in his middle or even early thirties, when he angles for a fat newspaper contract, lending his illustrious name to comments written by a ghost writer whose work is of minor value without the boost of someone-else's fame.

Often, sport generally suffers from too much money being available for participants, and from politics. These take no account of the enjoyment of players, but unwarrantably use highly-publicised sports as barometers of national prestige. Brazil is currently the top footballing country. To argue that Brazil is therefore a better country than Ecuador is baloney. It may not even be a better footballing country. If the folk of Ecuador enjoy their games more, I would regard them as a better football-playing country than the world champions. After all, games are primarily for enjoyment.

One big game only has escaped the general deterioration. There is no money in British hockey. No country, at least around Britain, can use the sport as a short cut to national prestige. Here in Britain hockey is an ideal game, sound, sane and healthy in spite of, or perhaps because of, its having a financial struggle. When I came back to hockey as a writer, after a long absence, the game was essentially the same as when I was playing it thirty or more years earlier. Oh yes, there had been changes. The ball could no longer be stopped by a boot, without incurring a penalty. A player could no longer indulge in the fiendish practice of hooking his opponent's stick. Such beneficial changes did not alter the essential character of hockey. It remained a game solely designed for the enjoyment of everyone participating in it—players, officials, spectators and writers.

I prefer cricket as a game, but in the past dozen years I have felt much more at home, been much happier, and had much more enjoyment in the company of hockey than cricket people. Nobody in the former has had any selfish axe to grind; nobody has had anything tangible to gain.

The leading player's reward is the honour of representing his country, the pleasure of occasional tours abroad, and fame strictly limited to a small circle. But that comparatively small circle is one of friends, as it once was essentially also in our other games and sports.

The writer returning to hockey could hardly fail to notice the game's spirit. In other games since the war, players in general have been avid for praise but resentful of criticism. I'm a critic, and have occasion to criticise. As in other games formerly, the men in hockey take praise and criticism as they come, and apparently bear no resentment about the latter, so long as its expression is honest.

None perhaps has been more critical of the England selectors and their admirable chairman, Harry Lewis, in recent years than I. It has not been all one-sided. The chairman in good humour gets some of his own back with a cunning dig at me when he speaks at a club dinner to which I also, surprisingly, have been invited. It might be expected that such antagonists would become hostile to each other. And so they might in other, debased, games. In hockey the reverse has been the case; the outcome a friendship which I should hate to forfeit. Harry Lewis, I think, is typical of those who keep hockey as a true game in England.

How long in an alien world can we keep hockey as it is to-day? During the 1963 international tournament in Lyon it was disturbing to read a remark by *The Times* correspondent about whole-time players of certain countries. Since then our own absorption in the Olympic Games and the extensive preparations we have made to fit out a medal-winning team have been equally disturbing. Is this our start on the downward slope? Are we beginning to put success in international company above enjoyment of the game? A paid secretary has been appointed by the Hockey Association—a wise move, for hockey needs thorough promotion to keep its head above water in days of continually increasing costs despite the promises of politicians. It would, however, turn out badly if it encouraged hockey people to think primarily about raising money to finance winning expeditions into the realms of international rivalry.

Already I have heard it suggested that the English schoolboy team should subsequently be kept in being as a side to be trained for such a purpose. Nothing could be more contrary to the spirit in which our hockey is now played and conducted. By all means let us compete internationally and strive for playing perfection, but let us take that competition in our stride. Let us fashion our international side within the existing framework of the game. Ample scope for improvement exists, without in any way changing the pattern of a game, based fairly and squarely on the clubs.

Traditionally the first three months of each season belong to the clubs.

I believe it is vitally important to the retention of the game's character that they should continue to have the first half of the season to themselves. Deprive the clubs of their leading players for representative matches before the New Year, and you risk breeding a new type of player dedicated to the winning of honours—a player without the club spirit, which is the heart-blood of hockey.

In 1963 the British clubs were pillaged of their best players week-end after week-end, for training sessions, trial games, home international matches and the Lyon tournament. Club hockey was disastrously disrupted. And, we have to admit, at the year's end we had precious little to show for all this misapplied energy. Britain were no better off internationally than if the season had been allowed to take its normal course. If we had anything to show, it would not have impressed me particularly, for I think less of winning medals than of preserving the last British game to survive as a true sport.

What was the value of all those special events—Lilleshall, Nottingham, Lyon and the like—when Britain continued to find her selectors in Scottish Highlands, Welsh mountains and university cloisters? My goodness, surely we should not start to alter the pattern of our game before making all the possible improvements in our existing international set-up, which is rooted in the present framework of the game. Special team-developing ventures are in any case valueless, when those who choose the teams are so out of touch with the game that they select two forwards who are not good enough for their county team and ignore the five who are.

A dozen gold medals would not compensate for the sacrifice of hockey's present character and spirit. In Britain—a country bedevilled and bewildered by its politicians, driven off the roads by a Minister, and refused rail travel by one of his henchmen, whose inhabitants console themselves with the noise of Beatles—hockey is something well worth preserving and enjoying.

9

INDIA HAS LOST GROUND

ASHWINI KUMAR

President, Indian Hockey Federation

A lot has been said recently about the deterioration in the standards of hockey on the Indian sub-continent. It is not my intention here either to defend the existing standards of play or to laud or decry our past glory in this game. What I would like to do is to recapitulate here some of the salient features which have given Indian hockey a unique place in world sport, and add a few random reflections.

As is well-known, hockey in India was introduced in various cantonment towns by the British Army a couple of decades before the advent of the twentieth century. To begin with, it was played in a rather crude form but, somehow, captured the imagination of the people and soon spread all over the country. Even then, few could have foretold that this game would take such a hold and would, one day, win for India a place on the map of world sport.

Calcutta gave the lead in the formation of hockey clubs in 1885, and soon other parts of the country followed suit so that the growth of State and local associations gave rise to the need for an All-India body which could effectively control the game. A few associations banded together and established the Indian Hockey Federation in November 1925 at Gwalior.

The new Federation soon got down to work and, in 1928, selected an All-India team to represent India in the Olympic hockey championship in Amsterdam. At the first attempt India established itself as the foremost combination in the world, and won the coveted Olympic gold medal. India continued to dominate the Olympic scene in the succeeding Olympics, winning in 1932, 1936, 1948, 1952 and 1956. Then in 1960 it was robbed of its world title by Pakistan, and our only comfort was that the title had gone to a part of the world which, not so very long before, had been associated with us in our quest for the world title.

It is frequently mentioned by critics these days that the present-day Indian technique of playing hockey is not constructive, is not direct in its approach, and usually results in low scoring at the expense of a stolid defence. Perhaps some of this criticism is true, but to label all Indian players, organisers and coaches as dull-witted and not capable of changing the pattern of play to suit prevailing conditions would be unfair. Indians generally perhaps do not realise that the standard of hockey all over the world has risen tremendously in the last decade. To-day, the hockey population of the world is almost four times greater than it was in 1936. In parts of Europe the game is nowadays played as a summer sport, and no longer do so many players contend on snow and ice-bound winter pitches. Indoor hockey has also come to stay. New hockey nations have been born—Kenya, New Zealand, Australia, Japan, Malaya, Poland and Korea to name a few. The art of dribbling, scooping and flicking which was, perhaps, our close preserve is now commonly practised all over the world. Above all, the game has become extremely fast and calls for one hundred per cent physical fitness in the players. In the circumstances, one cannot judge the present-day Indian standard of play by a yard-stick which is thirty years old.

On the other hand, it cannot be denied that to-day hockey in India is no longer a premier sport. The reasons for this gradual decline are not far to seek. As a sport, hockey is not a part of the "big business" racket. It cannot offer a five-day glamorous "Test" fare, in which thousands of spectators can throng as if they were witnessing a festival. For some unknown reason it lacks the popular hold which football has on the public, and does not possess a box-office appeal which can support fabulous cash prizes for players and professionals.

Despite all this, Indian sportsmen still do play a lot of hockey—perhaps for the reason that India has been tops in this game for a long period in the past.

Another factor which has been responsible for our technical excellence at hockey is the wiry physical frame of our players which this game requires. Unlike football, brawn is always at a low premium, for to play hockey efficiently one has to eschew all violence and subordinate robust tactics to skill and agility. Perhaps it is the elimination of strong-arm methods which has made hockey less popular with the masses, who now want gladiators sporting in blood and thunder in the arena. One thing is certain, hockey will never be able to present a sadistic fare to the public as "all-in" wrestling does!

Until recently the usual method of learning hockey in India was simply by playing it. To-day, however, there are a number of schemes in operation all over the country whereby national coaches travel round instructing potential players in strategy and technique. The young player has a much better chance of being educated out of his weaknesses and this is as it should be, because the standards are no longer so low that one can play in a happy-go-lucky fashion and still remain supreme.

For a very long time in our country we neglected proper instruction of our players, even in the basic principles. It is for this reason alone that we find that, although other nations have progressed tremendously, we are still clinging to what we possessed some years back. No wonder, therefore, that we are getting hard knocks in the international field. It is true that nature occasionally produces a prodigy like Dhyan Chand, but ordinary players have to learn how to play games the hard way, just as they need to be educated in the various complicated processes which go to make our social set-up. Other countries have made great use of instructional films and large quantities of illustrative literature, and have paid coaches to give practical lectures and demonstrations as aids to the learning of the game. Till recently we did nothing in this direction—we clung on to whatever we had and did not produce a single national coach.

During the last twenty or thirty years we have sadly neglected our playing pitches and grounds; national competitions no longer draw crowds to enthuse and encourage aspirants. The wherewithal of hockey, i.e., hockey sticks, balls and other equipment have become so expensive that the vast majority of people who live in our country can no longer afford to play the game on a scale which can be termed as national. Perhaps if we eradicate all these disadvantages I have mentioned, India may get back on the road to recover some of the ground lost in the past decade or so.

10

JOHN CONROY

ZULFIKAR GHOSE

Hockey Correspondent, *The Observer*

If John Conroy had been a cricketer or a footballer he would have been as much a part of the popular imagination and native folk-lore as England's Len Hutton and Stanley Matthews. Instead, his emergence as one of the greatest British hockey players and his subsequent retirement from representative hockey have been noticed only by followers of the game.

He hit the headlines all right: "Britain Needs Conroy" said *The Guardian*, "Conroy in Class of His Own" said *The Times*. They were just two of the innumerable headlines with which hockey followers during the 1950s were familiar. In 1958 *The Observer* called him "the most dazzling player in Britain". Earlier, in 1952, when he played for Britain at the Olympic Games in Helsinki, the captain of the Indian team which won the gold medal told him, "You could have played for us if you had lived on in India." No higher praise could be given to any hockey player.

John Valentine Conroy was born in 1928 in the Central Province of India, of Anglo-Indian parents, being the seventh of thirteen children. His hockey career was quite sensational, beginning with the muddy yard of his home town and reaching climaxes at the Helsinki and Melbourne Olympics. In the 1951–52 season alone he played for the Army, the Combined Services, England, Great Britain *and* Europe. At the age of twenty-four, it was like winning the Nobel Prize with one's first novel. And yet Conroy did not start playing hockey seriously until he came to England and joined the Army; what is more, it was an accident that he took up the game at all.

Although he played hockey in his childhood and early youth in India, it was in England that he properly learned the game. He began playing when he was three years old, using a piece of wood for a stick and a wooden ball. He played with Sepoy children, three or four to the side. When he went to a boarding school in Nagpur at the age of six, his hockey for five years was limited to beating a cork ball around a pitch. It seemed a primitive attempt at self-entertainment, but even so Conroy was advanced enough skilfully, when he went to St. Lawrence

John Conroy

School in Mount Abu, to get a place in the school team straightaway. This was his first experience of playing for a full team, and some of his opponents were not eleven years old, like him, but adults. He remained at Mount Abu till he was seventeen, but while he continued to play hockey there, he was never formally coached.

Conroy came to live in England soon after the end of the Second World War, and joined the Army—for no other reason than that his father had been in the Army—to become a regular soldier. Hockey, however, was far from his mind at that time. He did not even know if the game was played in England. One day, however, he had to report to his sergeant-major.

"Are you from India?" the sergeant-major asked.

"Yes," replied Conroy.

"Do you play hockey?" enquired the sergeant-major.

Conroy muttered a rather hesitant affirmative, and the sergeant-major said, "Well, you're playing to-morrow afternoon."

The match was against a local R.A.F. side, and of the six goals which his Army team scored, Conroy netted five. Such a performance was inevitably noticed, and he was at once invited to play for his Corps' side, R.E.M.E. He made an excellent debut, and in his five years as a member of the team they did not lose a match.

In 1950 Conroy joined a London club, Mid-Surrey, and he has played for them ever since, being made an honorary life member of the club in 1958.

His selection for England was the greatest thrill of his life. For Conroy was an Anglo-Indian, and the England of the early 1950s was far from ready to absorb players from the Commonwealth even if one of their parents had been a true Englishman.

This was perhaps the necessary spur which contributed to Conroy's greatness. To take the place of an Englishman, he had not only to be as good, but considerably better. He worked hard to be just that, and even when he had been selected, there were people who frowned at his appearance in the England team. But prejudice finally broke down in the face of Conroy's glorious performances, and his selection for Great Britain followed. He went on to represent England thirty-two times and Great Britain twenty-three times.

After the 1956 Melbourne Olympics he went to Canada with the notion of importing Japanese goods; the business did not come off, and he worked as a labourer. A year later he returned to England, and within two weeks was gratefully received back into the England team.

By 1960, however, the selectors thought Conroy's powers were declining, and he was omitted from the British team for the Rome Olympics. This was generally considered to be a blunder as, in fact, it proved to be.

Conroy has always been an opportunist in the circle and has a wonderful goal-scoring record, but like any other great inside-forward in either hockey or soccer, it is his ability to create opportunities for his team which has been his most important contribution. He was so far ahead of his rivals as a tactician that there is no doubt his omission from international hockey was rather premature.

Conroy was irreplaceable and already he has become a legendary figure and his name a synonym for top-class performance. Any great player makes a lasting contribution to a game, revealing a profounder aspect of it than one had been accustomed to, and so it was with Conroy: he brought a new approach to British hockey, making dribbling a refined art, giving body swerve and feinting a dramatic usage. It is a measure of Conroy's greatness that we continue not only to recall his rhythmic movements in the field but also to judge new forwards by the high standard he established.*

* *The above story was adapted by Zulfikar Ghose from his own article originally printed in The Observer.*

11

THE PATTERN OF THE RULES

M. G. COWLISHAW

The evolution of the game of hockey during the past thirty years or so can well be appreciated by a study of the changes made in the rules during that period.

Three principal considerations have always been in the minds of the rule-makers; first, to improve the skills required; secondly, to open up and speed up the play; and thirdly, to counter abuses.

In 1938 hooking of sticks and the intentional use of the body (except the hand) to stop the ball were forbidden, thus putting a higher premium on stick-work. Since then the five yards line has been opened up to seven yards; the circle enlarged; the twenty-five yards bully abolished; and the penalty bully replaced by the penalty stroke. Penalty corners have been varied, to provide more chances to score; umpires have been given powers to penalise intentional infringements by defenders outside the circle, and the penalty stroke instituted to deter deliberate fouls in the circle. All these changes were brought about gradually, with the full support and approval of the players.

In making these changes, the International Hockey Board consistently placed more responsibility on the umpires to judge "intention", while the speeding-up of play has necessitated much greater concentration and quicker reaction, especially when the advantage rule is to be well operated. At the same time the deterioration in the code of sportsmanship has made umpiring very difficult.

What other alterations are on the cards? The universal adoption of the "Indian" type of stick has radically altered the style of play. It is much easier to play the ball on the left of the body, and this tendency will have to be dealt with when it leads to obstruction, possibly by the

A men's International in England. England v. *Wales. Hurlingham Park. London. April 1964. Dick Constable England's centre-forward, about to score England's fourth and last goal after a pass back from the goal-line by Derek Miller (extreme right). The 4,000 crowd are crammed into the back of the stand to avoid the rain. L–to–R: Poole (background), Page (head visible), Corby, Constable, Morris, Savage (Welsh goalkeeper), Prosser, Thomas (head visible), Wilson (6), Whiteway, Sutton and Miller.*

(*Photo. Anthony Hallas*)

A women's International in England. England v. Scotland. Wembley (London) March 1964. England right inner, Pamela Stinchcombe, throws up the spray in the Scottish circle. England won 3–2. L–to–R: J. Calder (foreground), Stinchcombe, Parry, Bryant, and Scottish goalkeeper, H. Weir.

(Photo. Central Press)

elimination of such play altogether when an opponent is within striking distance.

As long as the majority of hockey players want to play in the worst months of the year, the development of the finer arts of stick-work is likely to remain fairly static, but one thing could and should be attended to—the game should always be played on grounds of full width. An extra five yards might be added with advantage, making the pitch sixty-five yards wide. Forwards cannot develop proper approach work to the goal when cramped for space in which to manoeuvre.

When the Board were experimenting with the free hit instead of the twenty-five yards bully, it was suggested that the hit might be taken either at sixteen or three yards from the goal line. Sixteen yards was decided upon but it seems to give too great an advantage to the defence. This might be reduced to eight yards, which seems a reasonable distance, but the free hit should always be taken from outside the circle.

The paucity of goals in the 1960 Olympics leads to consideration of widening the goal; a very simple operation, only requiring a new cross bar. The reason for a goal being four yards wide is obscure, but the addition of another three might might lead to more goals and, after all, that is the object of the game!

There is, however, a much more serious problem, that of attitude of the players, and perhaps even more importantly of their coaches, to the spirit of the game. At one time—not so long ago—deliberately to foul in the circle was not done; nowadays the approach is: "Will a foul pay or not?" The rules of hockey were not designed to cope with such an outlook, and umpiring is not based on such an approach. It is quite possible that the rules will have to be rewritten to cope with these changes in ethics—a deplorable state of affairs perhaps—but unavoidable.

12

THE HISTORY OF OLYMPIC HOCKEY (1908-1960)

PATRICK ROWLEY

Hockey Correspondent, *Exchange Telegraph News Agency*

Shrilly a vibrant fanfare of trumpets pierces the air echoing round and round the vast stadium, and the Olympic flag with its five interwoven circles—the symbol of united continents—is unfurled on the highest mast. On the green veld in the centre of the stadium thousands of athletes look up in expectation. Suddenly the earth throbs its silent protest as cannons resound, and the air is filled with the vibration of beating wings as thousands of pigeons are released to take messages of goodwill to the far corners of the earth. As the birds circle for the last time above the packed arena, a choir breaks softly into an anthem, the voices swelling into a crescendo that fills one with deep emotion.

Then all eyes move to the entrance of the stadium as a lone athlete in white strides onto the red shale of the track, proudly carrying the

Patrick Rowley

burning Olympic torch. The last of a team of runners who have carried the torch from Olympia in Greece, the site of the ancient Olympiads, he runs the last lap before the solemn silent crowd, little sparks of fire cascading from the torch onto the red shale. He stops on a dais overlooking the vast throng; raises the torch to the sky, and a great flame leaps up as the sacred Olympic fire is ignited—destined to burn night and day until another Olympiad is over.

The opening ceremony of the Olympic Games is moving and awe-inspiring pageantry. Its ymbolises the wonderful ideals on which the Games were re-started in modern times. Thousands of great athletes from countries all over the world, of different races and creeds, black and white, come together to strive their utmost against each other at various sports. All are joined together in a spirit of great comradeship and each one is movingly affected in some way by the opening ceremony. Some are fired with the spark of greatness; others overwhelmed, destined to strive in vain. Yet, for all the memory of having taken part will never fade.

The modern Olympiad was not always the magnificent spectacle it is to-day, with the exploits of the best athletes from all over the world watched, through television, by millions. When hockey was included for the first time, at the IVth Games in London in 1908, it was a very different story. Modern science had not brought us many of the things we take for granted to-day. Only twenty-two nations were able to take part in the Games held at the stadium known to-day as the White City. There were many fine performances, particularly by the American and British Empire athletes, but few heard about them, and it was only because of the moving drama when Italy's Dorando was assisted half-conscious towards the finish of the marathon that the world was stirred at all by the Olympics.

The rest of the Games were already over when the hockey tournament started in late October. Only six teams had entered, the four United Kingdom countries, France and Germany, and most of the players arrived in London, stayed two or three days to play their games, and left for home after a pleasant but slightly unusual week-end.

For most of the players, the games were just additional internationals. England was drawn against France; Scotland against Germany; while Ireland and Wales received byes into the semi-finals. The English were favourites, for they had had the better of their matches with the other home countries, and although the game was spreading rapidly in those days, the continental countries had not played hockey long enough to compete with the founders of the game.

The first-ever Olympic hockey match was played in beautiful weather on October 29, 1908, and was between Scotland and Germany, who were represented by a club side, Uhlenhorster (Hamburg), who remain, to this day, one of the best German clubs. The pitch, which had been subjected to a tremendous battering in the weeks beforehand, was not at all conducive to good hockey. Scotland won 4–0 and the honour of scoring the first Olympic goal went to their inside left, Ian Laing, who surprisingly never played for Scotland again. The continental challenge ended when England then beat France 10–1. In the semi-finals England, whose team had been practically unchanged for four seasons, adapted themselves far better than the Scots and qualified to meet Ireland, who had beaten Wales 3–1.

There were only 5,000 people in the huge stadium for the final, but for the first time in the history of hockey, everyone sensed it was an important occasion. England confirmed they were the outstanding team, by inflicting their heaviest defeat up to that time on Ireland, winning 8–1. In their three matches they scored twenty-four goals, and all agreed that England's centre-forward, Stanley Shoveller, was the best hockey player in the world.

It was twelve years before hockey was again included in the Olympics. There was insufficient support for the game in 1912 (Stockholm) and the Berlin Games were cancelled because of the First World War.

The world had not recovered from that war when, in 1920, the Olympics were renewed at Antwerp (Belgium), and only four countries, England (Great Britain), Belgium, Denmark and France entered the hockey tournament. There had been no international hockey for years, and most of the competitors were earning their first caps. Again the hockey was completely divorced from the rest of the Olympic Games, and this time the tournament was decided on a league basis, everyone playing everyone else. England's great centre-forward, Shoveller, was still going strong although nearly forty, and the continental sides could find no answer to his brilliant play. England won her first two matches by defeating Belgium 12–1 and Denmark 6–1, but their final match against France never took place. A story is told that on the evening before the game, the last of the tournament, the French took their English rivals "round the town" with the idea, it is uncharitably suggested, of getting them "sewn up". It seems that the English players were rather better at this than were their hosts, for the following day the French, hit by illness, scratched. Great Britain, represented by England, was awarded the gold medals, and Denmark was placed second, ahead of Belgium.

Four years later, in Paris, hockey was again omitted from the Olympics because of limited support, but interest in the game was growing fast, and it was clear that some sort of international body was necessary, to unite the sport and to be responsible for the organisation of the Olympic hockey tournaments. It was on the initiative of a Frenchman, Paul Leautey, that the Fédération Internationale de Hockey (F.I.H.) was founded on January 7, 1924, with seven founder countries—Austria, Belgium, Czechoslovakia, France, Hungary, Spain and Switzerland.

By 1928, when the Olympics were due to be held at Amsterdam, this number had been doubled and ten of the fourteen countries entered for the games, five of them, including India, and the hosts, Holland, for the first time. The great disappointment, however, was that England (Great Britain), was absent. Several opinions were voiced at the time as to why Britain did not enter. Some said it was because the Olympic tournament was held in May after the British season, and this meant it interfered with lawn tennis and cricket commitments; others that Britain had suddenly become anti-competitive. However it is far more likely that the real reason was that British officials, who were responsible for founding the International Hockey Board to administer the rules of the game, did not recognise the F.I.H., which Britain had to join to compete in the Olympics.

The outstanding game in the pools was that between the hosts, Holland, and Germany, which Holland won 2–1 after a thrilling match. The Germans played Haag—considered to be the best centre-half in Europe at the time—at centre-forward, and paid for this tactical error. Their true worth was clear when they beat Belgium 3–0 in the third place match for the bronze medal.

India and Holland topped their pools and the increase in interest in hockey was clearly demonstrated when 23,394 spectators, easily the biggest crowd that had ever watched a hockey match until that time, saw the final. The spectacular Indian side were firm favourites after gaining sweeping victories in their pool, but the crowd supported Holland strongly. It was a fast, clean game which frequently brought prolonged applause from the spectators. India, with several injured players, took a long time to settle, while the Dutch surprised everyone by playing superbly. They were weak in the circle, however, just as nearly all the European teams were in those days, and India led 1–0 at half-time. In the second half the Indians really came into their own, and Holland were beaten 3–0 and saved from a heavier defeat only by the brilliance of their backs, Tresling and de Waal, and goalkeeper Katte.

Just as a centre-forward had left an indelible impression on the mind in the previous Olympic tournaments, so it was at Amsterdam. The Indian centre-forward was a 21-year old, Dhyan Chand, who enthralled the spectators with his brilliant play.

Once again the hockey tournament had been played at a different time from the rest of the Games, but it was a wonderful moment when the Indian, Dutch and German teams lined up facing the score board, to be presented with their gold, silver and bronze medals. As the national flags were hoisted, the British national anthem was played, and the first great Olympic hockey tournament movingly came to an end.

If anyone thought India's 1928 victory was a hollow one in Britain's absence, India had no chance to prove otherwise. Although their team returned home from Amsterdam via London, they were regrettably not offered a game against either a Great Britain or England side—a ridiculous slight that has been repeated several times since.

The world, and America in particular, was at the height of a financial depression when the Xth Games were held in Los Angeles in 1932. Country after country withdrew until only three hockey teams were left—India, Japan and the hosts. India, who had produced an even better team than in 1928, were in a class of their own against the "new boys," and whipped Japan 11–1 and U.S.A. 24–1. By now, Dhyan Chand had his brother, Rup Singh, playing alongside him, and against America Rup scored twelve goals and Dhyan seven.

India were a wonderful side; they made the game look simple and beautiful as they raced through their opponents' defence, with the ball always under superb control. Chand himself had become a veritable magician, and the performance of India's team was voted the outstanding exhibition of skill in any sport.

The Japanese also created a fine impression and they took the silver medals by beating the United States 9–2. It was obvious that they intended to learn as much from the Indians as they possibly could and studied their rivals even at training.

Most Olympic Games are remembered for some special feature. Amsterdam had seen the introduction of women competitors, and Los Angeles provided the first Olympic Village. Competitors of every sport were housed together, so that hockey players were able to rub shoulders with the more publicly boosted personalities of other sports.

Each Games also produces its own atmosphere, and there could not have been a greater contrast than that between the Los Angeles and Berlin Olympiads. By 1936 Hitler had been in power for three years and the Games were a great opportunity for him to impress. Everything was done with military precision and for the glory of the Fatherland. Elaborate welcoming plans had been laid on for each of the visiting teams; players were lavished with gifts; and Hitler was thrust down the throats of everyone. Hockey players, the majority of whom are used to a back seat, were almost overwhelmed; they even found a special stadium had been built for the hockey tournament, which gave spectators an ideal view of the little white ball.

Hitler was also determined that the German competitors should dominate the games, though America, and Jesse Owens, in particular, had other ideas. Statistically, there did not seem any reason why Germany should not improve two places on their previous appearance in the 1928 hockey tournament and carry off the hockey title. So when Germany stepped out to meet India in a practice game on July 17 before the Games started, they were determined to undermine the morale of the Indians. They could not have been more successful, for robust tactics paid off and they won 4–1, thus ensuring a far greater interest in hockey at the Games.

The Olympic regulations had been altered so that each team should play a minimum of three matches and a maximum of six matches during the tournament and as twelve teams had entered, three groups of four were formed, based on a ranking list drawn up by the F.I.H. India, Germany and Holland were seeded, in that order, and as two teams went forward to the semi-finals from Holland's group, that was the toughest.

The top seeds duly qualified for the semi-finals, together with France. India, reinforced by the arrival of Dara Shah,* who was flown to Berlin as a replacement after India's practice match defeat, trounced France 10–1 in the first semi-final, while Germany gained revenge for their defeat by Holland at Amsterdam by winning the other semi-final 3–0.

There was terrific tension before the final, and this was increased when heavy rain caused the match to be postponed. As the following day was the last day of the Games, the match had to be played in the morning, and Dhyan Chand says in his autobiography *Goal* that for the first time the Indians were not sure of victory. Both teams took the field to tremendous applause, the German giants looking enormous beside the slender Indians.

There must have been many who thought David could not slay Goliath that morning, but the Germans, not for the first time, made a tactical blunder and, in their confidence, tried to play the Indians at their own game. The Indians, seeing their chance, bided their time and allowed the Germans to exhaust themselves. At the interval India had slipped into a 1–0 lead, and when they put on the pressure the Germans became very ragged. Art triumphed over brute force, and India went on to win 8–1, the greatest final victory in the nine Olympic hockey tournaments to date.

So once again the Indians stepped up for their gold medals and Dhyan Chand, who had scored six goals in the final, and goalkeeper Richard Allen, who had only conceded one goal in five matches, each pocketed their third.

Altogether 184,103 spectators watched the hockey over the period of twelve days of the tournament, and the stadium was always well filled. Holland took the bronze medals by beating France 4–3 in the third place match, but the peculiar group system did not give the impressive Japanese or Afghan teams an opportunity to test their skill against the Dutch.

* *Pakistan Team Manager 1964*

Chand and Allen could well have gone on to gain their fourth gold medals at Tokio in 1940, but the Second World War put a stop to the Olympics, and it was not until 1948 that the world's greatest sportsmen came together again in blitz-damaged London.

Before the Games took place at Wembley, the British Hockey Board was formed from the four countries making up the United Kingdom and affiliated to the F.I.H., a step that meant, at long last, that India and Britain could meet in the Olympics. In Germany's absence, the F.I.H. seeded India, Britain, Holland (Netherlands) and the newly-formed independent state, Pakistan, in that order and, because of withdrawals, the teams were again divided into three groups. The four seeded teams duly reached the semi-finals, though Britain were surprised in their first game by Switzerland's defensive tactics and had to be content with a goalless draw.

Both the semi-finals were great matches. India, for the first time in the history of the Games, were lucky to win, scraping through 2–1 against the Netherlands who surpassed themselves and probably deserved a draw; while Britain had to make an all-out effort to beat Pakistan 2–0. So the argument of twenty years was about to be settled—"Were the Indians better than their original teachers, the British?"

In the vast Wembley stadium which had been packed in the days beforehand to watch Zatopek win the first of his gold medals in the Athletics, Fanny Blankers-Koen speed to three "golds", and Gailly be passed by two other runners as he struggled round the last lap of the marathon, 25,000 came to see the hockey final. The crowd seemed much smaller in the vast stadium and were so far from the field that the players must have felt very remote.

It was in this unreal atmosphere that this match of matches took place. The heavy and bumpy pitch favoured the British style of play but the Indians, whose average age was twenty, adapted themselves quicker than the home team and went on to win by four goals to nil. So India were not only Olympic champions but world champions too.

The result was not really surprising, for the British played a similar type of game to that used by the continentals in previous Olympics. This held no hidden terrors for the Indians, who were continually presented with the ball when British passes went astray, and were thus able to keep their opponents on the defensive for the greater part of the match.

Pakistan were expected to win the bronze medals by beating Netherlands, for they had defeated them 6–1 in their group. However, their third place match was drawn and Netherlands proved to have the superior stamina in the replay, winning 4–1.

Four years later at Helsinki (Finland) the same four teams reached the semi-finals and again India triumphed, though it was the Netherlands whom they beat in the final.

Only one pitch was available in Helsinki, and so the F.I.H., against their will, were forced to agree to the tournament being held on a knock-out principle. Twelve teams took part and a preliminary round was held to eliminate four teams and obtain eight quarter-finalists. The four 1948 semi-finalists were the teams excused the preliminary round, and they reached that stage again by playing only one game—a very unsatisfactory affair. India and Pakistan convincingly beat Austria and France respectively, but Britain and Netherlands got through by one-goal margins against Belgium and Germany. The eight teams eliminated played in a consolation tournament some way from Helsinki.

Olympic history was made when Poland and Belgium had to replay a match as the Belgians had used sticks over the regulation width. Poland, who lost the first match 4–3, won the replay 1–0, and went on to reach the consolation final, in which they were beaten 4–0 by Germany.

Back in Helsinki India confirmed her superiority over Britain in the semi-finals by winning 3–1, and Netherlands, playing very soundly, again beat Pakistan, this time 1–0.

In the final the Netherlands decided to play with only three forwards up, but the plan failed, for India scored at regular intervals and led 4–0 at half-time. The Dutch reverted to an orthodox formation in the second half, but India, for whom their captain and inside right, K. Singh (Babu), was outstanding, were still superior and finally won 6–1.

One disturbing feature at Helsinki was the prevalence of rough play. Many put this down to the tournament being held on the knock-out basis, but it certainly appeared necessary for a more uniform interpretation of the rules to be made by the umpires.

India's success at Helsinki was their fifth in succession, and their reign as world champions had lasted twenty-two years—probably a longer period of superiority than any sporting team had ever had before. By 1956, when the Games were held in the Southern Hemisphere for the first time, at Melbourne, probably a great many people had decided that they were unbeatable. They won again but, by the end of the Melbourne Olympiad, that myth had been destroyed.

Melbourne undoubtedly staged the first truly world championship, with teams for the first time from every continent in the world. The standard was higher than ever before and only India, ridiculously put in the same group as the three weakest teams, had any "easy" games.

The only notable absentees from the games were Netherlands, whose team was withdrawn in protest against the Hungarian uprising. Once again the top seeds—India, Britain, Pakistan and Germany—reached the semi-finals, but not without some heartburning in the British and German camps. Britain, in a group with Australia, Kenya and Malaya, won through only after a play-off with the hosts.

The first semi-final between India and Germany was a very poor game, spoiled by the defensive tactics of the Germans, who were extremely rough. The Germans brought their inside right back to make a fourth half-back, hoping to score a break-away goal and hang on to their lead. By half-time the Indians must have been very worried, for while their opponents had failed to score, so had they. The relief early in the second half, when India's captain Balbir Singh did find the net, was very clear. It proved to be the only goal of the game, and for the first time India had failed to score more than one goal in an Olympic match. It was a disappointment quickly to be repeated.

Great Britain's semi-final with Pakistan was probably one of the best games of hockey ever played in the Olympics. Pakistan by now were a truly formidable side, but Britain probably had as good a combination as they had ever fielded. The Pakistanis, profiting from some suspect umpiring, were two up by the interval, but Britain pulled up to 3–2. Then for a glorious fifteen minutes the British team played like the best side in the world, but they could not score again, and for the first time India and Pakistan had qualified to play each other.

The rivalry between these two nations, whose players only nine years earlier had all been Indians, was very great. A grim defensive match took place and India scored the only goal at a disputed penalty corner. Pakistan had a similar "goal" disallowed, and the umpiring on the whole marred the game. There were many who doubted whether the result was fair. It was clear, however, that the rest of the world was beginning to catch up with the Indians, and that their world supremacy was in jeopardy.

In the third place match, Britain's often brilliant John Conroy was badly injured midway through the first half, and Germany won 3–1.

The eight teams eliminated in the groups took part in a classification tournament and, as a result of this, each team was given a ranking position for the first time. The Australians in their first-ever Games were awarded fifth place.

The physical and mental strain for competitors was great in Melbourne, but in 1960 at Rome, under the burning Italian sun, it was even greater.

Twenty-seven of the forty-four nations affiliated to the F.I.H. applied to take part in the games, but eleven had to be turned down because the International Olympic Committee had ruled that only sixteen countries could compete at the games in team sports. The F.I.H. tried to have this rule rescinded because they considered it against the Olympic ideal, but the same rule still applies today.

A welcome innovation at Rome was the drawing of lots for the forming of pools, and the introduction of quarter-finals. As a result of the pool matches, the four quarter-final matches were: India *v.* Australia; Kenya *v.* Great Britain; Pakistan *v.* Germany; Spain *v.* New Zealand. Australia and New Zealand qualified after play-offs with Poland and Netherlands respectively. It was the first time that Netherlands had failed to win a silver or bronze medal in their five Games appearances.

The improvement in world standards was quite clear when all four quarter-finals were won by single goal margins. India, Britain, Pakistan and Spain won through, Britain only after the longest game of hockey ever played. In torrid heat they battled with Kenya for fifty-seven minutes of "sudden death" extra time before Saunders-Griffith scored the all-important goal.

The two semi-finals, final and third place matches were all decided by a single goal too. Britain again went down by only 1–0 to India, and Pakistan defeated Spain by the same score. Spain proved their fine performance was no "flash in the pan" when they defeated Britain 2–1 in the third place match, to ensure a new name appearing on the medal winners' list.

India were no longer firm favourites to win the final, for Pakistan had lifted their "world" crown two years earlier when they had drawn 0–0 with India and won the Asian Games title on goal average.

If one expected an entirely defensive game again between the two great adversaries a surprise was in store, for Pakistan went straight on to the attack. It was a courageous move and it paid off, for they scored after thirteen minutes. It was a superb effort. Hamid, a tactical genius, created an opening in the Indian defence and slipped the ball through for his winger, Noor Alam. The winger crossed to Nasir at the top of the "D", the ball was stopped instantly and Nasir flicked it at lightning speed into the far corner of the goal.

After that, defences dominated, but there was still much to delight the crowd. As the game progressed it became clear there would be no further score, and when the umpire finally blew the last long blast on his whistle, there was a tremendous roar. India's long Olympic reign was over and Pakistan's captain climbed to the top of the rostrum—his team *Olympic Champions!*

The Olympic hockey title has remained in Asia for twenty-six years—the 1964 *Olympic Games are to take place in Asia for the first time.*

13

NOT A WORD ABOUT WINNERS!

MISS MELVYN HICKEY

Wimbledon, Worcestershire and England

Hockey is an amateur sport; and women's hockey is perhaps the most amateur of amateur sports. Men are much more interested, and quite logically, in who wins and who loses, in the final placings of the tournament or championship, in the top goal-scorers, the unbeaten sides and the possible "caps" for the coming internationals and Olympics. The majority of women hockey players when asked why they play the game will answer simply—because they like it. Women don't have to worry about the beer intake all the week, the long runs at the beginning of the season "to get fit", the necessary re-discovery of their lung capacity and the sudden cut down in smoking. For most of them it just means carrying on with their normal job—the housework, the office work, looking after the kids, doing the shopping, cooking the meals. They play for the love of the game and the fun it entails and there is not a word about winners! If they all went out there for an hour and ten minutes and cantered around changing sides, one might get the impression that the sheer joy of the exercise was sufficient reward. But of course results matter, and whilst it is all very noble to say, as a great many do and very sincerely, that they don't mind losing one bit providing it has been a good game, played in the right spirit and they've lost to a better side, there is and must be a very definite line drawn between the extremists—and which side of that line you are matters very much.

Personally I see no point in going out on to the field not caring whether my side wins or not—the whole object of the game is lost—and I can assure you that there was no such feeling as the English XI marched out on to the field in Baltimore (U.S.A.) in August 1963. Why, we would have felt unworthy to have been our country's representatives, and rightly so. But win or lose fairly and squarely—that's the aim; not by means foul and unfair, nor by deliberate abuse of the rules. If one accepts the game and a set of rules that govern it, I see no satisfaction in winning only by breaking them.

The England XI found themselves in Baltimore for the Eighth Quadrennial Conference and Tournament of the International Federation of Women's Hockey Associations. Sixteen international teams were there altogether, and also delegates from many of the member countries. It was hot and humid. It was the time of the year when all sensible people, if they could, got out of New York. We arrived. We stepped out of the plane, having left London Airport on a nice English summer's day (57 degrees F.), to be knocked back by a wall of heat. After the traditional welcome, we had a week in which to do what we liked. The hospitality, sight-seeing and friendships are everlasting memories of every conference. In New York there was the wondrous view from the Empire State building; the impressive skyline from Manhattan harbour; and later, the elegance and dignity of Washington and the Lincoln Memorial; the quiet cross-laden slopes of Arlington, and delicious lobster in Maine. But I am digressing—we soon got down to a week's practice at a camp in Maine. Then we moved on to Baltimore where the temperature dropped a little and the atmosphere became suddenly cosmopolitan and alive with hockey players arriving from as far afield as Trinidad and New Zealand, South Africa and Canada.

Inevitably amongst such a gathering there is contrast in everything. The teams' uniforms alone provided a colourful scene. Trinidad and Jamaica (how they loved the heat!) were in short tennis style skirts and shorts, Canada, Scotland and U.S.A. favoured tunics, and other countries wore either divided skirts or shorts. The blazers ranged from well-tailored hip-length box jackets, shortened versions of straight reefer coats, to the conventional school-girl type. Footwear was either shoes or boots (cleats if you're really U.S.), canvas or leather, bars or studs, stiff or pliable, heavy or light, striking or unobtrusive—but most of them seemed to be adequate on the somewhat bumpy, dry, not too close-cropped new grounds of Goucher College. There were many Indian-headed sticks in evidence; some half Indian, some good old English style. Everyone seemed happy with what they'd got—that's why they were using it, I guess. The goalkeepers' equipment varied from open-work slats on the pads to wicket-keeping type of pads and modified hockey versions, but no one goalkeeper I talked to seemed satisfied with the "kickers". Most of them had modified and reinforced them in some way. Perhaps women kick harder than sports goods manufacturers think!

There was none of the "we play for fun" spirit out there. Everyone was extremely proud to be representing their country, realising they were true ambassadors in every way, and determined to try harder than they had ever tried before, and not satisfied to finish second. This was not the time to be sentimental, indecisive, non-committal or modest.

There was no official result, no official champion team at the tournament—for everyone does not play everyone else. The policy of the International Federation of Women's Hockey Association has always been to further sportsmanship and playing the game purely for enjoyment and recreation. The competitive spirit has therefore been kept deliberately under control. Undoubtedly if there were a championship at stake the matches would definitely be played far more keenly; even so, tempers became frayed, play deteriorated and feelings were roused in some matches. England played six games, losing only to New Zealand (2–3); drawing with South Africa (1–1) and U.S.A. (0–0); and beating Australia (3–0), Netherlands (2–1) and Trinidad (1–0).

The different styles of play are fascinating. In the past it was England who set the style, England who sent her coaches out to other countries, England who won and England who was copied. This resulted in countries like South Africa and U.S.A., as well as our near neighbours, Scotland, Ireland and Wales, playing what became known as the English style of game. Continental countries like the Netherlands and Germany, now forces to be reckoned with, play a "continental" type of game very much influenced by the men's game and their male coaches. It is a fast, spasmodic, hard-hitting, stick-to-stick game. Our style is more flowing, longer "through" passes, less reversed stick play. There's good and bad in both, of course, and South Africa was the only one of the teams at the conference who appeared to have produced a style of play that contained the good points of both. They equalised in the last minute of their game with us and the match, the first of the tournament, was generally acknowledged to be the best seen at the conference.

But already teams are beating England: mainly because other countries have improved tremendously; but also because England has not the outstanding personalities that she had in her hey-day and also, I believe, because we must be ready to adopt the successful methods used and proved by our opponents and *add* them to our own game. The most important of these is obviously to use far more reversed stick play. No longer is it, or should it be, regarded as bad play and a sign of lazy feet. When I was taught, this was the case, and coaches and umpires alike had their whistles in their mouths the moment a stick was turned over, regardless of whether or not any obstruction was involved. We're a conservative lot in England, but gradually and steadily umpires are

being educated, and coaches are realising the importance of reversed stick play when used skilfully and knowledgeably. I believe it is the secret to our remaining one of the leading women's hockey-playing countries of the world.

14
WELCOME TO HOCKEY

Welcome thou game of doubtful joy,
  That all delight to play
All turn to thee, each fickle boy
  (The footer's stowed away).

Unfold before our wond'ring eyes
  Thy manifold delights,
The bully, foul, the merry cries,
  When stick on head alights.

How warm he looks—the man in goal
  (A kind of purple blue),
He dreams about the price of coal,
  And lets the ball go through.

How pleased is he with stick aloft,
  Who finds that after all,
The head which some have termed "so soft",
  Can stop a flying ball.

None frown a frown, none say a word,
  Good humouredly each chuckles,
To seem annoyed would be absurd,
  When banged upon the knuckles.

When sticks fly up and crack thin heads,
  When knees are getting crocky,
When stricken thousands seek their beds—
  What game is there like Hockey?

ANON,
Felstedian, 1901.

15

HOW TO SUCCEED AT HOCKEY AND STILL STAY HUMAN

NEIL FORSTER

Richmond H.C., England and Great Britain

Those unfortunates who knew me in my playing days may be expecting something controversial in an article under my name, but I am afraid the old fires are beginning to die down and years of banging one's head against a brick wall have had a dulling effect.

My hockey career started meteorically, spluttered uncertainly and finally subsided unnoticed. I was never a selectorial darling, but perhaps because of this, had a great deal of fun out of the game and acquired a fairly good insight into its administration and its play. There is a vast gap in my knowledge, however, in that I have never played regularly for a lower eleven in a club, and therefore I have probably missed the true flavour of the game: sad, because temperamentally (some might also say technically!) I am perhaps better suited for the fifth eleven than the first!

I did not play hockey in the Services (no one would select me), and started playing for my college at Cambridge University in 1948/49. I played for the university in my first season of hockey after leaving school four years before, obtained my first England trial the following year, and my first cap the year after—which perhaps confirms the excellent theory that players should not be rushed into internationals!

Therefore my experience is mainly of university, international and "top club" hockey, and it is in this sphere where the game, like most other amateur games in Britain, faces its main dilemma. The problem is whether one can compete at international level and still have those pleasures associated with the game which to some make it worth while. Do we really have to make the choice between nine o'clock bed and no vices or continuous orgies of drink and women or can there be some British compromise? I think the events of the past few years in most international sports have shown that the British temperament does not lend itself to dedication, if this dedication means a complete concentration on the game. In so many sports this has tended to produce an individualist who is so wrapped up in his own performance, and so convinced of his own superiority, that when something goes wrong he is temperamentally incapable of overcoming it and certainly incapable of admitting that there might be something in his own performance which could be improved. I think if one is going to play any game at top level there are certain heavy responsibilities in keeping fit and trying hard, but the man for the crisis is nearly always the man who has lived a fairly broad life and has learned to take the ups and downs of that life with a certain amount of sang-froid. By all means train and play hard, but repeated experience at the highest level shows that there are qualities of character which are just as important as fitness and technique, and that these qualities of character go with a balanced view of life. Perhaps one can go too far, but I would much prefer to have a couple of drunken Irishmen (though fairly sober at the time!) in a crisis than two dedicated schoolmasters. Also, the individual who concentrates on himself destroys the spirit essential in team games, and we all know that every great club side has been based on a sense of comradeship, which in turn is based on a flourishing and not always temperate social life: it is no less so at higher levels.

Having demolished the "dedication" faction I must equally condemn the "play for fun" boys. This attitude has led the British game into a stagnation since the war, which has been extremely damaging. Only in the past year or so have steps been taken to put the administration of the game on a proper basis, steps which should have been taken at least ten years ago. The failure of the Hockey Association to acquire a national ground at Richmond when it was available at such reasonable terms was disastrous, and sprang from the attitude of mind that, after all, "this is only a game we play on Saturdays and we do not want to get involved in large finance or anything sordid like that". If at that stage in 1953/54 the ground had been acquired and a good secretary appointed, how different the position might be now! This was a great tragedy to English and British hockey. Nonetheless we still have an absolute obligation to continue to compete in international events if only to show that we can do well and still remain human. Further, without the ultimate goal of international honours the incentive for the good young players dies and the game will die with it.

With a good secretary, backed by a sensible board of control, we can still compete and we can still win. The key to success in international competition rests on three things—the technique and ability of players; the selection of the right players at the right time; and leadership of those players when action is joined.

A lot of rubbish has been talked about the technique of players having deteriorated, but having played with several of the great pre-war players, I do not think it has. In fact, with the advent of the Indian stick actual stick-work has improved, although I do think that there is a deterioration in intelligent tactics, particularly amongst forwards. While, however, our technique has not deteriorated, it has fallen seriously behind other countries, and compared with them many of our players are technically and tactically incapable of carrying out simple manoeuvres. Concentration on team practice in recent years has been useful, but it has tended to obscure individual shortcomings, and it is individual coaching, even at international level, which is the prerequisite of team tactics. Individual coaching is particularly important in Britain because we mature very late, and in the key positions are not usually very good hockey players until we are approaching thirty or even over. Unfortunately by then many good and great players have either been discarded in the endless quest for youth or have been unable to maintain, with business and family commitments, the standard of fitness required. It is all the more important that such players should be used to impart the knowledge they have gained to the individuals who have taken their place. Of course, one of the reasons why we do mature late is because generally speaking our school coaching is not good. One has only to watch a small Indian or Dutch boy playing with a hockey stick and compare him with his British contemporary to realise that something is horribly amiss. There still seems to be a failure among schoolmasters to appreciate that the Indian stick has made many moves previously taboo highly fashionable, and the good old British idea of "playing for the team" must not be allowed to crush brilliant individual skill.

After technique one must have tactics, which involve intelligence and toughness, which involves character. Tactics involve intelligence because the really shattering moves are those which are *improvised* by players thinking faster than the opposition, and particularly by the ability of players to read the game several moves ahead so that they are in the right position at the right time. Character is in-born and is then tempered by environment. Nonetheless, the present club system does not always sort out the sheep from the goats in this respect, and while the County Championship was a step in the right direction, I think an intensification of club competition would bring out the best in players, without necessarily detracting from the enjoyment of the game. I have always thought, particularly now that transport is so much easier, that there should be a far more concentrated grouping of talent at club level, which may involve a return to the previous system of a fairly small circle of clubs attracting most of the good players and playing each other two or three times a year. This involves segregating the clubs into groups, which suggests a league system, but I am not yet convinced that a league as such is inescapable. I would prefer to see some other system of occasionally replacing teams in the top group by those that have consistently shown form in lower levels. At one stage I contemplated a sort of club "F.A. Cup" organised regionally on a knock-out basis, culminating in the champions of the regions playing each other to establish the "top club" of Britain. It might still be a good and stimulating idea. Whatever method is used I am sure an intensification of competition at top-club level is an essential pre-requisite of technique and character-building necessary at international level. At present the step is too great in Britain, whereas, in vivid contrast, the top clubs are of near-international standard in countries like Holland and India.

Assuming we manage to produce some reasonable players, we then have to face the hurdle of selection. This has been extremely weak over the past fifteen years, and I have wondered sometimes whether some selectors know anything about the game at all! My view is based on conversations with selectors and upon an assessment of the actions they have taken. Over the ten-year span in which I was involved in international hockey, the England selectors were blessed in having one back and two wing-halves virtually permanent fixtures, and I think from 1948 to 1957 employed only four inside-forwards: Fletcher, myself, Conroy and Borrett. Thus the team was virtually ready made, but on the other hand they signally failed to fill the other gaps and appeared to show a total lack of appreciation of the basic limits of certain players. In talking to some selectors after the game, I sometimes realised with despair that they had entirely missed the tactical point of the game and therefore often totally misjudged a man who played a subdued but vital tactical role; nor did they sufficiently study the conditions and opposition faced by each player in each match. When it came to Great Britain selections some farcical decisions were made. The team to South Africa in 1951 was a classic case, but I thought they had grown out of it until the selection for the Rome Olympics was announced. Here all the lessons of the 1956 Melbourne Games (of course, *nobody* who had been there was on the selectorial board!) were thrown aside, and a chronically unbalanced team was sent out. In addition, the basis of the team built up in practice was destroyed.

In fact, the standard in Rome was so low that the team did extremely well despite the selectors, and it would seem probable that a better selected side might have got through to the finals. However, to hold the semi-final place was a good achievement, particularly as after the 1956 Olympics so many good players retired or began to decline. Incidentally, I remain convinced that the 1956 British Olympic team was the best team in the world at that time (barring the Dutch team which did not compete), and with a little luck and drive should have won the gold medal.

Having knocked down the selectors, I must hasten to pick them up and dust them off. They have a thankless and difficult job, and they work extremely hard, mostly in their own time and at their own expense. The present trial system inevitably involves a huge amount of travelling and they are required to watch several games of very little utility from the selection point of view. The problem therefore seems to be to change the trial system so that fewer and younger selectors can be used. Ideally, the size of the selection committee (given that we would probably not accept a dictatorship) is perhaps five, of which one should be a chairman (somewhat older than the rest) and the others should be experienced internationals of recent vintage. The trouble is that such comparatively young selectors could not spare more than a few week-ends a year, and therefore I suggest that the present trial system should be entirely scrapped.

Players of actual or potential international value should be recommended from the various divisions and areas, and for this purpose each division would have a small selection committee consisting, again, of experienced international or divisional players, including some who are still playing. The players thus nominated, say forty to fifty, would be called together and put through a full week-end of trials under the eyes of the England selectors. In these trials the strengths and weaknesses of individual players would be fully explored, and the selectors would also have an opportunity of getting to know personally the characters involved. After making discards, a second week-end could take place—perhaps a fortnight later—and from this would emerge an England team of, say, fourteen players. This process could be completed fairly early in the year and then, I suggest, would be the time for the selected team to play matches against the divisions and other opponents, in order to acquire team work and give the divisions an opportunity to field a side. By the time the internationals commenced it seems to me that a pretty good side could be produced. Meanwhile, of course, as in all trials, the selectors would endeavour to watch certain players throughout the *whole* game and not just when they had the ball, in order to study their positional and tactical ability; and it would also be necessary to consult, particularly before finalising Olympic Games teams, club captains and others who may be aware of temperamental weaknesses. The final Great Britain selection could then play matches against the rest of England, Scotland and Wales, just as they would be required to play against the English divisions, before being pitted against the continentals or Indians.

Having got a side together, a manager and a coach are required, and it is these appointments which are vital. For Olympic games it is necessary to produce the spark which sets the team alight, and this is the manager's job, unless the captain is an exceptional character. The manager must be able to deal with men as well as boys, and must know his men well.

The coaching of an international side should, as I have mentioned earlier, be of two parts—the first being individual coaching, which is all-important, and the second being tactical coaching, which is itself dependent on the degree of individual talent available. As far as individual skill is concerned, there is no doubt that the Asian player is quicker of eye and wrist and, with the advantages of generally good and dry pitches has developed a ball control which we will probably in general not be able to rival. But the excuse that our pitches inhibit our skill is surely rebutted by the Dutch, who have consistently produced extremely good ball players on pitches which are often worse than ours. The problem therefore seems to lie in our school coaching and in the "hit and miss" style of many clubs. I am convinced, however, that tactically and physically we are in many ways superior to the Asian player, and that a combination of a fast open game with individual control can beat them. India and Pakistan have now developed a game which depends greatly on individual skill and short passing, so that it is very rare now to see a defence-splitting pass or a move of such speed that the defence cannot recover. The games tend to feature brilliant individual dribbling which we generally cannot match, but this should be amply countered by the precise execution of fast attacks based on quick intelligence and on our superior fitness, speed and robustness. But the key to this is basic control, because the faster the move the more control is required.

In defence we still produce world-class players and, since the war, I would put in this category Wyatt (who missed the best of his hockey in the war), Carnill, Robinson and Cockett (a little defensive, perhaps!). To them I would add now Davis and Neill (despite a little slowness on the turn), and I might add Walford if I had seen him play against top continental or Indian opposition. In goal Day could certainly rise to world-class heights and was—on these occasions—the best goalkeeper I've ever seen. As for forwards, there have been only Borrett (again partially a pre-war player) and Conroy, who learned his hockey in India and of whom it might be said he was world-class except against world-class! Fletcher* was talented, but, I think he would admit, not quite of world class. Bowden of Ireland was also very good, and O'Hara and Matheson a pair of backs approaching world class. Lastly,

* *Manager of Britain's Olympic team,* 1964.

there was Geoff Stocks—world class in almost any position—if he had wanted to be!

These players seem to stand out above the ordinary humdrum internationals, some of whom have been particularly bad. I think our failure to produce forwards is partly because of the strain thrown by our present style of play on inside-forwards, and the fact that, because of late maturing, players are often dropped before they reach their best or are no longer capable of retaining sufficient fitness to withstand the strain of inside-forward play.

But I see no real grounds for pessimism. Once we have completed the painful process of adapting ourselves in schools and clubs to the full advantage of the Indian stick—and this can be done by extensive use of indoor or hard pitches—then I think we will be able to hold our own at international level. I am talking of course of men's hockey, because British women's hockey still has to go through this painful process. We have qualities of determination and mental stability which others do not have, and we must not allow these qualities to be destroyed by an excessive dedication to the game, which produces just the opposite mentality. We need drive and fearless constructive criticism at all levels of administration, and we need, through the clubs, a keen and convivial spirit which will be produced by an intensification of competition on the field and of social life in the club. But we must move fast, because the lethargy of the last ten to fifteen years has meant that the game is in relative decline, and this process has to be reversed. It will not be easy, and it requires clear-headed and enthusiastic leadership at all levels. As for me, having so repeatedly and fruitlessly stuck out my neck during my career on such matters, I shall retire to my armchair in the hope that in the future the game will become so popular that I can watch it on television without having to get cold.

16

DHYAN CHAND—THE GREATEST PLAYER OF THEM ALL

R. SRIMAN

Sports Editor, *Times of India*

I had to go all the way to a distant hilltop in Rajashan, some three hundred miles from the Indian capital of Delhi to find Dhyan Chand, the greatest hockey player of all time—the legendary figure who played a vital role in India's Olympic successes in 1928, 1932 and 1936.

Dhyan, the Don Bradman or Stanley Matthews of hockey, is now India's national coach, and when I found him, at a hill-station clinic, the 58 year-old genius was teaching a handful of boys the finer points of the game. What I saw was one of the most startling experiences of my life. Chand appeared to give a gentle tap to the ball and, behold, the goalkeeper—no rabbit—nearly jumped out of his skin. The ball came searing towards him, then swerved like some Alec Bedser outswinger and ricocheted into the top corner of the net. Chand had "chopped" and hit the ball, all in one action. Then he asked one of the trainees to hit the ball from the wing as fast as he could. As the ball sped towards him, Dhyan, with a slight wrist action, diverted the ball past the goalkeeper.

Dhyan Chand

"Look, I'll score now with my back to the goal", he said, and, as a pass came from the centre of the field, the maestro, with his back to the goalkeeper, moved slightly to his left and hit the ball with the reverse side of the stick. The bewildered goalkeeper was again a helpless spectator.

Despite his age, Chand scooped, pushed, dribbled, and showed a hundred other tricks, in the manner of a true champion.

Dhyan Chand came from a family who had served for generations in an Indian Regiment and he learnt all his hockey in the Indian Army which he joined as a Sepoy. It will gladden British hearts to know that he received all his early encouragement from British Army officers, who quickly recognised his genius. Whatever the standard of the game, a surprisingly large number of Britons, not exactly known for their love of hockey, would always turn out if the dark, lissom Chand was playing.

Though born at Allahabad—Nehru's town—Dhyan migrated with his parents to Jhansi. He and his equally famous younger brother, Rup Singh, joined the Jhansi Heroes, and quickly this team became a dynamic outfit. Chand used to return to his home town on annual leave every year, and the occasion was something for celebration. For a month or so, there would be nothing but hockey at Jhansi—morning, afternoon and evening. The number of players the two brothers attracted to the game is legion.

Chand was first known to the world outside India in 1926, when he toured Australia and New Zealand as a member of the Indian Army team. Then, as in 1928 when he went with the Indian team to the Amsterdam Olympics, he became the idol of all who watched him. Even those who had had no insight into the game were fascinated by his amazing flexibility and manoevrability. The stick, on the continent, had been dubbed as something of a lethal weapon, but in Dhyan Chand's hands it was like some magic wand. If the ball had been glued to the stick, he could not have achieved a greater effect. Spectators began watching Dhyan Chand with the same stupefied amazement as children look adulatingly at the theatricals of the Harlem Globetrotters.

A thorough gentleman, unassuming and gentle, he was probably the most popular of Indian players. At a time when India's captaincy in any sport was offered only to those with some social standing, Chand, despite being an "other rank", took over the leadership of the team to take part in the West Asiatic Games at Delhi and, later, of the 1936 Berlin Olympic team.

Had the war not intervened the world would have seen much more of Chand. Such was his fame that in 1947/48, even though he was well past his prime, he was pressed into service on a tour of East Africa because the hosts insisted that he be included in the team. Incredibly he was still better than the best in India then, and he returned home top goal-scorer.

Chand is known for his unrivalled artistry, his matchless dribbling and his peerless scoring prowess, but his true greatness lay in his ability to part with the ball selflessly to the unmarked colleague near by. With rustic simplicity—he did not have much education—the great centre-forward would shout instructions to his colleagues at the top of his voice. He rebuked sternly on the field, but off it did not bear the slightest malice. In fact, his uninhibited frankness endeared him to all, and no one who played with him ever hung on to the ball a second longer than necessary. Therein lay not only his success but also that of those who played with him, particularly his younger brother Rup Singh, whom Chand is never tired of rating as a greater player than himself. "The gods have been kind to me," he once said, "but I am not half as good as Rup."

Chand retired from the Army as a Major, and now spends his time coaching coaches at India's National Sports Institute at Patiala in the Punjab. It would be too much to expect him to be as brilliant a coach as he was a player, but there can be no greater inspiration than to watch him, even today. Those who now preside over the destinies of Indian hockey pressed him into taking charge of the Indian team for the 1963 Lyon Tournament, with the result that the Indian team was voted the best in the festival, ahead of Pakistan!

Dhyan is still giving a great deal to the game, but, unlike leading lights in other sports, he has not had his due. Although the father of a family of eleven—he has had no "benefit", and has been unable to lay his hands on his life's savings in the Army Thrift Fund. When partition of the Indian sub-continent came with independence his savings, some Rs.15,000 were left with a treasury which became part of Pakistan. Chand is still in correspondence over this money, but a man to whom no problem on the hockey field was knotty during his playing days, is no nearer a solution despite the best efforts of friends on each side of the border. Some day, one hopes, this great and true sportsman will get his deserts.

17

DAD'S RAVING AGAIN

JOHN BARTLETT

East Grinstead H.C., Oxford University and Sussex

"Fred! I wouldn't go into the drawing-room if I were you, Dad's doing his hockey rave again."

"Poor old chap! Trouble with you, Jim, is you've no feeling for history and no imagination. I rather like listening to some of the stuff he comes up with. Exaggerates, though; hockey couldn't really have been like that only twenty years ago."

"What, all that nonsense about playing hockey for fun? You've got to take that with a pinch of uranium. Still, Mum says he's had delusions since he fell off the mono-rail coming back from Hurlingham after the 1975 Cup Final."

"Some game that must have been—wish I'd seen it. They were talking about it on steam radio in a scrapbook programme the other night—Tottenham Hotspur 5, Corinthian-Casuals 3—last time an amateur side got into the Cup Final, you know. That was the great Tottenham side of the mid 1970's. Dad says that when they got rid of the "hockey-for-fun" gang and encouraged professionalism, the game caught on like wildfire, swept the country, killed soccer in a couple of years. Mostly the influence of women, he says; in the old days they liked speedway, wrestling, motor-racing, odd sports with an underlying risk of death or serious injury and, of course, professional hockey with twenty-two superbly fit players all armed, brought them out in their millions on a Saturday afternoon. And they weren't disappointed. Lots of deaths in the early years of the professional game, and the gates went up and up—Tower Hill, Tyburn and Twickenham all rolled into one for five bob on a Saturday afternoon."

"'Course the Hockey Association nearly ruined it with that new rule of theirs last year. Remember, Fred? 'If a player shall premeditatedly slay or harm an opponent, having in the umpire's opinion raised his stick above shoulder level, he may, at the umpire's discretion, be asked to leave the field for a time considered suitable by the umpire.' Usual loopholes though, Dad says; always a bit woolly in their legislation, and in the first season after a new rule is passed there's always been a lot of blowing in the other umpire's half."

"Seriously though, Jim, the old boy comes out with some splendid reminiscences sometimes, doesn't he? Told me the other day that amateur clubs in the old days didn't train, prepared their own pitches, didn't get expenses paid and some even drank with their opponents after the game."

"Wouldn't do now, would it? Three nights training a week or not eligible for selection, government-subsidised stadiums, expenses plus, and egg and chips after the game, and into the chara. The social side of hockey has certainly gone for good. Dad says it was the sennapod-in-the-soup incident at the official banquet before the Irish match in 1969 that was the beginning of the end of the social side. Too much risk in conviviality the night before, if you're playing for a £500 bonus the next day."

"Another thing he said was that he used to go abroad with some team with a most peculiar name, pay his own fare, and actually stay with one of the foreigners they were playing against. Sounds very naïve, doesn't it?—but could have been fun."

"Still, I wouldn't go back to the old days, would you, Fred? The national side's been unbeaten for five years and they used to get some dreadful drubbings (in the old days). The way the national coach has trained those three Indians, two Germans, two Spaniards, an Irishman, a Dutchman, an Englishman and a Japanese into such a superb combination beats me! Did you see us beat Holland last Saturday? Marvellous—made me proud to be English!"

18

THE GAME GROWS UP

RICHARD HOLLANDS

Editor, *Hockey News*

In the autumn of 1963 the Hockey Association, having decided that its affairs had outgrown the compass of purely honorary officials, appointed a professional secretary, the first full-time paid official it has ever employed. After seventy-seven years—the Association was founded in 1886—hockey had ceased to be a spare-time sport and was facing up to the realities of existence as a viable activity, with a contribution to make to the education and culture of the country in the twentieth century. And about time too!

In origin, hockey is a very ancient game. We know the Greeks had a word for it. But in its modern form the game emerged out of the hustle and bustle and inventiveness of mid-nineteenth-century England, along with association football, Rugby football and a variety of sports and pastimes, not all of which have passed the test of time. Conditions in those early days were unfortunately not as favourable as they might have been for this offspring of an ancient stock.

Unlike soccer or rugby football, hockey cannot be played on any old piece of open ground. It needs smooth, firm, fast turf, on which the ball will run straight and true, and the speed and skill of the game can find full expression. The only grounds of that sort in existence at the time were cricket grounds, and they were available only in winter. So hockey became a winter game which, by rights, it never should have been, and—worse still—accepted a status of dependence upon cricket, dependence not just for so many pence and pounds, but dependence for the very means of existence, the good earth itself.

These two factors have largely conditioned its development in

England. The landlord-tenant relationship between cricket and hockey clubs which resulted has been a burden on the back of the tenants, and still is in a great many cases. Cricket clubs, like all landlords, took the most they could get by way of rent and other benefits, which sometimes included bar profits, and gave the least they could in exchange. The sacred square, invariably sited plumb in the middle of the ground, must be roped off and remain inviolate. It must include not merely the area between the popping creases, which is all that matters, but between the lines of the wickets and very often some yards beyond where, when May comes, the bowlers will in no time do ten times the damage that a wing-forward or half might inflict. The effect of this, in a great many cases, has been that the pitches which hockey clubs rent flanking the square are reduced to the minimum width permissible under the rules (fifty-five yards) and sometimes below that, whereas the maximum of sixty yards is indispensable to any club wanting to play good-class hockey.

Besides having to make do with narrow pitches, hockey clubs often find themselves unable to secure the thorough preparation of the ground essential to keep it in condition for winter use. More often than not, the groundsmen are employed by the landlords and pay little heed to the requirements of the tenant, however reasonable. The result is that grounds which would be playable without damage if properly cared for are declared unfit for use far too often, with consequent cancellations that react to the detriment of the hockey club membership.

Complaints to the cricket committee are likely to fall on deaf ears. So long as the "square" is carefully tended, nothing else matters to them. The fact that the hockey club may have to go without a match for their money is of no great concern beside the fact that the outfield remains unscarred. The hon. treasurer gets the rent just the same.

Short of cancellation, the best of hockey teams often have to play on pitches where the grass is too long, the worm casts have not been broken up, the surface has not been rolled and the marking is incorrect. The difficulty in acquiring pitches of the right size in the right condition, added to the unnecessarily high risk of cancellation, has created a strait-jacket which has restricted both the rate of growth and the tactical development of the game. Bad grounds are disastrous in their effect on the standard of play because the ball cannot be accurately controlled, and hit-and-run becomes the order of the day.

Why has such a state of affairs been tolerated for so long? Mainly, though not entirely, for economic reasons. The alternative to using cricket grounds was to buy other grounds and be prepared to meet the cost of draining, levelling, sowing, fertilising and maintenance, which in real terms was an expensive operation even in the good old days when a penny was a week's pocket money for a schoolboy and a shilling a soldier's pay for a day. No one was prepared to put up the money, and the welfare state was still a long way off.

Moreover, to remain free and sufficient to the day and game, with no financial commitment other than a weekly rent, suited the temper of the players and their times. Hockey in its early days in England was centred on a few of the more exclusive schools, Oxford and Cambridge Universities, and some of London's wealthier residential districts, Blackheath, Ealing, Molesey, Surbiton, Teddington and Wimbledon. Its members mostly belonged to the upper middle-class, and were fiercely amateur in their outlook on sport. To them professionalism was a dirty word and professionals an inferior breed. They remained so until the First World War swept some of the class-conscious cobwebs out of our heads for good and all.

About this time, too, football was shocking our grandfathers with the scandal of professionalism—it was then an amateur game—just as football shocks us to-day with scandals of a deeper dye. The hockey fraternity were determined no breath of this suspicion should blow in their direction. The Hockey Association was only six years old when the following words were added to Rule 1: "... and only clubs and associations composed entirely of amateurs are eligible for membership." At the same time a new Rule 12 was adopted in the following terms: "That no affiliated association, and no club belonging to the Hockey Association or any affiliated association, and no player or member of any such club, shall institute or take part in any hockey challenge cup, or prize competition ...", which has always been interpreted to include leagues.

Though this rule has been relaxed in a few specified cases—the most notable and recent being to permit the introduction of a county championship—it has remained in force ever since, and is still regarded by the Council of the Hockey Association as a cardinal principle. It has been instrumental in keeping professionalism out of the game, by leaving it poor and unattractive to persons having an eye to the main chance.

It has done more than that. It has also deprived the game of the stimulus of competition and the element of challenge, which to most healthy young men and women is at once the fascination and fulfilment of sport. Without that stimulus, hockey has drifted down a pleasant backwater, avoiding the seething waters of the main stream of sport but losing in the process vitality and enterprise and the pursuit of any recognisable objective. There being no competition, there was no incentive to improve the standard of play. Small grounds, bad grounds, what did they matter? You hit a little harder, ran a little faster, if you could. It was all great fun. What else mattered?

Did we not play the game better than anyone else anyway? And, indeed, we did more often than not: better that is than Ireland, Scotland, Wales and France, who up to the First World War were our only rivals, except for one encounter with Germany which ended in England's favour by nine goals to one!

When in the 1920s the Olympic Games threatened to disturb their peaceful backwater, the Hockey Association retreated still further into seclusion and withdrew from the Olympic tournament, in which gold medals had been won in 1908 and 1920. Olympic hockey, they thought, was unpleasantly reminiscent of those very cup and league competitions which they would not tolerate at home. But backwaters, though inviting to the casual visitor, have their dangers for those who linger too long. Life stagnates in them. In the twenty years between the wars, while England and Britain kept themselves to themselves, except for the occasional fixture against one of our nearer continental neighbours, Germany and Holland virtually eliminated England's long lead in the management and practice of the game. Farther afield, India were setting new standards of technique and teamwork evolved on the smooth and sunbaked pitches of a tropical land—standards which made them champions of the world for thirty years.

The astonishing thing to me is not that this happened but that hockey retained its hold in England, continued to attract enough of the youth of the nation not merely to make good natural losses but to provide for steady, if rather slow, expansion. It would not and could not have done so without intrinsic qualities that appeal to games players. I have been told many times by schoolmasters, who are also games-masters, that hockey stands very near the top in the popular estimate. Among reasons given for this popularity are that it satisfies the natural instinct to strike something, preferably a ball because that gives the best response; it satisfies also the strong impulse in most of us to be part and parcel of a team; it is fast and free and open; hands and feet, head and heart, all have their part to play, and the long and the short, the weak and the strong, meet on more or less level terms, subject only to fitness and stamina.

These are the qualities which account for the hold the game exerts on those who have once made acquaintance with it. Rugby is not a game for the frail or the fussy, and not even its most ardent supporters would, I think, claim that it is an intellectual exercise. In association football there is no place for the strength and skills of the hands, the most highly developed of the human limbs. Hockey has no such limitation. Its appeal is both physical and intellectual. It can be played by either sex and at all ages from seven to seventy, and if anyone thinks that to be an exaggeration I am prepared to give chapter and verse.

This is because the use of brute force is barred: "...There shall be no charging, kicking, shoving, tripping, striking at or holding an opponent by any means whatsoever . . ." Hampering or intimidating an opponent also incur penalty. So does hooking or striking at the stick. Skill and speed, stamina and accumulated know-how—these are the weapons of the hockey player. They combine on good turf and in the established framework of the game to produce a pattern of movement, swift, scientific and dazzling in its variety. Properly promoted and played by professionals on perfect grounds, hockey would present a splendid spectacle and football would have a rival for the allegiance of the sporting public.

Played as it is and will long continue to be, by amateurs only, it is still a fascinating game, well adapted to the needs of the second half of this century. Being suitable for girls as well as boys, hockey is the ideal game for the comprehensive schools now coming into existence in increasing numbers and destined in all probability to play a major part in the educational system of the future. This is bound to lead to the merits and attractions of the game becoming more and more widely appreciated and will add momentum to the normal process of expansion.

Before long hockey will require not one secretary but a permanent secretariat, and the game which started in these islands a century ago will be exerting its influence all over the Commonwealth and among many peoples of the former colonial territories of Africa and Asia, who are ready and willing to cultivate other links with Britain now that the political tie has been broken.

If the Hockey Association are to retain their voice in the councils of this growing game, of which they were the founders, Britain—and that means of course England as the greater part of Britain—must remain one of its leading exponents. That can only be done if the H.A. make up their minds upon the basic methods to be employed and the type of player to be encouraged. This is not so easy as it may sound. Until the last ten years or so coaching was unheard-of, and no accepted theory of the game had ever been committed to paper. Now, at last, attempts are being made to evolve a theory and set up a coaching organisation.

Committees exist for both purposes and, though committees are often long-winded, their very existence is a reminder that the problems will not solve themselves. The means, too, are now coming to hand, as a niggardly Chancellor grudgingly repays a few thousands out of the millions he has taken out of sport. I believe that so far as natural talent goes, England can hold her own with any country in the world, and that once this talent has been wedded to a sound theory and constructive practice of the game, the teams that represent England and Britain will again become the admiration of all-comers.

OLYMPIC GAMES. FINAL *Rome 1960. India* v. *Pakistan.* (*Photo. Associated Press*)
A thrilling moment as India's Bhola (stick aloft) is frustrated by Pakistan's goalkeeper, Abdul Rashid (12). Pakistan won 1–0 to end India's 32 year long reign as Olympic champions. L–to–R: Udham Singh, Noor Alam, Atif (3), Rasool, Bhola and Rashid.

NEW ZEALAND v. *NETHERLANDS. Olympic Elimination round game. Rome 1960. New Zealand's Abrams (left arm raised) covers his goal as a Netherlands shot sails over the crossbar. New Zealand's goalkeeper is Schaefer. The match was drawn 1–1.*

(Photo. United Press International)

19

HOCKEY FOR "THE COLLECTIVES OF PHYSICAL CULTURE"

Translated extracts from the introduction of *ХОККЕН НА ТРАВЕ* (*Hockey on Grass*) by P. EPIGINA and M. I. OREGOVA—an official Russian text book published in Moscow in 1955

Both the party and the state attach great importance to the development of physical culture and sport in our country. Physical culture and sport strengthen health, mind and character. They develop patriotism, collectivism, will-power and courage. All these attributes are indispensable for the citizens of the Soviet Union—builders of Communism.

Amongst many aspects of sport, games occupy one of the most important positions from the point of view of popularity and usefulness... Hockey, on grass, is a new game for our country.

It is true that Russia has known for long such games as "Kuban", "Kotel", "Lahon" and others, where players were chasing balls with curved sticks.

. . . Hockey forms part of the Olympic programme. Because of its character the game is ideal for the over-all physical development of the players.

Hockey does not require a great outlay on equipment. The game is bound to be popular in pioneer camps, collective farms, clubs, services, etc. One must expect in fact that hockey will find followers all over the country.

The rules have a lot in common with ice hockey, and therefore it should be quite easy for the players of the latter to pick up the principles of grass hockey.

This book is meant for the collectives of physical culture. In it we give the basic principles of the game. Its main object is to give both players and coaches some idea of the principles and techniques of the game.*

**Editor's Note: See ROUND THE WORLD, page 177.*

20

SELECTORS

AN INTERNATIONAL SELECTOR

This is a sad story; and in this writer's view, the selectors of both the Hockey Association and the Upper Sedgebury Grammar School Old Boys Fourth Eleven are as one.

Who selects the selector and what are his qualifications? To get on the list you must become known as a keen, interested type who often watches games; one who has sufficient money to afford the travelling expenses and one who can get time off. You do not necessarily have to be an ex-international or county player. This is certainly not just a sour conclusion after reading who has been selected for a particular match, for research shows some selectors have never even played the game!

If there is a vacancy, it is worth trying a bit of flattery on the other selectors. If there is no vacancy, some sustained criticism of the oldest and least popular selector is worth while—and with any luck you will be in.

The process might cost you a few drinks, but never mind. Once you are a selector any candidate for selection will always rush to buy you a drink, except after the last game of the season, when it is surprising how mean they become. At this stage the experienced selector can turn with fruitful condescension to lesser mortals, who will always buy a drink for the privilege of talking to you or telling you how they used to play or whom they would select.

What is a selector's philosophy? It's a thankless job and he must realise from the start he can never be right: at best, he can do only what is expected of him, but since different people have different expectations, even that is well-nigh impossible. He must realise, *ab initio*, that he is there to be shot at and—have no illusions—everybody will certainly shoot and probably undercut.

How does he select? He has twenty-two players to watch. If he umpires, he must restrain his concentration from wandering because his professional standards get the better of him. He must not take an interest in the result. Does he ponder on the pitch—too grassy, too soft or dry, level here or bumpy there? You usually find in Britain that trials are held in the mud and wet of January or early February for internationals to take place in late dry March.

Let us give the selector a mere five minutes' concentration on Colours' outside-right—which is too much anyway, because that would mean 110 minutes for the whole twenty-two players. How does the winger position himself? Does he blend with his inside-right; is he getting good service? If he is getting bad service, what would he be like with good? Is his opposing half in top form or is he off-colour? Is he on form but frustrated by the inefficient back behind him? Is the umpire penalising him wrongly; has he a cold, has he quarrelled with his girl-friend, is it just indigestion, couldn't he sleep last night because the central heating in the hotel was too high?

Has the selector a cold, a headache, jaundice or, as it's a cold day, is nature calling him or is it just raining and his shoes are leaking?

What does it matter? A fifth eleven goalkeeper could tell you that Whites' outside-right is better than Colours'. It's as simple as that.

Now for the actual selection. It is absolutely incredible what strange ideas your co-selectors have. Besides, player "A" is a jolly nice chap; you have the advantage of knowing him well, he plays for your club and for your county; and as for that chap who thinks "B" should be chosen, well, it's probably more than a coincidence they both come from the north. (If you are English, for north read North Wales or North Scotland. Because of the political situation, you must on no account read N. Vietnam.)

Well, after a little bit of feeling from the others, broadmindedness on your part, and sometimes complete exhaustion, a team is chosen. You disagree completely of course, but *esprit de corps* and all that, means you must pretend otherwise and that the selection committee's choice is in fact yours. The really infuriating thing this time is the centre-forward. If you have to be overruled, you feel as a selector you ought at least to be allowed to tell him: "For Pete's sake, tackle back or follow up" or something. But you are not allowed to. That is probably the coach's job. His views differ from yours and from those of your moronic colleagues. He is going to order them to play the 4, 3, 2, 1, 1, 0 formation.

What about dress? During the trials wear your oldest and warmest clothes, especially the latter, because it is sometimes just a little cold in January. The scruffier your clothes, the easier it is to escape recognition. This may enable you to overhear—incognito—the opinions of spectators or players, which is a great help when you do not know what to do and cannot wait that long to read the views of the recognised hockey journal. On "the day" your clothes should be your status symbol. A shooting stick, a sheepskin jacket, immaculate tweeds, your country's floral emblem in the buttonhole; perhaps a cigar. A bowler hat and a despatch case are quite out of place.

If you go by car do not take one of the players. He may get an unguarded opinion out of you (damages for slander can be penal), and when you are on your own you have to be a bit thick-skinned to let him buy you a lunch. Besides, the co-efficient of ego satisfaction increases directly with the audience, and if you get a warm glow from an audience unit of one it might be as well to consult a psychiatrist. By train and with your selector colleagues, travel first-class. As between you and the team it helps build up an aura of remoteness. Without your colleagues, be condescending and travel with the players.

Finally, your retirement? Life gets a bit sad when the first thrill has worn off. You can't enjoy a match and cheer your side. You have to keep note of how the left-half is shaping, if the inside-left is tackling back into the gap and all that jazz. At any dinners you are usually pushed off to the end of the table or the side, next to the local club's assistant match secretary, auditor or groundsman. Any pretty young girls at the dance go for the callow youth and especially for "C", who played a shocking game and doesn't seem to care. Someone is talking about technique with the Indian-type sticks. You can't stand the sight of them, and thank goodness all your hockey was played with a proper English stick. You still feel that wrench at your back when you tried to flick the ball that went behind the goal. Golly! It must be nearly fifteen years since you gave up playing, and then you'd had a pretty long innings. You don't mind buying your own drinks now, and it would be rather nice to sit back and criticise those other chaps. In fact, it might be downright enjoyable.

21

THE BEST OF BOTH WORLDS

DICK DALUZ

Mid-Surrey H.C., Surrey & India

It is an accepted fact by the hockey-playing nations that India and Pakistan are the finest exponents of the game in the world, and the question often poses itself: "Why are they so superior?" In my opinion, the answer is very simple—their players are completely dedicated to the game from an early age.

Up to 1960, hockey in India was not taught, and no official coaching organisations lectured in schools and clubs; individuals learnt by trial and error—pushing, hitting, flicking, and dribbling, both at walking pace and then at top speed. Dribbling a ball for hours gives a strength and flexibility of wrist which enables one to acquire a high degree of efficiency in ball control.

There is a universal tendency among boys during play to take on the mantle of the international stars of their country. Just as in England one can overhear kids professing to be a Ted Dexter or a Jimmy Greaves, so the children of India can be heard at play vying with each other to be like the hockey "greats", Dhyan Chand, Rup Singh, or Penniger. To a passer-by, the fantasy surrounding these childish aspirations might sound quite amusing, but they show an instinctive leaning towards higher levels of sport. It is uncanny to see how the boys acquire varying degrees of dexterity with the stick and smooth body control.

The players graduate from the common to the schools, where the game is played every day for three to four months of the year. The keen rivalry fostered by inter-house matches and games against neighbouring schools gives the beginner his first baptism of competitive hockey and an added incentive to acquire a prowess comparable to their international idols. The goal of each one is the attainment of his school first eleven colours, while at the same time the boys learn to discipline themselves by playing as a team rather than as individuals.

On leaving school, boys automatically gravitate to those clubs which hold pride of place in the highly competitive field of First Division hockey. To many the transition proves far too great, but some go on to provincial level and take the steps toward reaching their boyhood dream of representing their country in an Olympiad.

My introduction to league hockey was in 1939, when I played for St. Joseph's College in Calcutta's Second Division for one full season. The following year saw my debut in the Premier League. For me this was a very auspicious year, because in my first game I played against the redoubtable Calcutta Customs, who were at that time one of the leading hockey-playing teams in India, including no fewer than eight current internationals.

Hockey in India is played on the same basis as football in England, with league and cup matches, which add to the interest and are a prime factor in India's superiority in this field of sport. The league in Calcutta is made up of five divisions, each with between eighteen to twenty teams. About a fortnight before a season starts, players report to their clubs for a daily training routine. These sessions, which last for an hour or more, are rigidly enforced, players having to find a very good reason for missing them.

The league is followed by the usual run of cup matches, culminating in the choice of a team of fourteen players to take part in the Inter-State Tournament.

This is held at a different venue each year—usually in one of the principal cities of India—and teams from all over the country assemble for a fortnight to do battle for the coveted prize of Champions of India. The championship is run on a knock-out basis, and 40,000 or more spectators a day flock through the turnstiles to watch the cream of Indian hockey players displaying their talents before the critical gaze of the selectors. To a player who is having his initiation in this grade of hockey, the sound of thousands of wildly cheering partisan hockey enthusiasts is quite an ordeal, and to come out of it unscathed is a great achievement.

The tournament is given tremendous coverage in the newspapers, as indeed are minor matches. This is an excellent feature of Indian and Pakistani hockey, as both the public and the selectors are constantly aware of the potential of various players. As a result, several have risen from the obscurity of lower-grade hockey to the Premier League and on up the ladder.

My introduction to international hockey was in 1941, when preparations for the Palestine Games were in progress. Selection meant that two of my boyhood dreams were realised—one to see and meet Dhyan Chand, the other to play for India. I discovered that in the first trial the great maestro was playing for the opposition. The outcome was a close-up of the wizard, which left me in no doubt as to my inadequacy as a player. However, with guidance and encouragement from such players as J. Gallibardy, G. Nyss and C. Tapsell—whose names were already household ones—I was lucky enough to retain my place as an international.

With the outbreak of the Second World War, there was a decline in the standard of Indian play which, I believe, can be partly attributed to the waning of interest because the Olympic Games were temporarily suspended.

Everyone in India welcomed the news that the Olympics were to be resumed at Wembley in 1948. Olympic year in India has a special significance, the hockey played being of the highest quality because each player is straining himself to the limit in order to attain his colours. As the fortnight for the State Championship approaches, tension reaches fever pitch. Every morning and evening players can be seen out on their own, doing training stints in their bid for perfection. Hockey enthusiasts throughout the country make daily predictions on the composition of India's team, while the aspirants for this supreme honour strut around like peacocks, enjoying the adulation of the hockey masses, and preening themselves before the selectors.

This is unfortunately a time when politics enter the field of sport. Selection is made by vote, and each State is concerned in obtaining the greatest number of votes for its own players. In racing parlance, this would be called "jockeying for position". The minor Provinces are usually outvoted by the larger ones unless there is a player of exceptional ability who cannot be overlooked. The merits and demerits of players are tossed about, and the selectors are under constant pressure from the States and, for that matter, from the Press.

At the end of the Provincial Tournament, twenty-two names are announced of those who are to go into strict training for six weeks prior to embarking for the Games. To all players with aspirations, the announcement is a merciful release from the months of strain and tension, although to some it is the end of the road.

During the next six weeks, all the players are housed in one camp, to facilitate the daily training routine. No player is permitted to leave the camp, except on Sundays, which are rest days. The coach knows he cannot teach his charges the game, and his main objective is moulding them into a cohesive body, with a singleness of purpose that will be beneficial to the side. Training hard together, a camaraderie soon springs up between the players, and this goes a long way to building team spirit which is such an essential quality of a great team.

Training is divided into two periods confined to the coolest parts of the day, the morning session from five till seven, and the evening from five to seven, the players having the rest of the day to themselves. The morning session is devoted to attaining peak physical condition, and is divided up into half-hour classes of P.T. exercises; dribbling with and without a ball the full length of the pitch, practice at basic principles such as stopping, hitting, pushing, flicking, etc., and perhaps tactical talks. To some, the exercise of dribbling the ball down the pitch may sound quite relaxing, but when done in a crouched position twenty times or more without a break it can be absolute hell!

The evening training consists of a full game played between the twenty-two players for ninety minutes without even a half time. This continuous play is of immense value, because each player is then able to play full stretch for the official seventy minutes without really being overtaxed. After the game the rest of the evening is taken up by talks between the coach and players. Here, suggestions are made and various theories put forward for the correction of faults noticed during the game; exercises involving co-ordination between half-backs and backs, and half-backs and forwards, are repeated over and over again until there is complete understanding between all departments. Knowing that all his moves will be anticipated and that he will never have to look up to see where his companion is creates a wonderful feeling in a player and means that the game can be played at a much faster pace.

As the six weeks draw to a close, there is a distinct air of depression in the camp because each player knows that five members will be denied their Colours. After training so hard and living in harmony for such a long period, it is really a bitter blow to be left out of the final reckoning.

I was one of the unlucky ones in 1948 and was bitterly upset at missing the trip to the London Olympiad. I determined to regain my international place, and four years later my dreams were realised when I was chosen for the Fifteenth Olympiad which was to take place at Helsinki in Finland. The tournament was held on a knock-out basis, and it is history that India retained her world mastery and won the gold medal for the fifth successive time. Helping India to another fine success and taking part in an Olympiad was a most wonderful experience.

While I was in Europe with the Indian team I became increasingly aware that life for a person like myself was very different there from that in India and I could not help but be impressed by what I saw. I did not need to dwell for long to realise that this was for my wife and family and, one year after taking part in the Helsinki Games, we emigrated to England.

People these days talk about what they can get out of sport. I have always thought that hockey is a game to be enjoyed. I shall ever be grateful that I took part in the Olympics, but I am even more indebted to the game for giving me the opportunity to see the European way of life.

I joined the Indian Gymkhana club in London, for it was good to be amongst people I knew, and at first I was content playing against only mediocre opposition, for I had had my fill of top-class competitive hockey.

I was asked on numerous occasions by the British international, John Conroy, to join his club, Mid-Surrey, one of the leading London clubs, but it was only in 1958, after I had played as a guest against Oxford University, that I decided to agree. The wonderful spirit shown by the team, both on and off the field, impressed me tremendously and was a factor in my move to become a member of the club, of which I am now proud to be captain.

I very soon realised after a full season with them what I had missed during my first five years in England—the tremendous social side, which goes a long way to promoting friendship among players which, in turn, leads to friendly rivalry on the field. After joining Mid-Surrey, my post-Olympic decision to retire from competitive hockey was altered. During a very convivial evening at my club, I was asked (and I am told, agreed) to play for the county. Surrey did me the honour of awarding me my colours, and I very much regretted having refused to play for them for so many years. It is a great pity that the clock cannot be put back.

Having played ten years of hockey in England, and having watched, played with or against most of the leading players, I marvel that the British team has maintained a high standard in the international field—for the game is played under appalling conditions. British players can never hope to match the Indian or Pakistani players in stickwork and ball control until, and unless, the game is played in conditions conducive to good hockey.

Competitive hockey in Britain is confined to divisional and county games, interspersed with international matches between the home countries. With no league or cup commitments to contend with, a vast majority of players accept the game merely as a form of relaxation. I would not for a moment suggest the game should be run on a league basis because conditions are all against such a move, but without the incentive that competitive hockey fosters, it is extremely difficult to attain a standard comparable to India and Pakistan who play the game daily.

Countries like Holland, Germany and France—to name a few—are now taking a far greater interest in the building of their national teams, and if Britain is to maintain her high position in the world of hockey, then there has got to be a completely new approach to the game. Week-end training sessions are not enough; time has to be found for an intensive training course to enable the members of the side to form themselves into a cohesive body, which is absolutely vital for winning.

Since 1953 the game in England has made tremendous advances both in style and technique. Having such fine players as Howard Davis, John Neill, Jimmy Deegan and Mike Corby, it should not be difficult to mould a side capable of winning against any opposition. To do this the players have got to be provided with adequate training facilities. There are indications that the game will one day rank with others in importance, and it is hoped that soon the introduction of all-weather pitches will enable players to acquire the speed and dexterity to match India and Pakistan.

Only then will Britain find youngsters trying to emulate the great players she undoubtedly possesses. So far not one British player has copied John Conroy, who has been weaving intricate patterns with his stick for over a decade.

22

TRAINING FOR WAR

JORGE PARSONS

President, A.A. Argentina de Hockey

In several books written by old time settlers and colonizers of the land known to-day as the Argentine Republic, references are found to a game played by the Araucano Indians which is not unlike our present-day field hockey.

It was known as "chueca" (meaning the twisted one) and derived its name from the stick with a twisted end which was used in the game. The ball was made of leather, but nothing is said about the interior composition. The field of play varied in size depending on whether four, six or eight players per side took part, but the standard size appears to have been one hundred paces in length and ten paces in width, the back line at either end constituting the goal line.

The game was started from the middle of the field and if, during play, the ball went over a side line the game was re-started in the middle of the field. When a team scored two goals the teams changed ends, much in the same way as the teams change ends after each goal in modern polo. When a team that was losing, say 2–0, crossed their opponents goal line, the score did not become 2–1 but 1–0. The first team to obtain a three-goal advantage was the winner of the game.

The Araucanos considered "chueca" to be an important feature of their lives because they felt that it constituted an excellent training for general fitness and for war if necessary. The young women of the tribe practised a modified and less rough version of the game.

Challenges were issued between different tribes or groups of the Araucano, and the game was usually played on the field of the challenger, who was expected to play host to the visiting team and its entourage. Two moons was considered a long enough period for the preparing of the team, and during that time the players lived apart from the tribe, slept in the open air on the ground, did not touch alcohol and, in addition to practising daily, made long forced marches.

On the day of the game there was heavy betting between the supporters of either side, the wagers being food, skins, blankets, sheep and even horses. Everyone who wished to do so could witness the game, except pregnant women whose heavy condition, it was felt, might be transmitted to the players, thus slowing them down.

According to descriptions, the game was very fast and violent, and injuries were frequent and sometimes serious. This was not surprising as the art of the game was to keep the ball in the air as much as possible.

23

BRITAIN'S MINORITY SPORT

JOHN CONROY

Mid-Surrey H.C., England and Great Britain

Since 1948 Britain has set itself the task of bringing back a hockey gold medal from the Olympic Games. In fact this goal has receded and, since winning the silver medal in that year, other countries have been overtaking us. It is time to cast aside the air of innocent bewilderment and ask ourselves bluntly: "What's wrong with British hockey?"

The obvious excuses are that we have bad weather, that we play the game when both weather and pitches are at their worst, that the game is not popular and we have not enough money. Now, were the game more popular more money would be provided for better pitches and we could play the game all the year round. Hockey in Britain is not popular because it has never been taken to the public: we have always expected the public to come to us, and have cried out in amazement when only three thousand watch an international. Now we find our standard in comparison with other countries is slipping. Apart from public support we need more serious training of more players. But we have no money available, no national pitch and too few players worth training.

There is, too, the sad fact that you have to have a reasonable amount of cash as a player to play the game at all, especially at high level.

Without the goodwill of various people to whom I shall always be indebted for their kindness and influence I, for one, would never have been able to play international hockey. To-day fortunately more players can surmount the financial barriers of club fees and expensive tours. But, even then, to play hockey in Britain at all you must hold one of certain trump cards; a university career, a period in the Services, a childhood in India, a hockey school background. To make top class at least two of these cards are required.

In the past Britain has depended very largely on three sources for her players—the universities, the Services and Europeans returning from India. The universities and the Services are the only institutions which provide the facilities and the time necessary for training to peak fitness. With the end of National Service the young men entering university are two years younger both physically and mentally, and two years less experienced than they were, having had three instead of five years hockey at the tax-payers' expense, while the Services themselves have far fewer players. The number of players from India has almost dried up since the post-independence "bulge". It is imperative then to find new sources of good players to maintain the necessary numbers.

To begin with, more people must be encouraged to play hockey. At present only a few boys' schools include the game in their curricula; these are mostly fee-paying schools, and are therefore of themselves restrictive, but it is absurd to suppose that people who have not been to "posh" schools or to universities will not make good players. It would be ideal, though difficult, to "sell" hockey to the local education authorities as an alternative to association or rugby football—a more realistic approach would be to encourage clubs to take on beginners and run junior teams. At present, to my knowledge, there is no club which does this. Were more boys brought into clubs when still at school the demand for facilities would arise in the schools themselves. Junior teams are an investment in the interests both of the clubs and national hockey.

Standards could be raised in the clubs as they now exist by more competitive games on Saturdays. A few years ago, after much stormy argument, the County Championship began and has soon proved its worth. This venture should now be followed by a knock-out tournament between clubs—as is the practice in many other countries. The main argument against such competitions is that they might produce a rougher type of game, but among English sportsmen I think this is most unlikely. It would certainly produce more tenacious players and stricter umpires and more energetic and enthusiastic play. There would be more spectator support—support which would be invaluable when we have to ask for contributions to the Olympic fund. The system of tournaments should be used at every level; including that of the junior sides which I have suggested. Sundays, of course, would still be free for the informal games which are part of the British hockey players' life.

At national level there is also room for the game to be sold more effectively. If we aim as high as a gold medal, we obviously believe the game we are playing is worthy of public notice, yet how often is good hockey provided for public consumption? Hockey has remained a participants' not a spectators' sport. Now the time has come to take it to the public. Television could be used much more. For example, it could have helped to pay the £400 which the Indians recently asked for as expenses to cover their visit to Britain. These Commonwealth players would love to play in the original home of the game but we have never yet been able to entertain them, although European countries from Poland to Spain have done so. In this, I feel, we have missed a golden opportunity to popularise the sport and to educate our own players in world standards. I often wonder how high the status of the game would be to-day if we had accepted the Indian style when it was first shown to the world in 1928.

Hockey is a closed book to most people in Britain. They have not chanced to enter the milieu in which it is played. This is an accident of society, but what of the barriers which cut across the hockey playing circle itself? The late Dermott Findlater, that great benefactor of Irish hockey, once pleaded at a dinner for selectors to talk to the players they have dropped. Ten years later no selectors ever do this as far as I know. When I was dropped from the team for the Rome Olympics a great deal of speculation appeared in the Press, much of it of an unpleasant nature. On writing to the selectors for a clarification of the position, I received a curt note to the effect that selectors do not give reasons for their decisions.

To an extent they are justified. But a great deal of good could come from constructive criticism and comment by selectors and from making public their reasons for preferring certain types of play. In this way they could give the team more useful homework to do, polishing up the various points and so using training time much more efficiently. At all levels a great deal more use could be made of old players. At present their advice tends to be handed over informally over a pint of beer after a game or at a club dinner. Were they used officially from junior to national level we would eliminate the great waste of knowledge and experience which is now taking place. With skilful training and a high spirit of competition boys could graduate through an efficient network towards international hockey.

Hockey in Britain is in the preserve of a minority. If we believe that we can be good enough to win a gold medal then the game must be opened up to more people. Hockey cannot maintain its standards unless those who are involved in it go out to meet the public at least half-way. We need more money and we need more players—we can only get these if we get wider support. We must drop what, looked at objectively, is a social barrier. To those of us who have had endless pleasure from the game since the war, it will be something of a sacrifice, but the time has come when we must either surrender our tight little private circle and be more outward looking or we must accept that hockey in Britain is a social routine of which internationals are just an incidental extension.

24

LET'S MAKE HOCKEY A SPECTATOR SPORT

STAN IMER ("Cyclops")
(Extract from *Hockey Circle*, July, 1963)

With very few exceptions, individual hockey clubs and their associations in Australia seem quite content to be regarded as playing a sport which no one wants to watch. Australia has a reputation for being a sport-loving nation, and the picture of ourselves which we like to see, overseas especially, is that of a country of sporting champions and sporting spectators.

When one gets down to analysing this very pleasant myth, one finds that it might apply to some sporting pastimes but it certainly does not apply to all. We have a record in amateur tennis second to none, but spectators stay away from the Australian and State Championships in their thousands—indeed, one suspects that the crowds which turn out to see the Davis Cup series rarely ever see another match. In Melbourne, Australian Rules football has a record following at all times, but in some states the same game is very small cheese.

If you examine all the other sports, you will find that mostly they conform to the same pattern of having a few centres of real interest but fade-away in other places. It is no coincidence that the two winter field sports that are played widely in all states are genuine international games. They have the same universal rules and a player could step in, or a spectator watch, in any part of the world without even knowing the language.

But here the similarity ends. Large crowds watch soccer and can enjoy it and understand it without knowing much about the rules. If they want to appreciate the finer points of what's going on there are very few rules to understand. Can spectators watch hockey and understand it as easily? Obviously not, because by comparison the rules are very intricate; because all too often decisions are not based on fact but on the umpire's opinion; and because the ball is very small, moves quickly, and some of the best play cannot be seen to advantage from the sideline.

It is also a fact that our soccer friends have exploited their natural advantages to the fullest and have promoted their game vigorously to draw in the crowds. Isn't it a fair hypothesis, then, to assume that hockey administrators should strive even more vigorously to overcome the so-called disadvantages and put hockey before the public? I don't think we have done much about it.

Basically there are two sides to this problem. The first is that the game must be made less technical and easier to follow. The second, but related problem, is to attract public interest. As to the first, I can already hear the conservatives pleading "don't fiddle with the rules". Isn't the present state of affairs the result of merely "fiddling" with the rules year in, year out—with never once a serious review of the whole character of the rules and of the game? Why hasn't some responsible body been conducting controlled experiments with such things as a two-man off-side rule, complete elimination of the bully, elimination of the seven-yard line and, perhaps, playing with sticks two and a half or three inches wide? Don't imagine for one moment that I would advocate bringing in all these changes at once—if at all. But it is easy to imagine that hockey could be a simpler, safer, more spectacular game *without* losing its basic character. As I see it, too much of the trivia in hockey has been wrongly regarded as traditional character to be preserved at all costs. For example, the bully, which has no real connection with general play, is the thing by which we are best known to non-adherents—but best known does not mean well known—"Hockey one, Hockey two, Hockey three" is used in derision! Our forefathers copied the three-man off-side rule from the rules of soccer as they then stood. Soccer abandoned the three-man rule fifty years ago to open up the centre field and shift the emphasis from defence to attack. In our wisdom we have retained it, and it is the cause of deplorably crowded, jostling and negative play, especially when the attacking back game is used. A two-inch stick might have been wide enough last century when the game was played by staid gentlemen (they couldn't possibly move fast in those uniforms), but surely a slightly wider stick now would give greater control, with speed, to the advantage of hockey as a spectacle.

One could go on arguing a case for these and other changes. Some of them no doubt will come in time, while others may not work out as well as can be expected in theory. Who will ever know if no thought is being given to it and no one is experimenting? To date, the International

Hockey (Rules) Board has reviewed the rules as a gentle academic exercise for lawyers, and seems intent on resisting real change, although it is prepared to elaborate at length on the hidden mysteries of the existing rules.

Change never comes from the top; it must come from pressure from grass roots. If we are happy and content to have most hockey played in back paddocks, to finance inter-state matches out of our own pockets, to do without international visits because we have no money, obviously nothing need be changed. If, on the other hand, we do need spectators at local matches, at inter-state matches and at international matches, because spectators mean interest and they mean publicity and they mean money in the coffers, our attitudes must change.

25

THE SHAMROCKS ARE COMING

NORMAN BROWNE
Beckenham H.C., Kent and Ireland

Early on the afternoon of October 4, 1962, a Boeing 707 Jet of Irish Air Lines took off from Dublin Airport for New York. There was nothing unusual about this, but for those interested in the game of men's hockey, history was in the making, for it was the first time a men's hockey team from the British Isles was to cross the Atlantic ocean.

The Shamrocks, a team of Irish hockey players, seventeen strong, accompanied by eight wives, an umpire and Mr. Louis Bowers, President of the Irish Hockey Union, were about to leave these shores to take part in the Privateers Hockey Festival near New York. This was not an international team and indeed it was not intended to be. It could best be described as a collection of hockey players who could afford both the time and the money to indulge in their favourite sport in a country that all were keen to see.

We had to touch down at Shannon to pick up further passengers but more important for us, to collect a consignment of Irish whiskey which was waiting for us in the Duty-Free shop at the airport. The Irish may lack subtlety on the hockey field, but plenished with alcohol they become shrewd and scheming.

A large Irish whiskey firm had been persuaded to give us a more-than-generous amount of this accursed vintage in order that we might boost the sales of their product in the States. Each person in our party found a cardboard container awaiting collection—in each were several

The England team which drew 1–1 with Ireland at Nottingham in October 1963. L–to–R: (Standing) D. Wilman, C. Langhorne, M. Corby, J. Cadman, B. Christensen, I. Ireland. (Sitting) C. Jones, J. Neill, H. Davis, D. Miller, P. Fishwick. Only Christensen was not selected for Great Britain's Olympic team in 1964.

(*Photo. Anthony Hallas*)

40th Anniversary of the F.I.H. (Fédération Internationale de Hockey). The President, L. J. Quarles van Ufford (Netherlands) addresses members of the Federation at the Hotel de Ville de Paris. On the right—R. Frank (Belgium) Hon. Sec., J. Daubresse (France) Founder, J. de Aguilera (Spain) Founder, A.Demaurex (Switzerland) Founder.

bottles of whiskey. In this way export tax was avoided within the limits of the law. There were obviously some thinkers on our side!

Half an hour later, as the giant aircraft was racing down the runway for take-off, a door in the tail plane flew open and what was to prove a wonderful hockey tour nearly ended before it had started. We all returned to the duty-free shop and fortified ourselves for the second attempt to get off Irish soil, while repairs were being carried out.

Fortunately all went smoothly until we reached the Customs at Idlewild Airport. Although we managed to talk our way through, we did get more than a few suspicious looks when we tried to explain away the whiskey, especially a two-gallon bottle that was to be presented to our hosts. It was at this juncture that we discovered that we were not in the U.S. to play hockey but to play field hockey. One Customs official roared with laughter when we tried to explain to him about our sticks—he couldn't imagine how we manage to play hockey on grass.

Our hosts, the Privateers, took us from the airport straight to the headquarters of the Festival at Rye, Connecticut, some fifty miles out of town. There we were briefed about our comings and goings for the next twelve days by John Rote, an Oxford Hockey Blue in 1946, who organised the festival so excellently for the Privateers. The single members of the party were put up with American families near the ground, and the married couples at The Pickwick Arms which, much to our disgust, was a perfect replica of an English-styled hotel.

The festival, unlike those in England, stretched out over twelve days, with rest days scattered here and there. Each team played all but one of the others, which made five games in all. The Shamrocks had two extra fixtures which were outside the festival—one against Blind Brook Polo Club and the other against a Combined Embassies XI in Washington. The Washington trip absorbed two days and was the highlight of the tour. There we played a team drawn from all the embassies but mainly comprised of Eastern gentlemen helped along by a few Americans, and one John Campbell whom we all had known in Dublin. The game was played before a crowd of schoolgirls and in a temperature well into the nineties. We won comfortably (3–0) and that evening were entertained by the Privateer goalkeeper, Edward Lifmann, at his sumptuous home on the outskirts of the city. It was on that evening that the gap in the standard of living between the U.S.A. and the home countries was most obvious. It was a tremendous party, followed the next day by a tour of the magnificent city.

The fixture against Blind Brook Polo Club, which we won 6–0, will be remembered not for the hockey but for the state of the pitch. Nothing even in the Bog in Ireland was ever as bad as this, but it suited the Irish style of play. The ball was lost in the mud on several occasions, and this I hadn't seen since my schooldays in Dublin.

Large American cars surrounded the field of play, horns blaring at every incident. Despite the playing surface, the setting was wonderful, the pitch being surrounded by heavily wooded countryside. The colours of the leaves during this autumn needed to be seen to be believed.

That evening we were entertained to a barn dance in the Polo Club pavilion—a great party where we were introduced to this exciting form of dancing and to a deadly potion they called Rum Swizzle.

Back in New York, the first game we played in the festival proper was against the Field Hockey Association of America Selection which was in fact the U.S. Olympic team in the making. This match was drawn, as was the game against the Privateers on the final day. The Privateers game was by far the best and was notable for the fact that a running commentary on the play was given over the loudspeaker system for the benefit of those spectators new to the game. This we thought was a most interesting innovation and one which might be most helpful at times in this country! We lost to the Toronto Field Hockey Club of Canada 1–2; and beat North Jersey, U.S.A., 2–1; Bermuda Hockey Association 3–1, which gave us a tally of two wins, two draws and one loss—the best record of any of the teams present. Unfortunately we did not play the Fédération Royale Marocaine de Hockey (Morocco).

During the festival we managed to squeeze in frequent trips to New York. On one of these occasions the team was given a reception by Mr. Robert Wagner, Mayor of New York, in the City Hall. The Shamrocks also managed to see New York from the top of the Empire State Building, do a river trip round Manhattan Island, visit Radio City, and—most exciting of all—have a conducted tour of the United Nations building.

Near the end of the tour it was the Shamrocks' turn to entertain, and we gave a party for all the other teams. That night a large hole was made in our whiskey reserves, but Americans, Bermudans, Canadians and Moroccans are unlikely to forget their introduction to Irish whiskey and Gaelic coffee.

We were only in the U.S. twelve days, but we managed to cover a lot of ground both on and off the hockey field. I should think we had no more than three hours sleep a night during this period but it was well worth it—an experience that all those who made the trip will remember and cherish forever. Long may there be hockey tours and festivals to visit!

26

THE GENTLE GIANT—JOHN NEILL

HARLEY GELLING

In spite of what may be termed the handicap of a mild manner and the contrasting build of a Rugby forward, John Whitley Neill (born May 15, 1934) is one of the all-time great defenders of English and British hockey. Since his first appearance for England and Great Britain in the 1957/58 season he has been an undisputed choice for both.

Although his fifty odd caps have been exceeded by his illustrious predecessor, Denys Carnill, and his present captain, Howard Davis, to many observers Neill is the greatest of them all. By Indian standards, he is one of the two British players who can be considered of world-class to-day. Almost majestically commanding, there is controlled power in everything he does. He looks as if he will never make a mistake and he rarely ever does.

Neill's introduction to the game was at Amesbury School, Hindhead, and he continued playing hockey at Rugby. In those formative schooling years, he invariably and not surprisingly played centre-half. When he started work as an articled clerk in the accountancy profession, he joined the London club, Southgate, and his first games for them were also as the midfield linch-pin. However, in the 1953/54 season, when Tim Abell came down from Oxford University where he had been captain and centre-half, Neill was converted—with notable perception—to right-back by Southgate, who can thus claim some of the credit for his future glory.

His county career began with an appearance at centre-half for Surrey "A" but his first divisional trial for the South was at right-half. An appendix operation delayed his first divisional appearance, but it was inevitable and in 1957/58 he began to use the Indian-type stick regularly; switched to left-back; was selected for the South and also took his first steps towards international recognition. An outstanding performance for the Rest in the final England trial put him firmly on the way, even though he had the disappointment of being England's twelfth man for the entire home international programme.

Then the fates took a hand. With the help of National Service deferment, Neill went on the English Hockey Association's tour of South Africa in the summer of 1958. He proved his versatility by playing in five positions on the tour, but it was an injury to John

John Neill

Strover in the first Test (drawn 2–2 at Port Elizabeth) that gave Neill his great chance. He came into the second Test team as right-back and laid the foundation for his future by playing a notable part in England's 3–2 victory. He kept his place for the remaining two Tests (both drawn) and also for the solitary international against Kenya (won 6–4 at Nairobi, on the way home).

On his return he was "called up" in the Royal Artillery and, like his

father (a retired Lieutenant-colonel—Royal Engineers), he became an officer. Games for Surrey, the Army, Combined Services, and England meant the 1958/59 season was an eventful one for him, and it culminated in the award of his first cap for Great Britain against Belgium at Hove. The next season was also a full and demanding one, with trips to Poland, and the Munich International Tournament. Neill was well and truly established, and it was no surprise when he was selected for the 1960 Olympics at Rome.

In Rome's tremendous heat the British defence as a whole played magnificently, and Britain surpassed themselves by reaching the semi-finals, though they had to be content with fourth place. Neill, by that time, had skill, tactical appreciation, a wonderful eye, a useful turn of speed, and probably the best tackle in the game. As the greatest forwards dribbled towards him, one could not help comparing his delayed strike with the simple majesty of a cobra's kill.

Since Rome, Neill's contribution to the game has been greater than ever, particularly as captain of Cheshire and the North, and vice-captain of England and Great Britain. He had moved north just prior to the Rome Olympics to take up his present post as a brewery executive at Warrington, and he was the backbone of the Cheshire side which reached the county championship final in March 1961. Over the past four years he has been the mainstay in both the English and British defences, proving just as dependable when switched to left-back before the Tokyo Olympics, to fill one of Britain's major problem positions.

In whatever position, and wherever and at whatever level he plays, John Neill always gives his best. His skill, temperament and sportsmanship are an example to all.

27

LOOKING BACK ON LYON

JEAN NOEL

The last stragglers trooped out of the Stade Municipal de Gerland and drove back along the wide cobbled roads into the wonderful old French city of Lyon, situated at the confluence of the Rhone and Saône rivers in Central France, and the world's biggest hockey tournament outside the Olympic Games was over.

Twelve countries had taken part in the tournament, including the four that had reached the 1960 Olympic semi-finals in Rome—Pakistan, India, Spain and Great Britain. Each had played seven matches in nine days, a tremendously tough programme requiring reserves of mental and physical stamina such as few had had to face before.

As at the January 1962 Ahmedabad Tournament, no official classification was made, which, in my opinion, was quite wrong, for sport means competition and there is no real rivalry without final placings. As might have been expected, the festival was barely started before unofficial tables were being drawn up by everyone. But while it had been possible to draw a fair comparison of the teams in Ahmedabad because each team played all the others, it was not so easy in Lyon where each country played only seven games.

India's first place was undisputed, although its team never reproduced the formidable mastery it displayed on its own soil at Ahmedabad twenty-one months earlier. Even so, they scored more goals and conceded fewer than any other side in the tournament.

Germany (Deutscher Hockey Bund), a superbly drilled side, were deservedly runners-up and Netherlands finished third despite the presence of the Olympic gold medallists, Pakistan.

India and Pakistan agreed to take part in this tournament on condition that they did not have to play each other, for neither master likes to play the other unless compelled to do so at major championships. Both appeared to be put out by the conditions at Lyon. Teams like Germany and Holland were quite at home on the converted soccer pitches, but at first the Asians found them anything but suitable, and they did not take too kindly to playing under floodlights. Pakistan took some time to settle into something like their best form, but India deserved every credit for quickly adapting themselves. They shared the honours in a grim 1–1 draw with Germany on the first day, but Kranich's goal was the only one scored against them throughout the tournament.

Pakistan started with a goalless draw with Spain and then, on the second day, in the unaccustomed aura of the floodlit stadium, were beaten 2–1, their first international defeat for seven years.

People began to ponder whether the European teams had at last closed the gap and were nearing the standard of the Asians, but by the end of the tournament, India had quietened those thoughts.

Nevertheless, Germany and Netherlands earned their second place ahead of Pakistan. Of the leading teams, Germany had to face the severest fixtures. They were the only side to hold India, and they beat Pakistan 1–0 in the final match of the tournament, despite playing with ten men after Kranich had been injured early in the game. Netherlands did not have to play India, but after their wonderful victory over the Olympic champions, the "Oranges" were beaten 3–1 by Great Britain, who shared with Pakistan and Spain the ignominy of being the most disappointing teams at Lyon.

The splendour of the fast moving, quick-thinking Dutch against Pakistan, and their agony when facing Britain in teeming rain, was the most characteristic feature of this festival of contradictions. I call it contradiction when Spain, after drawing with Pakistan, were beaten 1–0 by Italy; and France lost 1–0 (a penalty stroke) to India and shared the points with Germany, only to be overwhelmed by a British team just recovering from defeat by Belgium.

HOW THEY FARED

	India	Germany	Holland	Pakistan	Belgium	Japan	France	Gt. Britain	Spain	Canada	Italy	U.S.A.
India		1–1				4–0	1–0	2–0	4–0	3–0	4–0	
Germany	1–1		0–0	1–0			0–0	2–1	4–0			7–0
Holland		0–0		2–1		1–0		1–3	0–0	2–0	7–0	
Pakistan		0–1	1–2		1–0	2–0		3–0	0–0			7–0
Belgium				0–1		0–2	1–3	1–0	3–2		3–0	4–0
Japan	0–4		0–1	0–2	2–0		1–0			1–0	3–1	
France	0–1	0–0			3–1	0–1		0–3		2–1	3–0	
Gt. Britain ..	0–2	1–2	3–1	0–3	0–1		3–0					7–1
Spain	0–4	0–4	0–0	0–0	2–3						0–1	8–0
Canada	0–3		0–2			0–1	1–2				1–1	2–0 1–1
Italy	0–4		0–7		0–3	1–3	0–3		1–0	1–1		
U.S.A.		0–7	0–7		0–4			1–7	0–8	0–2 1–1		

The title of the unluckiest team in the tournament surely went to the Belgians. Rarely have I seen a side dominate as they did in the second half against Pakistan, and throughout their matches with Japan and France, and still lose each time.

The British team lacked forwards, and only a few of their players were up to the high standard required. Much more had been expected from a side that was good enough to take fourth place at the Rome Olympics. Their best quality was undoubtedly courage, but that is not enough in such a high-class tournament; clever stick-work and sound tactics are also useful.

Japan confirmed the excellent impression its young team left in Ahmedabad, but Italy, Canada and United States, as expected, were too weak to provide other than a minor role. Canada was playing hockey outside North America for the first time in its history and can look back with some pride at its performance. It lost only twice by more than a one-goal margin, and by defeating United States qualified as America's representative at the Tokyo Olympic Games.

Looking back I cannot help thinking that India, Germany and Netherlands earned their final placings by fine team work. If I had to select a Tournament XI from all the many fine players I watched, I should be very tempted to name mostly Indians. Dharam Singh, who incidentally scored a hat-trick with short corner shots against Spain, Charanjit Singh, Mohinder Lal, Joginder Singh, Peter, Patil and Darshan Singh are all players with skill, stamina and intelligence. Others who caught my eye were three brilliant goalkeepers, Garcia (Spain), Miwa (Japan), and Dobigny (France); Munir Ahmad Dar (Pakistan), Neill (Great Britain), and Nonn (Germany) at full-back; Davis (Great Britain), Greinert (Germany), Anwar Ahmad Khan (Pakistan), and Iwahashi (Japan) at centre-half; the German wing-halves Krause and Ferstl; wingers Woeller (Germany), Krol (Netherlands), Roersh (Belgium), the fantastic Khalid Mahmood (Pakistan), the mercurial Keller (Germany), the subtle Takana (Japan), van Vroonhoven (Netherlands), Bernaert (Belgium), and Schuler (Germany) at inside-forward.

Umpiring was neither better nor worse than it always has been and always will be. Several penalty strokes were awarded, and it was clear that most of those officiating accepted their responsibility and did not hesitate to inflict the severest sanction. This is a good way of protecting hockey, which could easily die from a disease whose characteristic is the defensive game played to excess with the use of all lawful and unlawful tricks. Let umpires continue to grant penalty strokes as often as necessary, it will keep hockey clean!

A lot of "sticks" were allowed, however, and at penalty corners the defenders were allowed to cross the 25-yard line too early on many occasions—the Indians being the worst offenders. This latter problem

FINAL TABLE (Unofficial)

		P.	*W.*	*D.*	*L.*	*F.*	*A.*	*Pts.*
1.	India ..	7	6	1	0	19	1	13
2.	Germany ..	7	4	3	0	15	2	11
3.	Holland ..	7	4	2	1	13	4	10
4.	Pakistan ..	7	4	1	2	14	3	9
5.	Belgium ..	7	4	0	3	12	8	8
6.	Japan ..	7	4	0	3	7	8	8
7.	France ..	7	3	1	3	8	7	7
8.	Gt. Britain ..	7	3	0	4	14	10	6
9.	Spain ..	7	1	2	4	10	12	4
10.	Canada ..	7	1	2	4	5	10	4
11.	Italy ..	7	1	1	5	3	21	3
12.	U.S.A. ..	7	0	1	6	2	36	1

will have to be solved in a more satisfactory way by those responsible for the rules.*

Judging from the amount of "sticks" at Lyon, all internationals these days seem to have learnt their hockey on the golf course at St. Andrew's. Some umpires enforced the "sticks" rule strictly and earned the displeasure of the crowd by continually blowing their whistles, while others, with a wary eye on the crowd, punished only the most blatant cases. The Rules Board have another problem here, for the sticks rule will have to be made uniform.

Lastly a word about floodlit hockey. The experiment of playing one of the six matches each day after dark was very interesting. The matches definitely attracted the biggest crowds and, with the impression of tremendous speed accentuated, the games appeared to be more exciting than usual. Nevertheless, the lighting in the Stade Municipal de Gerland was not of a high quality and made things difficult for both players and umpires. I personally feel the hockey ball is too small to use in artificial lighting. As I left the dark, empty stadium on that last October evening I could not help thinking that the good old sunlight, even when scarce, still seems better than any other light for the game of hockey.

* *Editor's Note: The rule was amended in May* 1964. *The defending players must remain beyond the half-way line now.*

28

"LUCKY DAI" DAVIS

DAVID MORGAN

B.B.C. Midlands Hockey Correspondent

Few who have seen Howard Davis play hockey will deny that he is one of the great ones. His stopping, hitting, concentration, fitness and uncanny anticipation make him stand out, even amongst the world's best players. His dedication makes it so easy to play alongside him, but if "Dai" Davis, captain of Great Britain, England, the Midlands, Staffordshire and a Bacchanalian, is one of the world's great players, he might also well be called "Lucky Dai" Davis.

Born on September 24, 1932, at the village of Breseley in Shopshire, he played wing-half in the Felsted School first eleven for two seasons before joining the North Stafford Club in 1950. After only four games in the second team, the club first eleven centre-half fell ill and Davis took his place. He had the tendency of most schoolboys to try to do too much on his own, but vociferous criticism from the club president soon put that right. He progressed so well that in the next season, when the regular county right-half, Robert Hollinshead, developed influenza, Davis was brought into the team at the last minute. When he recovered, Hollinshead found himself playing at full-back.

Davis's guide and mentor in these early days was the former England centre-half, John Wootton, who was also captain of Staffordshire and the Midlands. This was the era of such skilful midlands half-backs as Tony Robinson, Paul Ledger, Peter Curle, and John Wheatcroft. Davis soon learnt a great deal.

In the 1952/3 season Wheatcroft was out of action, and Davis was selected for his division and played right-half against the North and the South. Later in the same season he appeared in the first England trial.

Although not selected for the final trial that year, his Midlands team-mate, Ledger, the England centre-half, developed influenza just before the game, played only in the first half and Davis, who was reserve, played in the second.

In July 1953 he was called up in the Royal Armoured Corps and played hockey for the Army and the Combined Services before being posted to Germany where he played for the British Army of the Rhine. In April 1954 he played right-half for the first England "B" team against Netherlands "B" at Amsterdam, before returning to the family pottery firm in Staffordshire.

Early in 1956 he was again chosen for the Midlands—this time at centre-half between Ledger and the Scottish international C. K. R.

Howard Davis

Vartan. England trials followed, and at Guildford on March 24, 1956, Davis first played for England against Wales.

It must have been a nostalgic occasion for, although born in Shopshire near the Welsh border, he earned the nickname "Dai" because of his Welsh mother, his surname, his command of the Welsh dialect and the inimitable "Dai and Blodwen" jokes in his after-dinner speeches. It was said that he was the only player on both sides who could sing the Welsh national anthem in Welsh and English!

Fortune even smiled on his British career, for when he was invited to an Olympic training week-end early in 1955, Owen, the Welsh centre-half and first choice, was unable to attend. Davis took his place, and at Melbourne in 1956 began a career at centre-half for Great Britain that was to earn him a record number of caps.

Since 1961 he has also captained England, but throughout his career he has remained as modest, enthusiastic and good humoured as he was when he first played club hockey in Stoke-on-Trent.

He will tell you that every game he has played has been enjoyable, but recalls especially the 1956 British side that might have won the gold medal at Melbourne but for a crop of injuries; the 1960 game with Kenya that Britain won 2–1 after fifty-seven minutes of extra time, and a glittering display by the fine 1956 England side which defeated Scotland 7–0.

Few English sportsmen are held in greater respect, for he insists that hockey is played to be enjoyed, and in doing so he has helped to bring to Britain the Indian stick and to foster the new spirit of adventure. He is Staffordshire's finest ambassador, having played a tremendous part in their proud record in the county championships, and will be remembered as player, captain, tactician, broadcaster and a champion of club celebrations and anniversaries. Never happier than in a tough Olympics match, never more popular than when playing inside-left for his club at the Llandudno Easter Festival.

The true test of his splendid service to British hockey will be found in the future, when players at all levels will recall with pride that they once played with or against Howard Davis, so nearly a Welshman, so clearly one of the greatest British players of all time.

29

A GLANCE THROUGH MY LIBRARY

BILL MALHERBE

(*a South African who owns the world's biggest collection of hockey literature*)

A cynic once remarked that hockey, in common with many other games, did not actually require any "literature"—why, most players apparently regard even a casual perusal of the book of rules as superfluous!

Be that as it may, hockey, which only crystallised in its modern form in the late 1880's in England, already had its first fully fledged handbook by 1895. Shortly afterwards a weekly magazine catered for the needs of the men's game, and in 1899 *Hockey, Historical & Practical* was published, a most comprehensive work.

Two years later Edith Thompson started a magazine for women's hockey, *Hockey Field*, which, except for breaks during the two wars, still flourishes and is today going from strength to strength under the guidance of the world's foremost women's hockey personality, Marjorie Pollard.

After the 1914/18 war the popularity of the game saw its spread overseas gain momentum, and good books were published in Holland, Germany and the United States, where women's hockey gained a firm foothold at the colleges.

Between the wars new magazines sprung up. *Hockey World*, which had such an influence on the game, first appeared in 1922; Jan Hoven started *Hockey Sport* in Holland (1931); Hec Cormie launched the live-wire *Hockey Circle* in Australia (1933), and the women's section of the United States Field Hockey Association issued *The Eagle* (1937).

After the last war, Leonard Podger resurrected *Hockey World*, but it lacked support and died quickly. It was not replaced in England until 1951 when Richard Hollands established *Hockey News*, a magazine of quality, that promotes hockey today. *Hockey* was published in Germany, Rudolf Dreisilker being the driving force behind this magazine, while *Indian Hockey* is now well on its way to the completion of its first volume.

Today we can list literally hundreds of hockey publications, ranging from slim pamphlets to stoutly-bound learned treatises, whose contents give sound information on every aspect of the game. Russia has produced a first-rate text-book, and almost all the European countries have furnished works on hockey, notably Holland, Germany (East and West) and Spain.

Naturally, as on any subject, certain books overshadow the rest and, perhaps, *Hockey in Ireland*, written by T. S. C. Dagg in 1944, is the one most likely to stir the blood of the true hockey lover. It is the story of how the game developed in the Emerald Isle, and how Irishmen played their part in carrying the game to the four corners of the globe.

H. F. Battersby's 1895 book *Hockey* takes the place of honour as the first book on the game, but *Hockey—Historical & Practical*, written by Smith and Robson only four years later, is incredible in that it contains just about everything the authors could lay their hands on. Herbert Bourke's 1907 *Hockey—The Game That Grows* (a Spalding publication), positively bubbles with enthusiasm, and in 1909 Eustace E. White's *The Complete Hockey Player* was, in fact, just that.

Then books came thick and fast and, with authors like Eric Green,

E. A. C. Thomson, Kate Lidderdale, Harry Haslam, Stanley Shoveller and Marjorie Pollard, they could not be anything else but first class. Philip Robson's *A Manual of Hockey* in 1934 was a little gem, and in 1938 a milestone appeared when D. S. Milford's *Hockey* was published, a book that became a standard work in many countries.

Britain easily leads the field in the number of publications and, since the last war, has produced some excellent books. Most of them are still obtainable, but it is noteworthy that overseas countries are now publishing their fair share of hockey literature. The Americans write the most detailed technical works, largely because they stem from college lectures, while, lately, India has produced a number of books on umpiring from the pens of Santosh Ganguli and Gian Singh which have been translated into Dutch, Polish, Spanish and Japanese. The German books are very thorough and valuable works, and their official handbook is by far the most attractive and informative.

With hockey now firmly established throughout the world, many clubs, associations and national unions are celebrating their long and happy careers, and these are increasingly being marked by the publication of commemorative works ranging from small, nostalgic pamphlets to impressively bound and lavishly illustrated volumes.

30

THE DEVELOPMENT OF WOMEN'S HOCKEY

HILDA M. LIGHT

Chiswick, Middx. and England; Past President of the I.F.W.H.A.

Organised women's hockey as we know it started in the United Kingdom in the 1890's and was played mainly by university students. The first national association was formed in Ireland four years later and their lead was quickly followed by England, Scotland and Wales.

The game soon took root and began to spread to the continent, and the idea of an international federation, though it did not materialise at the time, was first raised in 1900, mainly with the object of working for uniformity of rules.

After the First World War, the game began to make tremendous strides, with the interchange of visits between clubs and international teams overseas, and in 1922 Mrs. Heron Maxwell, then President of the All-England Women's Hockey Association, put forward the idea of forming a body to include all national women's associations. Two years later, after an international match at Merton Abbey between England and the United States of America, a meeting was held with Mrs. Heron Maxwell in the chair, at which it was agreed to go ahead with the project, draw up a constitution, and submit it to twelve countries known to be interested.

These preliminaries took time but, in 1927, the inaugural meeting of the International Federation of Women's Hockey Associations was held in London, presided over by Miss Edith Thompson (England), at which a constitution was submitted and adopted.

The founder members were Australia, Denmark, England, Ireland, Scotland, South Africa, U.S.A. and Wales. It had been hoped that other continental associations would join, but as these in almost all cases were sections of mixed associations, who were themselves occupied in building up the Fédération Internationale de Hockey (F.I.H.), none came in at that time. Nevertheless, the I.F.W.H.A. went ahead, Miss C. J. Gaskell and Miss W. A. Baumann (England) serving as the first president and hon. secretary respectively, with Mrs E. B. Krumbhaar (U.S.A.) as vice-president, and Miss E. M. Alexander (Scotland) as hon. treasurer. It was decided to hold a council meeting annually and to arrange triennial conferences.

The first conference was held in Geneva in July 1930, when two exhibition matches were played, despite the summer heat! The U.S.A. proposed that a tournament should be arranged in conjunction with future conferences, and a committee was appointed to consider its rules. Ever since then the Federation has worked for uniformity of rules, and the subject has been debated again and again.

Three years later, in Copenhagen, under the patronage of H.R.H. Princess Margaretha, six of the eight member countries sent teams while, in addition, Germany and Holland accepted invitations, and a composite team from overseas also took part. Each team played three matches. The committee that year expressed the hope that, at some future date, the game would be played everywhere under one code of rules, but it was felt to be impracticable at that time. In the meantime it was decided that international matches should be played in accordance with the rules of the hostess association.

The third conference took place in Philadelphia (U.S.A.) in October 1936, under the patronage of Mrs Eleanor Roosevelt, and again six national teams took part in the tournament. Tours were arranged for the visiting teams, and these proved such an outstanding success that they have been included in each of the succeeding meetings.

The I.F.W.H.A. was making progress and women's hockey was on a sound footing. Nevertheless, contacts were maintained with the men's international federation, the F.I.H.

At the first of the conferences, in 1930, the possibility of collaborating with the F.I.H. had been discussed by representatives of both sides. The main points at issue were representation, subscriptions and the exact definition of the word "country". The F.I.H. ruled "one country—one vote", with equal subscriptions, and maintained that Great Britain was one country with Ireland as a separate entity. This was unacceptable to the I.F.W.H.A., which considered that an association with a large membership could give greater support than one with a small membership, the latter being affiliated in their body as an associate member. Bearing in mind the tradition and organisation of the game in Great Britain, the suggestion that the three home associations should be regarded as one was felt to be unrealistic and was refused, although it was felt that the scale of representation might be lowered.

Although nothing tangible had come of the early contacts between the two federations, the F.I.H. set up a women's committee, and in 1931 the two sets of representatives met in Paris. Concessions were made on both sides, but the F.I.H. refused to recognise the I.F.W.H.A. on an equal footing or the absolute independence of women in their internal organisation, and so the two federations went their separate ways.

Closer links between all the women's hockey-playing countries were forged at a meeting between the two committees in Amsterdam in 1948. Most of the women's sections of the continental associations joined the I.F.W.H.A., which was a wonderful step forward, greatly strengthening the association.

The fourth conference was due to be held in England in 1939 but had to be cancelled at the last moment—due to the outbreak of the Second World War, with the Australians practically aboard their ship. Because of the war, the federation was more or less laid up in lavender until 1948, when England renewed her invitation by offering to hold a conference in 1950.

Recovery after the war in Europe was slow, and England had to cancel the invitations, but South Africa stepped into the breach and a most memorable meeting was held in Johannesburg. After the 1950 conference was over, the six national teams which took part in the tournament travelled to many parts of the Union and Rhodesia, being affectionately known as "Hoffa's Circus", after the organiser, Miss Hoffa, then hon. secretary of the I.F.W.H.A. and of the South African Association. It was at this conference that the parade of teams with flag bearers and, that most popular feature, a variety evening with each team contributing an item were instituted.

An approach had been made in 1948 to the Olympic Games Committee for the inclusion of women's hockey in the 1952 games. This was refused and it was unanimously agreed at Johannesburg that the I.F.W.H.A.'s triennial conferences, tournaments and tours were far better suited to women's hockey than anything offered by the Olympic Games, with its necessary limitation on the number of participating teams, knock-out method and short duration. A few years later it was decided to hold conferences every four instead of every three years, in order to avoid clashing with the dates of Olympic meetings.

In October 1953 England was at last the hostess country, with H.R.H. Princess Margaret as patron. The meeting at Folkestone was blessed with incredibly good weather, and sixteen teams participated. Following the conference, the F.I.H. honoured the All-England Women's H.A. with the award of the Leautey Cup, given annually to the association contributing the most outstanding work to the game.

Nineteen fifty-six saw the conference in Australia, where Sydney University proved a most excellent centre. Ten associations sent teams —a magnificent turn-out considering the immense distances involved, and the tours following the conference covered all the Australian states and New Zealand, while teams in their travels to and from Australia also played in Ceylon, Fiji and Curaçao.

At Sydney it was decided to appoint Miss K. Watkins (England) as hon. affiliation secretary. Membership had remained at its eight founder members for some ten years before the influx of members in 1948/9, but now stands at twenty-six, to a large extent as a result of Miss Watkins's work.

The question of a code of rules for international matches was re-opened by Belgium at the 1956 conference, and a draft code was prepared for consideration. At the seventh meeting in Amsterdam in 1959 this failed in its object though, with some amendments, it was adopted for use at conference tournaments. This was undoubtedly a step towards realisation of the original ideal which can be achieved only with the willing agreement of all member associations, the federation having no power to enforce decisions.

Fifteen teams took part in the Amsterdam tournament, and tours were enjoyed afterwards by six of the more distant countries who visited Great Britain and Ireland and several European countries.

The 1963 conference and tournament was held at Goucher College, Towson, Maryland, U.S.A., and for the first time everyone was accommodated under one roof, enjoying the wonderful facilities of an American university. Sixteen national teams and a composite team, the International Wanderers, took part, Jamaica and Trinidad/Tobago making their first appearances.

As at all conferences, new officers were elected, the new president and hon. secretary being members of the country due to stage the next conference. The period of service of officers has always been limited so that fresh minds can be brought to bear on the problems facing women's hockey. This system has drawbacks, particularly in regard to the growth and diversity of the present membership and, in America, it was decided to institute the office of an hon. general and conference secretary who would be eligible for re-election. This, it was felt, would provide more continuity and strengthen the administration.

Looking back over the years the I.F.W.H.A. has given to hundreds of hockey enthusiasts the opportunity to see much of the world. Each national association has organised the conference for which it was responsible in its own traditional way, with excursions to special beauty spots and places of historic interest. Constant features have been recognition and entertainment from state and civic authorities and, above all, the unlimited friendliness and hospitality extended.

It has always been the policy of the federation to further sportsmanship and encourage playing the game for enjoyment and recreation. With this object in view, it has sought to keep the competitive spirit strictly under control and its tournaments, by design, have never been organised on championship lines. This has undoubtedly contributed to the friendly atmosphere which has characterised its meetings. Those who were fortunate enough to attend the conference at Philadelphia will recall the remarkable sermon preached by the Rev. D. Newton at the conference service, the theme of which was "contest without conflict, rivalry without rancour, and struggle without strife". This might well be adopted as the motto of the I.F.W.H.A.

31

4-2-3-1

BILL VANS AGNEW

Beckenham H.C., Kent, Scotland

Who devised the first formations in hockey? Was it some Greek sage with a passion for uniformity: a military tactician who also introduced the game to India: or was it a mathematics master who believed in practical demonstration? Whoever it was, he was allowed to interfere with an opponent's stick and put his foot to the ball whenever he liked. His playing days must also have ended long before these practices were abolished.

That same genius probably never saw an Indian-style stick, and certainly never knew how well he taught the game to the Indians who chastised the British tourists in 1964. But Rugby football and cricket have had their changes, and even dear old England has innovated quite a few. Who started bodyline bowling?

Most people have taken it for granted that a hockey team consists of five forwards, three halves, two backs and a goalkeeper. On occasions one back is played like a deep centre-half, and in the early 1900's some London clubs successfully adopted the formation of four half-backs and no goalkeeper, but otherwise there has been a marked lack of interest in altering the status quo.

I have always wanted to experiment, never having been happy with the normal line-up, which I felt gave far too much licence to the opposing inside-forwards. I wanted them to be marked tightly and to eliminate the dangerous change-over of the back, which has always made the defence vulnerable to a through pass down the middle.

A psycho-analyst undoubtedly would have affirmed that my antipathy to inside forwards originated from my younger and more athletic days which I spent at centre-half flitting from one inside to the other in search of the ball.

The first chance to experiment came in 1954. Scotland had drawn with England and were to play Holland in Amsterdam the next day. The idea was for the wing-halves, my brother and myself, to mark the inside-forwards, and the backs to mark the wings. It was not a success, and after two goals had been scored against us in ten minutes, we conformed.

It took a long time to eradicate this memory, and it was nine years later that the 4–2–3–1 formation was conceived, by the union of association football's 4–2–4 system and the hockey off-side rule. The midwifery was conducted by the London club, Beckenham.

There was a shortage of inside-forwards throughout England at the time, and this was also the case at Beckenham. The lack of time in which to train or produce new ones meant that the rest of the team would suffer from this shortcoming. The alternative was to re-position the players to take the maximum advantage of their capabilities. Thus the 4–2–3–1 was born, and not for the purpose of conserving the failing resources of the author as was popularly rumoured amongst his contemporaries.

4–2–3–1 means four forwards, two link-halves, three half-backs and one back. The forwards play as two wings and two insides, the latter having to be very mobile and cope with the centre-forward's duties as well. This means that attacks down the wings can be made by two fowards as a pair rather than by a solitary outside forward. The insides, unlike their orthodox counterparts, are not expected to tackle back far, thus reserving their energies for attack.

The defensive duties of the insides are taken over by the link-halves who mark the opposing inside-forwards; back up their own forwards as an attacking centre-half would do; and also act as relay stations from their own defence.

The wing-halves play a rather more defensive role, very closely marking the opposing wings. The centre-half shadows the opposing centre-forward, which means that the forwards of the opposing team are marked man for man—unlike the orthodox formation, which allows the centre and inside forwards plenty of room.

The lone back plays on his own twenty-five line, moving laterally across the field rather than up and down. His job is to cut off the through pass, and he gets surprisingly little to do in comparison with usual full-back play.

What are the advantages of the system? Firstly, one has better control of the game, due to the increase in depth of positional play, with less movement. Passing is much shorter and more direct and the long hard hit, vulnerable to interception and often unstoppable, is no longer necessary. Secondly, the defence is tighter, the opposition forwards have much less rope, and usually find it difficult to brush off the close attention of their markers. The vulnerable change-over of the backs, which has always struck me as a very poor method of defence, has gone, while the long through pass should be a gift to the deep-lying back. Thirdly, the work load is now much more even. Players have a smaller area of the field to cover and therefore the ball is made to do most of the work. In fact, the ball can be passed backwards with more certainty, even to the goalkeeper, who can originate attacking moves.

It is surprising how easy it is to play the system, provided there is a will to apply concentration to the method. A five-minute pre-match talk with the famous festival side, Tramps, at a very pleasant Easter tournament at Bad Kreuznach, produced an excellent result after two disappointing performances.

Does it work? The Beckenham results before and after we adopted the 4–2–3–1 show a small increase in goals scored, and a decrease of one-third in goals conceded. The teams were virtually the same, with the exception of a few shinier scalps and a slight increase in girths among the defence!

Everyone enjoyed playing it, and our learned and vocal supporters increased in number and noise, most of them being favourably impressed. As for the team, they learned to think more about their positional play on the field, and all became better players for it. Our opponents produced many plans to counteract the formation, all of which were different, but it was pleasant to know that they even thought of a way to beat us. Perhaps the greatest compliment was paid by the English coach, who produced a two-page résumé on the formation before we played his club.

The Cambridge University team of 1962 had a very successful season playing 4–2–3–1, and several other teams tried it, including the Ladies of Aberdeen University. Are you square, too?

32

OFFICERS v. SERGEANTS

ANTHONY ARMSTRONG

An extract from *A Military Omnibus**

Our football match with the sergeants is, of course, such a serious business that it is practically a religious ceremony; our annual hockey match with them, however, provides merely comic relief. It is, in fact, treated so lightly that the men are not even given a half-day off to watch it. This means that your touch-line audience is confined solely to those men who are either sick, excused duty, just off duty, just about to go on duty, on duty near by, or merely happen to be passing: in fact, a bare two hundred, instead of the usual two hundred and thirty!

The standard of play among the members of the two teams naturally varies considerably. On the one hand there is Lieutenant Holster, a star player, who wears a shirt like a coat of arms, canary-coloured gloves turned back from the wrist, and white tape round his stick in no fewer than three places; while in contrast to him is Sergeant-Major Magazine, who thought hockey was a game till he was given a stick to play it with. Between these two extremes are players of every degree of skill, such as Lieutenant James, who plays fairly regularly; Captain Bayonet, who hasn't played since school; Quartermaster-Sergeant Fourbytwo, who knows the rules but can't play the game itself; Sergeant Grenade, who can play the game itself but doesn't know the rules; and Lieutenant Swordfrog, who can obviously play golf. Then there is Sergeant Haversack, who has a stick but can't play, and Corporal Foresight, who can play but hasn't a stick—a deficiency due to his having been raked in to complete the officers' team at the last minute in place of an absentee. It results in his being put in goal, where he is allowed to kick. Finally there is Lance-Corporal Scabbard, who has been appointed referee more by virtue of a very powerful whistle than because of any deep knowledge of the laws of the game.

With a mighty blast, like a factory signal, play begins, and the forgetful Sergeant Grenade, omitting all formalities of the bully, drives the ball with a masterly tee-shot straight from the centre of the field

* *The above article previously appeared in "Punch".*

through our goal. Deafening applause results. Ten minutes are then wasted while Lieutenant Holster explains, first to our opponents and then to the referee that by the rules it isn't a goal; after which five more minutes pass while the referee explains to the touch-line crowd. The impression finally left on the touch-line is that it is rotten luck on Sergeant Grenade and that there is some sort of a clique against him, led by Lance-Corporal Scabbard. Being very tenacious of the right of free comment on all matters of public interest they refer to this belief through the remainder of the game.

Play is uneventful for some while after, till Lieutenant James, stopping a high one with his hand in front of our opponents' goal, drives it through, about two inches from the goal-keeper's head and at thirty miles an hour—a magnificent scoring shot. A piercing blast from Lance-Corporal Scabbard's whistle, however announces it as a free hit to our opponents for "hands". When the matter has been adjusted, the officers demand another referee while the sergeants demand another goalkeeper, Sergeant Haversack having left a message to say he has suddenly remembered he was orderly sergeant and has had to go. Captain and Quartermaster Ledger comes forward and says he can just spare the time to referee; and after a hot meeting of all the sergeants, the junior lance-sergeant present "volunteers" for the vacant position in their goal-mouth.

Further play up to half-time consists of a series of brilliantly organised movements by Lieutenant Swordfrog, Lieutenant Holster, and Captain Bayonet, all of which are foiled by Sergeant-Major Magazine at right-back. Sergeant-Major Magazine has spent most of his spare time going about swinging his stick at the end of a long arm, like a Neanderthal man called out to defend his home, and his tactics when at close quarters are somewhat primeval. His method of stopping a rush seems to be (*a*) to step on the ball and sink it deeply into the ground, (*b*) to sweep his attackers' legs from under them with his stick, and (*c*) to fall over on top of them afterwards. Any purely technical brilliance on the part of his opponents is thus apt to be dimmed; for Sergeant-Major Magazine is no gossamer. Counter-attacks by our less conscientious members on Sergeant-Major Magazine's shins are without effect, as he is discovered afterwards to be wearing a pair of bayonet scabbards under his stockings.

The score at half-time is two to the officers and one to the sergeants, the latter scored by Sergeant Grenade, who swept the ball up into his midst at the half-way line and by a magnificent rush bore it with him through our goal, and incidentally through the net, no one having been able during his advance to penetrate his protective screen and take it from him.

Midway through the second half a very knotty point arises. During a mêlée in our goal-mouth, Sergeant-Major Magazine, who has broad-minded ideas on the position of right-back, drops his stick. It is at once picked up by Corporal Foresight, the officers' goal-keeper, who hasn't one. Sergeant-Major Magazine demands it back, but Foresight, throwing discipline to the winds, asserts that possession is nine sections of the Army Act, and that he has won it in fair fight.

Sergeant-Major Magazine puts him under arrest. Corporal Foresight appeals to Lieutenant Holster. Sergeant-Major Magazine thereupon puts him further under arrest, and Foresight appeals to Captain Bayonet, his company commander. Captain Bayonet sends off for a copy of Queen's Regulations to find out what to do, or rather—since nothing is just *done* in the Army—what action is to be taken, or procedure to be adopted, in the case of hostile weapons captured from the enemy during battle. The Adjutant gives it as his opinion that it is a nice point; Lieutenant Swordfrog is appointed Prisoner's Friend; and we are just about to unravel the affair when a whistle blast announces that Captain and Quartermaster Ledger has decided it is time. Thereupon the whole question is at once complicated by Private O'Jector, who timidly appears from the crowd and asks for his "stick back, plase, sorr—the wan which the sar'nt-maer borrered from my kit."

The inquiry is therefore adjourned for further witnesses to be called, and for the evidence to be reduced to writing.

Careful, you might have hit me!

33

LOOK AHEAD, BRITAIN !

ALEX BANNISTER

Daily Mail, England

Hockey is too fine a game, in my opinion, to hide for long under its present cloak of modesty—a modesty that goes to absurd lengths. As an outside admirer, so to speak, knowing how other games speak up for themselves, I wonder just how much hockey suffers from a prim aversion to many forms of publicity. A field game as fast, skilful, and as exciting as hockey can be, deserves far wider public support. And the English public could be reached.

Take Britain's achievements at recent Olympics. Their hockey men could hold their heads high—which is more than can be said of many of the much-vaunted and publicised athletes. Yet, I suggest, few of the general public could answer the snap questions: Where did Britain finish? Who were the players? For that matter, how many could name one English international in any period?

Modest space is given to hockey in the so-called quality papers—which is preaching to the converted; but for the rest, with their mass appeal, hockey is virtually ignored.

I do not believe for one moment that the game would be vulgarised, or its many splendid traditions endangered, by increasing popular interest. To my mind that is the logical outcome of natural growth and expansion. Nor would the game's pure and much-envied amateurism, which remains an oasis in a desert of sports materialism, be endangered if the one obvious step were taken to set up league competitions on a regional basis. The success of the county championship lends support for this argument.

Further, I suggest, weekly competitive play would sharpen standards, and automatically lead to an improved international side, which serves as the shop window of any sport.

If club matches began to mean something, hockey's recognition as a leading game would not be long in coming. Newspapers would certainly give more space, and there seems to be scope in television.

Surely hockey can offer more than many of the sports regularly televised and at the same time, make considerable financial profit. To judge from some of the unimportant events which are given wide and long coverage, television has far from exhausted its range of sports.

There were many arguments and protests raised in cricket against the gamble of a knock-out cup competition. How empty they were proved to be; and I am sure a knock-out cup competition for hockey would be similarly successful and popular in England. Is there a valid reason in these modern days why such a gamble is against the interests of the game?

In the running and organising of a knock-out competition—yes, in addition to the leagues—hockey would not be faced with many of cricket's vexing problems—such as the hazard of the weather and over-crowded fixtures. Internationally, the formation of an under-23 team is admirable (even though it is a copy from soccer). The appointment of a paid secretary of the English Association suggests an awareness of problems, but it is high time that British hockey "thought big". Let it be wildly imaginative. A few failures won't hurt, but harm must come if there is no quality of dare. All games must either go forward or backward; there is no standing still.

As I write, Britain is getting its expected hiding in far-off India, and some words by Australia's secretary-coach, Mr. Charles Morley, carry special significance. He has, I read, promised to retire from office twenty-four hours after achieving his life-long sporting ambition—an Australian hockey victory over both India and Pakistan. For thirty years he has studied the tactics and methods of teams and players from the sub-continent and he says (so rightly): "Once you have beaten them you know you have a hockey team."

In terms of numbers Australia is a relatively small hockey-playing nation, but if there is one country capable of ending the invincibility of India and Pakistan it could well be Australia.

There are several reasons. For the most part Australian grounds are dry, the climate is good. Australians, too, take a great pride in national achievement—a quality capable of taking them far in any sport, once the basic skills are conquered. It is possible that even with their natural ability to play all games well and confidently the Australians could never quite equal the agility and dexterity at top speed enjoyed by Indians and Pakistanis. But Australians have an uninhibited will to win, reservoirs of determination, and perseverance, which could more than equalise any marked differences of skill.

In a short while Australia has travelled far. Until 1956 their only international opposition was an exchange of visits with New Zealand. Yet at the Olympics at Melbourne in 1956 they were fifth out of sixteen teams, behind India, Pakistan, Germany and Britain. At Rome in the next Olympics, Australia were beaten by only India and Pakistan, and in a tournament at Ahmedabad, which attracted twelve entries though not one from Pakistan, they were third, below India and Germany.

So it is clear Britain faces not only growing competition from Europe in the future, but from Australia. Britain cannot afford to mark time if her place in world hockey is to be maintained.

I see no reason why—as cricket and soccer have done so often in the past—the best coaches cannot be hired to raise domestic standards. Every year British footballers and cricketers fan out to all parts of the world to impart their knowledge to eager learners from school to international level. Several of the Olympic soccer players at Tokyo were coached by Englishmen.

Is it not time that British hockey reversed the trend, and invited the top Indians to organise their coaching? This is no reflection on Britain's coaches, who do invaluable work in their own time, but Britain should try everything; she has little to lose but the whole world of hockey to gain.

34
FESTIVAL

NEVILL MIROY

Royal Navy & Middlesex; Manager, Folkestone International Hockey Festival

No hockey season in Britain would be complete which did not culminate in a festival. All over Britain, and on the continent for that matter, festivals are held, and thousands of players travel as Tramps, Ghosts, Llamas, White Mice, to indulge in the game they love and have a jolly good time. Nothing typifies the spirit of the British player better than a festival. No leagues and cups here, no bitter rivalry; it doesn't matter a hang if you win all your games or lose all of them, one does one's best.

My wife and I have the privilege of running the Folkestone International Festival which is held at the seaside resort on the South-East coast of England every year. It is probably one of the best known festivals in the world, for teams from America, Argentina, India, South Africa and most of the European countries have taken part over the past fifty odd years.

It is privately organised, and was given to my wife and me by my father-in-law, the late C. F. H. Wagstaff, as a wedding present. Some present! In its earliest days a few members of the local club invited some of their friends to Folkestone for the Easter week-end. There were four teams in 1906 and twenty-one in 1947 when my wife and I took over. To-day fifty-six teams take part, and in so doing bring to the seaside town over a thousand players, supporters, journalists and umpires. Some invitations are sent out two years in advance, and my wife is kept fully occupied attending to the thousand-and-one queries that arise eight months before the festival.

Nearer the time I have to arrange the programme and allocate the umpires, a most demanding part of the organisation. It might appear easy to make fixtures for fifty-six teams, but many questions arise—Have they already played during the season? Did they play each other last year? Are the two teams of reasonably even strength? Does an umpire see one particular team more than once and are his games arranged so that he is not on one pitch all the time? There are seven pitches all at the same venue—one of Folkestone's big advantages—and they are always excellently prepared by the local Corporation.

The increase in the number of teams has necessitated more and more umpires and since the war they have been invited from all over England. Many who have accepted have benefited greatly. In 1959 I asked two Dutch umpires to join us, and this proved such a popular step, practically and socially, that two men from a continental country are now invited every year. This is appreciated by the players, who thereby experience continental interpretation of the rules—unfortunately different from ours in several respects.

Each year I select one foreign and one home team as principal guests, offering one of them the attraction of playing against the Festival Eleven on Easter Day. An invitation to be a member of the Festival Eleven has become a very high honour, for the team is chosen from all those participating in the festival, and many a current international has had to be a spectator.

Possibly the greatest thing about a festival is the friendly rivalry in which all the games are played, and the opportunity it gives to meet new opponents. To play against a foreign club is always attractive to the English sides, and invitations are sent to selected overseas clubs every year. Each Olympic year we really try to "go to town", and the invitations are so worded that the foreign countries can, if they so wish, send their potential Olympic sides. In 1964 three such sides accepted invitations—Spain, France, playing as "Blue Devils", and Britain under the guise of "Unicorns". It is completely within the nature of the festival that both Spain and the Unicorns were beaten by Oxford University.

The social side leaves nothing to be desired, and it is a tribute to the resilience of the hockey players that, however late or early to bed, they give of their utmost on the field the next day, although it must be accepted that there are occasions on Easter Mondays when their skills are somewhat obscure.

It is inevitable that over the years many incidents take place which cause a certain amount of innocent mirth; some are now recognised as classics and are re-told with fresh exaggerations year after year.

One of the best remembered concerned the former British Olympic team centre-half, Frank Reynolds, who was noted amongst other things for his fine bushy moustache. Frank was due to play for the Royal Engineers, but he and his team were nowhere to be seen when one of their matches was scheduled to start. Then, suddenly, a roar of laughter rang round the field as Frank led out his team each wearing a moustache similar to his. So great was the amusement that it was close on half-time before Frank requested permission from the umpire to leave the field—his team had been playing with twelve men.

There are humorous incidents off the field as well. A visiting player, proposing the health of the Folkestone Corporation, admitted that a young shrub, now a large flowering bush occupying pride of place in his garden in the midlands, once adorned the Folkestone cliffside. The mayor was amused; not so the local vicar who, early on Easter Day, found the flag of one of the most famous hockey clubs flying above his church tower!

It is, of course, common to see souvenirs of any festival displayed in clubhouses; it is, however, difficult to understand how borrowers could hope to display the enormous hotel sign of the festival headquarters in their home pavilion. Yet somehow this large piece of wood, some ten feet by two feet, was unbolted and transported to London. At Charing Cross Station it appears that the students had a change of heart and decided to return the sign but, impecunious after the week-end, they couldn't raise the carriage fee between them. It was some months later that an intelligent attendant in Charing Cross Station's Left Luggage Office telephoned the hotel to say he was minding a large piece of merchandise, on which he would be quite prepared to waive the warehouse charges provided he could send same "Carriage forward."

A penguin caused me more bother. One of a pair made of stone that lived in one of the Folkestone bars it was "lifted" by a Service side who, in turn, lost it the same night to one of the London hospital teams. The following November, visiting the clubhouse of the hospital concerned, I learned the penguin had only the week before been "lifted", and it was one of a number of articles which had found a new home in London's Strand. A few days later I happened to read in the Press that King's College had been raided by students and certain souvenirs taken. I finally found the peregrinatory penguin high on a perch in a University of London students' common room. As some nine months had now elapsed since its initial wandering, the Principal was a little suspicious of my story—nevertheless, he was persuaded to allow this important and much-sought-after trophy to return to its rightful owner, and it was actually wheeled into the festival dinner the following year by one of the original borrowers and returned with due ceremony to its rightful owner. To-day the penguin, with its twin, adorns an old people's garden in Folkestone, where no doubt it bores to death the twin with its travellers tales.

On another occasion a hotel proprietor rang me to say he had lost his front door. Sure enough it had been unscrewed, lock, stock, and panels. We found it next morning blocking one of the goals on the main pitch and when, at considerable expense and inconvenience, I delivered it back and actually screwed it into its proper place, the proprietor never even offered me a drink!

Perhaps he didn't enter into the festival spirit, but the atmosphere is normally catching, and Folkestone is always a cheerful place at Easter. As I look out over the grounds filled with players and see and take part in the whole-hearted enjoyment of a hockey week-end, I know that all the heartaches and hard work have been worth while. Festivals have become integral parts of the hockey scene.

35

THE PRINCE OF CENTRE-FORWARDS—STANLEY SHOVELLER

DAVID MORGAN

B.B.C. Midlands Hockey Correspondent

Each succeeding generation throws up an outstanding personality in many fields of sport. In the early 1900's it was Stanley Howard Shoveller, M.C., the Prince of Centre-Forwards—the finest British forward there has ever been.

Shoveller can be compared with Stanley Matthews for his genius, dedication and skill. He was an elusive runner and a magnificent dribbler, often feinting, leaving an opponent leaning in one direction while he was busy beating the next. There was no more pleasing sight in hockey than one of his sudden and electrifying bursts that delighted his comrades, paralysed his opponents, and left the spectators gasping—a close corkscrew down the field, with little or no detour, and a quick push that usually meant a goal.

He dominated world hockey for nearly twenty years, from March 1902, when he scored against Wales in his first international, until March 1921, when King George V was attracted to Foxgrove Road, Beckenham, to see him in action for the last time against Ireland. Shoveller was the only Englishman to win two Olympic hockey gold medals, for he played in the victorious teams of 1908 at the White City, and 1920 at Antwerp, sweeping England to victory by scoring eighteen goals in five games.

Perhaps his proudest moment came when he was acclaimed by the players and officials of six countries at the Olympic banquet at the Hotel Russell in 1908. One and all subscribed to the view that he was the greatest player of all time, the highest and most finished product of the game.

His was the inspiration from which sprang the skill of some of England's finest forwards, and he was the nightmare of opposing centre-halves. Probably only one ever managed to "tame" him, and that was Irishman P. N. Murdoch, in Shoveller's last international in 1921.

"Shove" is easily England's top goalscorer, and only his business commitments prevented him from having the most caps as well. He failed to score for England in only three matches, his best performance being six against Wales in 1906. He scored five in a match three times and got ten hat-tricks. If this seems slightly mathematical, so were the problems of the umpires whenever he played for Hampstead, Surrey and the South, for he did not reserve his best performances for internationals.

He played his full part in administration too. He was hon. match secretary of the Hockey Association from 1906 to 1912, a vice-president of the H.A. from 1921 until his death in 1959, and an England selector with an eye for goal-scoring forwards in the thirties.

As an author on the game, his coaching articles provided the background at many famous schools. His seventy-one goals in twenty-nine games for England gave him every right to tell others how to do it.

"Shove" was no ordinary hockey player—he was a phenomenon at a time when hockey was developing into the world game it is now. He captained his country on many occasions and never failed to bring out the teams' very finest qualities by the sheer brilliance of his personal example.

In an era when goal-scoring seems to be a lost art, his record should be an inspiration for the world's centre-forwards to find a way through those packed defences again.

36

THE SANDS OF SEATON CAREW

GORDON WILKINSON

Secretary, Durham County H.A.

It is January 1963, the whole of the region is buried under twelve inches of snow, and the weather-man gives no prospect of clearance for weeks to come. Groundsmen stand at the doors of their equipment sheds, gazing out over the bleak scene of unsullied white, at the goal-posts standing silent, stark in the glistening, untrodden snow. The cutter and roller gather rust in the dark of the shed.

Match secretaries are weary of sending out cancellation notices; some do not even trouble to think of matches, and settle down to week-ends of television, children and crossword puzzles. Players tramp gloomily around the house, kicking the dog, and smoking to excess. Wives, at first happy at the thought of having a man around the house on Saturday and Sunday, now wish for a break in the weather and the clearance of the snow, so that their better halves can get out and become human again.

Near by, the wind from Russia whistles over the North Sea, whipping the wave crests into spattering white caps. The beach, washed by the tides, is the only strip of Britain clear of ice, frost and snow. The promenade is deserted save for a solitary figure clambering from the only car in the car park. He consults his watch and his tide tables. Soon his tasks will begin. The sea recedes as the tide sweeps south down the coast and the sand is left billiard-table smooth and glistening. A perfect canvas for the master's hand. The figure collects his equipment and, breasting the keening wind, steps on to the clear, smooth expanse. With measure, string and square and a large pointed stick, the grand design is drawn on the sand. Farther along the beach the same pattern is repeated—Jack Jemison, captain of Durham County Hockey Eleven and of Norton Hockey Club, has overcome the worst that winter could inflict on the hockey fraternity. Two pitches have been prepared for the early afternoon.

This was true, infectious enthusiasm. During that long, long winter of 62/63, the Norton club did not miss a single week-end's hockey. When distant clubs were daunted at the prospect of facing that wind off the North Sea, emergency calls went out and scratch elevens from neighbouring clubs in many combinations and permutations were hastily arranged. In the Norton clubhouse, boilers were lighted and water heated; doors were locked; players climbed into cars for the eight-mile ride to the sands at Seaton Carew, just north of the Tees mouth.

The deserted car park became alive with cars, players, "camp followers", umpires shook dusty whistles, and tentative, joyous trial blasts competed with the shrill of the wind. After the cosy misery of Saturday firesides this was true, adventurous, wonderful hockey. The ball ran true and stick-work became somehow easy. The near-zero air made running necessary to keep warm; even the umpire sprinted up the wing ahead of the winger. Of course, those nearest the sea edge kept a close eye on the advancing tide. It would be no great fun to find two or three inches of sea water lapping around the feet.

At half-time the game was switched to the second prepared pitch, a new surface unruffled and inviting.

Editor's note: Needless to say, the sands at Seaton Carew became the Mecca of Hockey in North-East England during that long winter. Matches started as early as 11 a.m., and other odd hours, depending on the tide times. Even the Durham County Association took up the lead set by Jack Jemison and Norton Hockey Club. Three "A" Eleven matches were successfully played on the same, ever new pitches. Norton, fit and in practice, did not lose a single match during that winter, and their goal average was astronomical.

37

A SONG OF HOCKEY

E. G. L. HOSE

Bromley H.C. and England

There is glory in the shooting of a goal,
  When the centre-forward's set;
  I have seen them break the net,
I have seen the daisy cutter and the roll,
  From a corner hit stopped dead,
  And with aim unerring sped
There is glory in the shooting of a goal.

  McKinley on the stump,
  Found glory "in a lump"
And Nansen had his pleasure at the pole;
  But taking things all round,
  You may bet your bottom pound,
There is glory in the shooting of a goal.

  When you hustle past the backs,
  By a series of tacks,
And you know you have the "keeper" in a hole,
  Or you hit like anything
  As it comes in from the wing;
There is glory in the shooting of a goal.

  Ho! the keeper-boy can't stop
  Those you get upon the hop,
But stands up there a-praying for his soul;
  When he finds it missed his eyes,
  He'll admit with glad surprise
There is glory in the shooting of a goal.

38

ENGLAND TAKES TO COMPETITIVE HOCKEY

DAVID WIGGINS

Hockey Correspondent, Sunday Times, *England*

"*A correspondent suggests that it would increase interest in hockey if a county championship were arranged on the lines of the Rugby Union Championship and the suggestion is worth consideration. As is well-known, a county championship takes place annually in the Midlands, and it has undoubtedly tended not only to increase interest in the sport but led to a material improvement in the character of the play.*"

Birmingham Post, March 29, 1899.

Fifty-eight years after it was first mooted, the Hockey County Championship began in England, in the autumn of 1957. Voices had been raised against it for many years, for the Hockey Association frowned on all forms of organised competition and feared that it might lead to practices incompatible with the game's admirable amateur ideals.

In fact, the institution of the county championship was very soon a great success and the game in Britain remains as wholly amateur as ever. It has had the effect, which divisional matches always lacked, of broadening the horizons of the game and bringing together counties which would not normally have met in serious contest: not counties from within a division, as before, but from any part of the country.

Before the 1957/8 season, local county matches were played in front of a handful of officials, a few dedicated enthusiasts, and, in the south, by those fortunate enough to enjoy their freedom on a Wednesday afternoon. Now, at an early stage in each season's championship, a noisy partisan band of followers attend the games and are very concerned about their outcome. It is almost as if hockey in England had begun a cup competition, and the draw for the early rounds is discussed earnestly before the season starts.

For a game which attracts only 3/4,000 spectators at an international in London, it was entirely gratifying in 1957 to find a thousand or more at Norwich on a bitterly cold day watching and supporting Norfolk against Warwickshire in the semi-final round. The edge of competitive play with its necessarily tougher methods is no bad thing in grooming players to represent British teams in international matches, especially abroad. It has sharpened their reaction to determined opposition but has not led to methods being adopted foreign to our traditions and ideals.

The advent of the county championship made quite an impact on sports editors. Those newspapers prepared to give some space to the game—and they are increasing slowly—very quickly fell for the new competitive line in hockey. Reporters who expected a quiet autumn afternoon at a club match six miles from home found themselves bundled off to Weston-super-Mare, or Coventry, or St. Annes-on-Sea for a group county championship final. The interminable round of trials tended to be overlooked and the pens were busily engaged on a game where the result really mattered to quite a few people.

But the best outcome of English hockey's most notable post-war innovation was the interest created by the championship among the smaller counties—smaller, that is, in population and in the number of affiliated clubs. Lincolnshire's initial success proved an ideal stimulus—a succession of wins by the big brothers might have had a depressing effect. In fact, Durham, Wiltshire, Norfolk and Hertfordshire have all made their presence felt in the first seven years and the honours have been well spread. Seventeen counties have reached the semi-final round in that time, and no less than fourteen in the past four seasons. Only Middlesex, who were losing finalists once and winners twice, have in any way threatened to hold the stage for too long, and when one considers the talent at their disposal it is indeed surprising that their record has not been better still.

Naturally there are snags about the championship but they are far out-weighed by the advantages. The standard of play in Britain has in no way been raised since 1957. Some would say that by spreading the best available players far and wide it is harder for the top performers to meet good opposition frequently enough. It is certainly true that only one southern county (and there are an uncommonly large number of first-class players in Kent, Middlesex and Surrey) can reach the semi-final round each year, and counties now select players without an "English" qualification. But our Olympic effort is a British one, and the Irish, Scots and Welsh have no county championships, though there is no shortage of cups and leagues in Ireland.

Of course the competition has further congested a heavy fixture list. Only the southern counties refuse to play Saturday matches, and in the rest of England, especially in the north, the clubs do not see their best players for weeks on end.

But this gives opportunities for many other members to play in a better class of hockey and it increases the interest in the county side if a club has a player actively engaged.

This competition must be encouraged. It has done more for the game in England in a few years than divisional, trial or home international matches have done since the end of the nineteenth century.

39

SATURDAY—AN OFFICIAL'S LAMENT

BRIAN LEWIS

Richmond H.C., London

Everyone, however modest, likes a little applause sometimes—our most Walter Mittyish dreams invariably culminate in rounds of cheers from an admiring populace; the actor taking his fifth curtain, the cricketer removing his cap as the crowd acknowledge his century, the captain bringing in his battered boat with all the ships in the river hooting congratulations—the applause is an integral part of the dream. In just the same way—even the poor hockey club official sometimes pines for at least a kindly word. Do I, captain of the second eleven, match secretary and ground committee representative ever get one?

This morning, being Sunday, I called in at the ground about half past eleven: the groundsman was doubtful, the pitch wet but recovering, so I over ruled him as usual and we hope to play this afternoon. It now being twelve I felt a pint or so might settle my Sunday stomach.

My centre-half and right-back were deep in conversation as I approached the bar.

"Not much of a game yesterday."

"No—we should have won all the same—no forwards, as usual."

"Well, the thing is, of course, if John weren't captain he'd be lucky to get in the fourth. Played a terrible game. I don't think he stopped it once in the first ten minutes."

"Ah, of course I wasn't there till after that. John was damn rude about it, too. All right for him, living down here, telling us to meet at the ground. I wonder how he'd manage if he had to get a bit of lunch and still get through the traffic from town by one-thirty. Five minutes walk for him and his wife to get the meal. Nothing to do but pick his kit up and get in the car."

At this point I wished my colleagues a restrained good morning; they changed the subject and I bought the beer. Walking home I must say I found myself a little upset. Nothing to do but pick up my kit and get in the car indeed. On a wet Saturday morning.

It had started quite well. When I woke up at about eight Jean was making the tea, the second had a full side and an association umpire lined up, the weather forecast was "very cold, with fog and snow later", so there was every hope of a warm, fine afternoon, and I'd had confirmations from all the clubs with which we had fixtures. The first telephone call came at eight-thirty. Captain of the first, two inside-forwards unable to play, and he couldn't do anything about it as he would be working away from a telephone all the morning. Would I please tell my two insides to play at home instead of with the second away? This didn't worry me too much—after all the first must have the best side available. I had the odd reserve up my sleeve, and now I could play centre-forward instead of left-wing—no one ever passes to the left-wing in the second eleven. So the first eleven captain rang off, still apologising and leaving me to have breakfast and get on with it.

Halfway through the cornflakes my umpire rings. He's very sorry, his wife has influenza, he can't manage to-day. This was serious; no hope of a replacement from the association at this stage, of course. There was one "possible", but he has no telephone, hates leaving the home ground when the first has a good match and lives three miles away. However, I hoped to make time to get over and talk him into it, put it out of mind for a bit and finished breakfast. Having got the coal in, done the washing-up and tried to mend the broken lock on the front door without much luck, I set about getting hold of the two inside-forwards for the first. After obtaining engaged tones on the 'phone from each (the first time either of them has even been out of bed before ten o'clock on a Saturday in living memory), I contacted both about nine-thirty. Both were happy to switch sides.

So the first was all right—all I had to do now was to find two of my reserves to play for me, organise an umpire, have a word with the groundsman, arrange a lift for my goalkeeper, who had been coming from town with one of the inside forwards—and my duties were done.

I normally have four spare each Saturday in my group; though I knew one was unavailable. Never mind, I rang him, got him first time, he would be delighted to play. Good.

Time, as ever on Saturday mornings, was slipping by remarkably fast. It was already quarter past ten and getting moderately urgent to fill my side but, just as I had a finger in the telephone dial, Jean called out it was raining. Well, it had been a dampish week, the ground was wet already and one of the visiting sides was coming about seventy miles; obviously I must cancel early or not at all. When I left the house on the way over to the ground it was one of those heavy, warm mornings, not raining heavily but dripping hard—the kind of day that normally stays the same until evening and puts a groundsman's heart into his boots. Our groundsman is very good but he is always inclined to scratch at the least sign of rain; even a heavy dew frightens him. It took nearly twenty minutes fast talking, the water dripping off my hat, to persuade him that we shouldn't do much damage providing the rain got no heavier. Even then, I had to promise "no play" should things get worse without, needless to say, the slightest intention of putting anything off. I should be safely off to my away game by the time the visitors arrived, and the first and third captains could sort it out for themselves.

Back at home I began to feel anxious—still one short, no umpire, nearly eleven and Jean needing the car by half past to visit the hairdresser. If I went over to see my potential umpire at once I could just manage it there and back by half eleven, but what about my eleventh man, and letting the visiting sides know the form about the ground? Obviously, the first essential was to tell the visiting sides. The "long-distance one" must know by twelve at the latest; with the other, there had been a shambles of a game last season, so a bit of tact was required.

At this moment, while still undecided which to do first, I had a stroke of luck. My goalkeeper, whose transport problem I had forgotten completely, rang me to say he had heard his lift was no longer on and would have to make his own way to the ground—not to worry about him at all. This was a nice change—a player prepared to arrange things for himself. When I first started hockey anyone without a car looked round, as soon as he knew himself selected, and found his own lift or travelled under his own steam by public transport. *Autre temps, autre moeurs*—nowadays the young men want it all laid on for them. I've known one or two not turn up at all just because a car was not arranged for them. Still, here was one cheerfully doing things for himself; even if he does let in about three soft ones a game, he's in the side for the rest of the season.

Recklessly committing myself to the certainty of an embittered civil war and malice domestic, I started the job of trying to get hold of a fixture secretary two counties away. After nine minutes—yes, nine solid minutes—the telephone operator, in that odiously condescending tone so many of them use to put the caller in his place, at last brought herself to answer just as I was about to tear the telephone from its socket. I suppose these operators know to a second how long they can get away with it before the caller goes mad, has hysterics or demands the supervisor. After five minutes more frustration, I got the number, to hear it was "fair pelting down in Oxford" and that my opposite number's telephone had been ringing the whole morning. Exchanging a few friendly commiserations on our hard lot we confirmed the game: if the rain got worse they would have to put up with a wasted journey. Next—that odd crowd we had a row with last year. Strangely their man was as nice as anything, agreed to bring his side over and was quite prepared for the match to be called off on arrival. Another job over and done—twenty past eleven. Now to sneak out to the car without Jean seeing me and off for the umpire.

So arrived the trickiest moment of my Saturday morning; talking a cross-grained, idle character into foregoing his quiet afternoon watching the first eleven, pontificating about hockey in general and umpiring in particular, and drinking far more than he should, and umpiring the second on a rough old track on a ground without a bar. Loud brass fanfares from his record-player greeted me at the door so I knew he was up. The "business" went much as expected—a few grumbles, but he agreed, and I promised to pick him up at one-fifteen. That meant five people in the car but only for seven or eight miles; even my springs should stand that.

I do not propose to go into the details of the trouble on my arrival home at ten to twelve. Nothing is more depressing than a domestic encounter, but I must admit I was unnecessarily provocative in insisting that the car be returned not later than one o'clock. Not surprisingly this raised the storm to an intensity reached only once before in my time. That was a rough one, too—all because I put out a tentative suggestion that we should come back from our honeymoon three days early to give me a chance of playing in the pre-season practice match.

The front door was slammed in a way that did no good at all to my repairs to the lock and I was left to contemplate the prospect of cooking my own luncheon, finding one more player and confirming that the rain hadn't yet washed out the second eleven game. Rather wearily I turned to the telephone again. Ten minutes afterwards, one full-back had flatly refused to play, and the other would only consent provided he were played in his normal position—left-back. Argument was no use and I got so fed up with him that I told him in the end we could get on without his valuable services and slammed the receiver down. I must have been more off balance after my row with Jean than I realised.

Almost in desperation I rang the third eleven captain, to find him in a great flap and two men short. Fortunately one place he needed to fill was left-back, so I gave him the name of my malcontent and quickly dialled the fourth eleven captain. Our fourth captain is always most helpful in such situations—he not only gave me the name of a player but, as the fourth were on the same ground as we were, promised to give him a lift over because of my shortage of cars. Needless to say the player, when I got on to him, was another back and I wanted a left-wing, but I talked him into it in the end, although he would be about as much out of place in the second-eleven forwards as a counter-tenor singing Siegfried.

There it was then—just half-past twelve, still only raining lightly enough to make play more than probable, and I had, at last, eleven men, even if four were backs, four halves and just two forwards.

I began to think about getting myself luncheon, but just as I had the knife poised above the cheese (I somehow always finish up with bread, cheese and beer on Saturdays—and I don't even like cheese), the extra-fifth eleven captain rings. Very sorry but he'd lost the name, address and telephone number, carefully given him by me earlier in the week, of the secretary of the club he was playing and didn't want to take his side over in case the game had to be cancelled. I gave him the number again, and for the next quarter of an hour the blasted telephone never stopped. Captain of the first—was everything all right?; groundsman—had I got the balls? (I had and would drop them off at the ground on my way); bar secretary—could I remember who ran the bar last time the first and third were at home together? No, I couldn't, his job, not mine; visiting side from Oxford—they were at High Wycombe, it was still pelting down, should they turn back? And so on and so on until, less than half a bottle of beer and two mouthfuls of cheese later, I heard the front door slammed and Jean was back from the hairdressers. Well, at least she hadn't crashed the car, nor had she got her hair done, but it was nearly one o'clock by this time so I grabbed my kit, remembered to kiss Jean goodbye, and was away. The telephone was ringing as I shot out, Jean shouted something from the window as I dived into the car. Nothing could touch me further; after the morning's fitful fever I could enjoy my game.

One thing I will say in my umpire's favour. He never keeps you waiting. After the usual trouble with traffic lights I picked him up at precisely one-fifteen, with a full quarter of an hour to go before meeting the rest of the side on the ground—nice time for a rapid one on the way.

The car park looked horribly deserted as we turned into it, but I always give a time well in advance of the real deadline so I wasn't too disturbed about that. The groundsman came hurrying over with a long face (it was still drizzling) to pick up the balls, and tick like a clock about using the pitches on a wet afternoon less than two months before the start of the cricket season. Long practice enabled me to talk him into, if not enthusiasm, at least acceptance: and when I looked round, the side now mustered eight and the fourth eleven were also gathering in strength with a most impressive number of powerful motor-cars in their ranks. Every side but mine seems to be stuffed with opulent cars. Five minutes later the fourth-eleven captain, with my eleventh man in his enormous vehicle, rolled majestically in. Nine men—with the goal-keeper going direct—left one to come; not bad at twenty to two, but where was my centre-half? As he is probably the best hockey player in the team and, more important, was due to take four others in his car, even I, for all my years of experience of crises, began to get nervous. I left it as long as I dared, but a decision had to be made; the fourth had ample room among their cars for my four chaps, and by five to two we finally got past the start line.

On the whole it hadn't been too bad a morning—just about average I would say—but, what with spending the first ten minutes of the game looking over my shoulder to see if my centre-half was coming and worrying as to whether I had deployed my forces to the best advantage, it is quite true my own play lacked its normal poise and assurance. Still, once the missing man arrived I don't think I was too bad. Exactly how

"Tell the fixture secretary I'd like a word with him—"

rude I was to the late-comer I can't quite remember but, damn it, he deserved a rocket. We were two down before he got there and he hadn't been on the pitch more than three minutes when he missed an easy stop on the edge of the circle, obstructed as he turned to chase the ball and it was a short corner. Three down.

We did get one back before the end, but with two halves and one fourth eleven back in the forward line we never really looked like saving it.

For the rest, I could enjoy myself. The evening was great fun. By the time I got home Jean had forgiven me and, *mirabile dictu*, not one man scratched for this afternoon's game. Now, if you'll excuse me I'll just go and get some luncheon—I've got to get over to the ground to open up the pavilion by two and I want to ring the university secretary about Wednesday's game. Oh, yes, and I must write to the festival people about Easter, confirm the fixtures for next week-end, drop a line to the Umpires Association, order half a dozen new balls . . .

40

THE INDOOR GAME IS HERE TO STAY

DAVID MORGAN

B.B.C. Midlands Hockey Correspondent

Since indoor hockey was introduced in Germany shortly after the Second World War, it has slowly caught the imagination of players in many parts of the world and in particular in Europe. It is different, it is exciting, above all it is sociable.

Tournaments quickly became popular in West Germany, and now every league organises indoor hockey championships for men, women and youth teams. International competitions attracting teams from Belgium, Denmark, Switzerland, Spain, the Netherlands and France are held in Berlin, Hamburg, Cologne, Munich, Wiesbaden and other centres. This is the natural consequence of severe winters when no play is possible for two months of the season.

Ideally, the game is played on wood, and the International Hockey Federation have authorised a set of rules in which the court is approximately forty yards by twenty yards, in two halves, with goals and rules similar to the normal field game. Teams are normally six-a-side and a game of two twenty-minute periods is more than the equivalent of a full-sized game outdoors. Naturally the ball must be kept on the floor, so only a push-stroke is permitted, and as four-inch boards on the side-lines keep the ball in play, the game is highly concentrated. Sometimes, in small halls, the court is completely enclosed and players may not enter their opponents' circle and may shoot from anywhere in their opponents' half. Substitutes are allowed—there is a "sin-bin"—no offside and no long corners. Most of the routine interruptions which occur in outdoor hockey have been eliminated, making the game popular with spectators but hectic for umpires.

In Great Britain the game was late in starting. Clubs near Birmingham played several knock-out competitions in 1961 at Digbeth Civic Hall. Then in 1962 the Herne Bay Club organised leagues for men and women in the Pier Pavilion. It was not until 1963, when a devastating winter prevented outdoor play for eleven weeks, that the game really caught on. Then many clubs were ingenious in finding suitable halls, though the size of the Army Drill Halls, Assembly Halls, covered swimming baths, gymnasiums and canteens often limited games to three a side.

The game is invaluable for stick practice because the ball bounces true and must be controlled in inches; it produces goal-hungry forwards who shoot on sight—hockey's biggest weakness; eliminates those terrifying swings with the stick; and inevitably quickens reactions.

Of course, it will never usurp the place of the outdoor game, but it is rapidly assuming an identity of its own, and there is plenty of room for bright young officials to take the initiative and organise indoor festivals, a national tournament, or international competitions.

41

PAKISTAN'S RISE TO WORLD SUPREMACY

SULTAN F. HUSAIN

Editor, Sportimes, *Pakistan*

It has often been said that the Indians have been Champions of the World in field hockey for over thirty years. It is true that India won the Olympic Hockey Tournament on her own in London (1948), Helsinki (1952) and Melbourne (1956), but before the partition of the Indian sub-continent in 1947, the teams that won the Olympic title on the hockey fields of Amsterdam (1928), Los Angeles (1932) and

Berlin (1936) were from a United India, and those territories which now comprise Pakistan supplied a considerable proportion of the players. The glory of these earlier victories must be shared in equal measure by India and Pakistan.

As a new-born independent state with a host of problems, Pakistan could not muster all her resources to organise her hockey between August 1947 and 1948 when the Fourteenth Olympic Games were held in London. Although an unknown quantity, Pakistan was seeded fourth behind India, Germany and Britain, and that is where she ended in the final reckoning. Her debut in the international hockey field as an independent state was thus inauspicious. The Netherlands beat her in a replay between the losing semi-finalists for the bronze medal.

Pakistan's second assault on the Olympic title at Helsinki in 1952 was as abortive as the first. Once again she lost in the semi-final—to Britain in the play-off for the bronze medal, but in between the two Olympics, Pakistan gained some encouragement. In 1950 she took part in the World Hockey Championship held at Barcelona, and shared the trophy with the Netherlands after a drawn final.

Soon after Helsinki, a change came about in the set-up of the Pakistan Hockey Federation and the new organisers put their heads together to probe into the causes of Pakistan's failures in the past two Olympic contests. They decided to form a high-powered Committee of Experts, consisting of former All-India Olympic hockey players, with the task of going into the past performances of the national teams and pinpointing the faults and foibles. Their findings were incorporated in a comprehensive and exhaustive report which, in course of time, came to serve as the blueprint for the new edifice of Pakistan hockey. The report did not make scapegoats of individuals or place the blame at any particular door. It only unearthed the mistakes made in the past and evolved a formula whereby they could be avoided in the future. A thorough and clear-cut policy was laid down for the guidance of those who were to run the Pakistan Hockey Federation, and detailed provisions for every situation which was likely to arise in the future were made.

The new plan was put into operation a couple of years before the 1956 Melbourne Olympic Games and the efforts of the new set-up quickly bore fruit. For the first time Pakistan reached the Olympic final and so assured herself of her first-ever Olympic medal. Although she lost to India by the barest of margins, her performance won her more than just an Olympic silver medal. Her display against India in the final marked her as a new power in international hockey. The solitary goal which gave India the gold medal was a hotly-disputed one. The circumstances under which it was scored are now part of hockey history. In a

Press interview after the Olympic Games, the then President of the International Hockey Federation is reported to have said that Pakistan was clearly the better side and that she was unlucky to lose to India by a goal which was wrongly awarded against her. The F.I.H. President clearly hinted that unfortunate umpiring decisions cost Pakistan the gold medal.

Her next big venture in an international contest was at Tokyo in 1958 when hockey was introduced as a team sport on the Asian Games schedule for the first time. Pakistan's tradition, established at Melbourne, was carried forward to Tokyo and she was awarded the gold medal by virtue of her better goal average (19–0 as against India's 16–1), although the Pakistan-India final ended in a goalless draw. There were many who did not give the winners full credit for their achievement. They called it a "hollow victory" because Pakistan did not beat India in the final. But the rules of the Asian Games contest were very clear on the subject. There was no provision in them for a replay and hence the gold medal was awarded to the team with the better goal average.

September 9, 1960, will go down in the annals of Pakistan hockey as a red letter day. Meeting India for the second time in the final of successive Olympic hockey tournaments, Pakistan reversed the Melbourne score and beat her by a solitary goal at Rome. This triumph won for Pakistan her first-ever gold medal in an Olympic team sport and added the Olympic title to the Asian Games crown which she had won at Tokyo in 1958. It was her greatest victory to date and a signal achievement. The dethroning of India as the Olympic champions had taken Pakistan twelve years and four Olympiads, and Pakistan could be regarded as the champions of the world in field hockey.

The Olympian heights reached had not been attained by sudden flight. It had been a tough climb to the top, and the success achieved was the result of hard work, for which the entire credit must be given to those who had laboured hard behind the scene—the organisers, the coaches and the players who had dedicated themselves to the task of placing Pakistan's hockey at the top of the international ladder. Much of the success achieved was due to the Committee of Experts report.

On return from Rome four years ago, Pakistan did not rest on her hard-won laurels. The Pakistan Hockey Federation were fully alive to the fact that it was not going to be an easy task to remain at the top. They were aware of the great advance made by countries other than Pakistan and India on the hockey field. After taking stock of the opposition which Pakistan was likely to face at Tokyo four years hence, the authorities prepared long and short-term plans soon after the triumph at Rome. The short-term plan was launched with the sole object of defending the Asian Games hockey title at Djakarta in 1962. An initial assessment took place soon after the National Hockey Championship in 1961 where the cream of the country's hockey talent was on display. Camps were set up and the nucleus of the team which was to carry Pakistan's colours at Djakarta was determined.

With the retirement of Major Hamid, the brilliant inside-right who had led Pakistan at Melbourne and Rome, another Army man, Major Manzoor Hussain Atif, was appointed captain of the National Team which made a highly-successful tour of Malaya, Singapore and Ceylon towards the end of 1961. More camps, trials and eliminations followed in 1962, and the selected team was sent to Kenya, where, for the second time, Pakistan won the Test "rubber".

September 3, 1963, was another landmark in Pakistan's rise to world supremacy in hockey. The traditional rivals, Pakistan and India, met once again in the final and a goal in each half sealed India's fate and enabled Pakistan to retain the title. It was a decisive and convincing victory which left no room for doubt regarding Pakistan's superiority.

Having discovered India's strength at Djakarta, Pakistan invited Kenya's team for a full-length tour, including five Tests. The Kenyans who had twice won tests against Pakistan in Kenya, found Pakistan very strong on her own grounds and were out-played in almost every match. With India and Kenya tested in turn, the next step which Pakistan took was to go over for the Pre-Olympic Tournament organised by France at Lyon in September 1963. The main object was to assess the advance made by the European teams since the Rome Olympics. Injuries to key players sustained early in the tournament upset the balance of the team and the world champions finished only fourth behind India, Germany and Holland in the final unofficial rankings.

Pakistan's overall poor performances caused great disappointment to her supporters at home and brought the wrath of the critics on all concerned. Treating the reverses at Lyon as a blessing in disguise, the organisers of Pakistan hockey galvanized themselves into action with the view to restoring Pakistan's fallen prestige and morale. An elaborate plan was drawn up, with two special camps under canvas, and a tour of New Zealand and Australia a month before the 1964 Olympic Games. The President of the Pakistan Hockey Federation, General Mohammad Musa, promised that everything humanly possible would be done to retain the Olympic hockey title at Tokyo.

42

THE FIRST INTERNATIONAL MATCH

Extract from The Irish Field, *February* 2, 1895

The first international hockey match has been lost and won, and Ireland has come out at the top of the heap, after a manner which will ever redound to the credit of the followers of the pastime in the Emerald Isle. The victory over Wales on Saturday was decisive, and if the Irishmen did only manage to chalk up three goals to their opponents nil, no one who saw the game will deny that they were several scores better than the "Taffies". That the pastime is flourishing in Ireland there can be little doubt, as witness the number of clubs which now owe allegiance to the Irish Union, and the growing popularity of the game speaks well for the energy and devotion of the few who have worked in the most praiseworthy fashion to foster it, both in the metropolis and the provinces.

To hark back to Saturday's match, everyone by this time knows, or ought to know, that Rhyl, a pretty seaside resort on the north coast of Wales, was the venue, which town boasts the possession of excellent hotel accommodation, a cosy little theatre, and a very fine pier, which latter however, was not much sought after by the visitors, seeing that snow and frost were pretty much on the spot. The team left Dublin on Friday night by the North Wall express boat, and with the exception of the talkative Walsh and Devlin, who accompanied the invasion as general engineer, every one of them felt the effects of the storm and were in a bad way when Holyhead was reached. Arrived on the ground the next day, the Hibernians, clad in green and white, were loudly cheered on stepping into the arena, which was as hard as nails. The home lot, who suffered by comparison with the Shamrock representatives in the matter of physique, also met with an ovation from the spectators, all of whom were supplied with cards giving a plan of the positions of the players, by the proprietors of our contemporary *Hockey*, with whom the idea of international fixtures originated. It was neatly printed in green out of compliment to the visitors, who greatly appreciated the attention.

Immediately hostilities were commenced—a regular snowstorm was raging at the time—the Irishmen, headed by Carton and H. Birmingham, swept down on the Welsh goal, which nearly fell to the first-named within a minute of the start. Over-anxiety to score lost the Hibernians several good chances, and after the home defence had been sorely tried, Hughes cleared, only to find Beckett passing out nicely to Carton, who renewed the siege with a fine stroke. The "Taffies" were compelled to concede a couple of corners in quick succession, but nothing tangible accrued, and subsequent to Mills grazing the cross bar with a high shot, Hughes and H. Evans came to the rescue, and the former, ably assisted by Parry, transferred play to the Irish end. They were dangerous for a moment only and Walsh and H. Birmingham quickly drove them back. The war was waged in the Welsh twenty-five for a long time, and eventually Carroll hit a brilliant goal from a difficult angle. The Irishmen, having tasted the sweets of success, now worked well together. Following a big stroke from Butler, Beckett again went away in grand style and notched the second goal for his side amidst much excitement.

Early in the second period, which the Shamrock entered two goals to the good, the home side were again having a bad time, and it may be said that they were in such a condition to the end. They were seldom dangerous throughout the half, while on the other hand, the Irishmen should have piled on the agony pretty thick were it not for defective shooting in front of goal. Within five minutes of the finish Beckett again distinguished himself by outpacing the home backs and hitting a magnificent goal. This was the only point notched in this period, and Ireland accordingly left the field winners of their first international by three goals to none.

Beckett was a long way the best forward on the ground, leading most of the aggressive movements, and he centred cleverly. Carton, too, played well, while H. Birmingham who got on as substitute for B. Hamilton, did splendidly, albeit his shooting was bad. Carroll was inclined to get out of his place and Rutherford was only fair. Ramsay did not at all come up to expectations, but then it must be mentioned, in fairness, that he suffered acutely in the passage and did not seem to have shaken off its effects. Walsh played a sound game and Butler throughout justified his selection, while Mills did all that came his way in creditable style. Dobbs was very solid and J. Birmingham in goal was a decided success. The teams were:

IRELAND: J. D. Birmingham (Palmerston); W. B. Dobbs, capt. (Dundrum), B. Ramsay (King's Hospital); J. E. Mills (Palmerston), T. M. Walsh (Palmerston), W. M. Butler (King's Hospital); P. Carton (Trinity College, Dublin), T. E. Beckett (King's Hospital), H. E.

Hockey in Tokyo. India v. Pakistan. Asian Games Final. May 1958. The Pakistan goalkeeper clears.

HOCKEY IN INDIA. The huge crowd at the opening match of the 1962 Ahmedabad Tournament see India attacking against Japan. When the picture was taken there was no score but India won 11–0, and went on to win the tournament.

Commemorative stamp, issued by Fiji to mark the first South Pacific Games in 1963.

Birmingham (Palmerston), H. E. Rutherford (Trinity College, Dublin), A. Carroll (Dundrum).
WALES: J. Evans (Rhyl); R. B. Jones (Huyton), B. P. Griffiths (Rhyl); J. H. Evans (Rhyl), Idris Jones, capt. (Sefton), Sergeant Edward Bennett (Chester Military); J. W. G. Casson and E. W. Powell (both Oxford Univ. and East Sheen), E. H. Parry (Rhyl), T. Evans (Rhyl), Hugh Hughes (Rhyl).
Umpires: W. N. Fletcher (Vice President of the H.A.) and W. F. Barnes-Ward (Manchester).

43
OVER THE DITCH

JOHN WAY
Reading H.C. and Berkshire Boars

The by-products of visiting a continental hockey festival are apt to remain with one for a long time, but, when fat heads have slimmed and astigmatism departs, the richer and more worth while memories remain.

For those whose command of French stops short beyond the ability to describe the location of their aunt's pen, a visit to the Royal Uccle H.C. festival held at Knokke-le-Zoute in Belgium can be a "humidifying" experience. The main thoroughfare of this casino resort proclaims details, on cross-street banners, of the Paques Tournoi, and in almost no time at all one is hobnobbing with the Mayor and Corporation at a civic reception in the town hall. After being topped up with Dubonnet, one quickly realises that the French, and all the Belgians, Dutch and Germans attending speak French, while the English speak only English. The initial stultifying effect of this shortcoming is soon lost when a dozen or so bucolic baritones trim the ancient rafters with a rendition of a song describing their father's acquaintanceship with one Lloyd George. Civic proceedings are rounded off with the presentation, by the Mayor, of a triangular-shaped plate, bearing the town crest, to each participating team, whereupon lengthy orations of appreciation are wound up with the English contribution which consists of an embarrassed spokesman chuntering glibly about his knowledge of the Gallic being confined to "Madamoiselle from Armentieres" and "Frère Jacques".

A visit to Holland, of course, presents no such language barrier if one discounts the complete inability to speak which can follow the tossing down of a couple or three measures of Bols. With one's tongue feeling like a yellow plush sofa it is tricky to be coherent, but, come to think of it, the Dutch language does sound as though it is spoken with swollen tongues.

The Hague, Bloemendaal, Zaandaam, Amstelveen and other names of repute in Dutch hockey circles conjure up, for many English clubs, happy recollections of games played in a similar style to our own and of hospitality unsurpassed. Almost from the time of arrival on Dutch soil one is accompanied by an adjutant, whose sole purpose is to guide, philosophise, befriend, interpret, sort out, scrape up, chivvy, chase and chaperon. These worthies knock up night porters, knock down high prices, sound reveille and become emaciated with the responsibility of shepherding approximately eleven of their charges to appointed hockey matches at appointed times. Among the dunes somewhere there must be a Dutch nursing home for Dutch Adjutants of Dutch Hockey Festivals. One always imagined that going Dutch meant standing your own corner. Don't you ever believe it!

44

BIRTH OF A HOCKEY NATION

TONY BOYD

Vancouver and Canada; Vice-President, Canadian Field Hockey Association

Perhaps it is true to say that few countries in the world face such enormous problems in the development and promotion of hockey as does Canada. Yet, in spite of them all, Canada qualified to play in the 1964 Olympics. It is an inspiring story!

Canada has a population of eighteen millions which, at first glance, appears to be adequate to support a strong hockey organisation and a high standard of play. This population, however, is strung out across the country in a strip which is over 3,000 miles long and not much more than 100 miles wide. Moreover, the climate over the vast majority of this area is rather unsuitable for hockey, being too cold in the winter and too hot (for Canadians) during the summer. Only near the Pacific Ocean coast-line in British Columbia is it possible to play during the winter months and thus avoid the intense competition for manpower among the various summer sports and activities.

This rivalry for manpower creates another major difficulty for Canadian sporting enthusiasts, such as is probably not encountered to the same extent in other countries. Virtually every country in the world is represented among Canada's population, each introducing its own traditional or favourite sports. Name any sport, and the odds are that you will find it being played somewhere over the 3,000-mile length of the country.

Hosts of other problems follow, or arise, as a result of these major complexities.

Only in British Columbia has the game existed for a sufficient length of time to develop stability and some tradition. Field hockey as it is known in Canada, to distinguish it from ice hockey, was introduced there in 1907 and experienced widely-varying fortunes for the next thirty years. Sometimes there were barely enough teams to form a league; at other times competition was quite vigorous. Nevertheless, only a few years ago, field hockey was relatively unknown and a little recognised sport in Canada—even to the extent that the West was unaware that the game was played at all in the East, and vice-versa.

Outside British Columbia, the game got off to a very late start. Toronto formed its first men's league as recently as 1954, and it was followed a year later by Montreal and then in rapid succession by Calgary, Edmonton, Hamilton and Guelph. The leagues in these cities boasted a maximum of four or five teams each. The lack of adequate facilities, good grounds, and the difficulty of arranging good competition and representative matches against other parts of the country, were the most serious problems. Grounds are a perpetual headache. In all cases, they are made available by the cities, but in both quality and quantity they leave much to be desired. Usually they are badly drained and bumpy. In eastern Canada one could frequently get down on hands and knees and count the blades of grass. This is probably a universal problem, but it does not help attract new participants to the game.

Several real enthusiasts were determined to see hockey progress despite all these difficulties, and in an attempt to provide links between the widely-scattered hockey-playing communities, the Canadian Field Hockey Association was formed in 1961, on the initiative of the British Columbia Association. Shortly afterwards, the world became aware of a new hockey nation taking its first furtive steps, when Canada was admitted as a member of the International Federation.

The new Canadian Association did not take long to make its presence felt. The first-ever East-West game was played in Toronto in 1962 and if the West, with their long tradition, expected to win easily they were rudely shaken, and emerged victorious only by the odd goal in five. Immediately after the match a touring party was chosen to travel to New York to play the United States in the countries' first-ever international. Canada lost all three preliminary games, but they learnt quickly and made a great start in their international career by winning the all-important match against the U.S.A. by one goal to nil.

Canada determined to aim for a place in the 1964 Olympic Games and, after applying, were informed by the International Federation that the Olympic play-offs for North and South America would be held during the pre-Olympic Tournament at Lyon in France. This constituted a great challenge, but a promising start was made, in raising a total of almost $17,000 (£5,800) towards expenses. Two inter-provincial tournaments and a second East v. West Canada tournament followed.

So on an historic day, September 22, 1963, the Canadian team left the Amercias for the first time. It had been decided to play a few games in England on the way to the French tournament, and when Canada lost 5–0 and 3–0 to two of London's best club sides, the prospects for a successful visit to Lyon did not seem at all bright.

Following that first taste of European hockey, the team travelled to the international tournament in trepidation, hardly being able to believe that they were about to be catapulted from small league play in Canada to the pinnacle of hockey competition against some of the best teams in the world.

Perhaps, aided by this feeling of unreality, the team proceeded to improve on all prior expectations—not through winning any more games than had been hoped for, but by keeping the scores to reasonable proportions. In fact only on two occasions were Canada outclassed.

A win and a draw against the United States secured a place in the 1964 Olympics—the main object of the visit—but not one of the Canadian players would deny that they gained the most satisfaction from holding the world's greatest side, India, who eventually won the tournament, to three goals. India scored once from a penalty stroke and their third goal just fifteen seconds from time.

The team received a great welcome on their return, particularly at Vancouver airport, where many lady players were present with the dual purpose of greeting the team and saying farewell to a visiting Australian team.

The Lyon results were well received in Canada and gained wide publicity, resulting in the game gaining greater recognition in home circles, and there has been a remarkable upsurge all across the country, with new teams and increased membership.

However, the officials still faced another great problem. Canada might have qualified to play hockey at Tokyo but would the Canadian Olympic Association send the team? To do so meant the C.O.A. having to re-make the entire Canadian team, re-allocating the number of places available to each sport, but finally, after several anxious months, the wonderful news came through—the Canadians would compete in the hockey tournament at Tokyo.

45

A LIFETIME OF SPORT

CHARLES E. NEWHAM, OBE

There was nothing in my early years to suggest the adventures which lay ahead. I first acquired the rudiments of hockey on the sands at a tiny seaside village just after the South African war ended in 1902. To-day, over sixty years later, my wife and I live in another delightful East Anglian village on the seashore, so the wheel has come full circle. Through my study window I look across two golf fairways to the cricket table and the hockey ground.

In the years before we were plunged into the First World War, there were occasional matches in the holidays and at Cambridge University, but hockey, at that stage, was just one of many games in which I was interested. Yet one thing did happen which was possibly a signpost to future activities overseas. For some unremembered reason, I umpired a few matches in Cambridge, including one or two ladies' matches and a local trial of some kind. I must have been terrified at the time, but the better for having to study the rules and their application.

After the war came a final year at Cambridge when I played and umpired from time to time. One cherished memory of those days is of a strenuous and hilarious visit with a scratch vacation side to a Bournemouth tournament, during which I succeeded in entering the display window of a leading departmental store and was sternly ejected. My interest in hockey was growing and I am pretty sure now that the beginning of a life-long friendship with Conrad Corfield, who captained Cambridge that year and played for England, was an important factor.

Cambridge days over, I left for India in 1920 to take up my first appointment there as Assistant Editor of the leading daily newspaper in the United Provinces, the *Pioneer* in Allahabad. While still settling down, I found myself on the committee of the All-India Hockey Championship Tournament and the All-India Lawn Tennis Championships. I was referee of the latter for one year and not improbably that had something to do with my being on the staff of the referee at Wimbledon two or three times in later years.

Both these championships were on the decline and were soon closed down or absorbed in the great surge of new developments everywhere. I did, however, both play and umpire in the national hockey championship, and thus had an early and salutary lesson that hockey in India was a very different proposition. "National Hockey Championship" was a rather pretentious title and, in fact, a misnomer. The files, dating from the foundation in 1899, remained in my keeping and are before me now, faded and mainly handwritten. The rules make it quite clear that this earliest of championships, however unwarranted the title, was as much a social as a hockey gathering, with dinner parties, receptions, dances, regimental tents and bands.

Modern umpires and officials may be amused to know that those early rules provided for two umpires, two linesmen, two goal judges (on request), substitution of players in certain cases by permission of the opposing captain and, finally, that in any case of dispute about the rules the secretary's decision was final. Those were the days, obviously!

After what might be termed a short induction period in Allahabad, I was transferred to our sister paper in Lahore, capital of the Punjab. This was the *Civil and Military Gazette*, on which Rudyard Kipling served for some years. So began happy years in a delightful city and province, with a host of friends and colleagues of all races. An era of intense development in every respect was just commencing and it was all most exhilerating and inspiring.

Only a few weeks had passed before the secretaryship of the Lahore Gymkhana Hot Weather Hockey Tournament was wished upon me as a temporary measure—which lasted two years. As the name may be found a little puzzling, it may be well to explain that the Lahore Gymkhana was the largest sports and social club in Northern India, and that the Punjab climate can conveniently be divided into two seasons, the hot weather and the cold weather. So this tournament was played in the former, just before the rains when the earth was baked and the heat was at its greatest. We played only in the evenings when a little "coolth" tempered the intense heat, but even so one was completely wet through and usually exhausted at the end of a game.

In 1921 I made some tentative soundings about the possibility of starting an All-India body, first mooted by Calcutta enthusiasts some twelve years earlier. Others were naturally thinking along the same lines, but the general reaction was that it was a little too early to foster and launch an All-India scheme when there were so many parts of a vast country, Provinces and Indian States, in which hockey organisation did not exist or was only rudimentary.

In the Punjab we settled down to tackle our own immediate requirements and the Punjab Hockey Association was founded. I had the honour of being its first president, and remained so until my transfer to Delhi seven years later. In this development, as in many others, tribute must be paid to the sage advice and warm support of a lifelong friend, Guru Datt Sondhi, later Principal of Government College—a great sportsman who is still a leading figure in the hockey, athletics and Olympic fields.

What was happening in the Punjab was happening all over India, and the enthusiasm for development and organisation was far from confined to hockey. Much the same story can be told of cricket, tennis and athletics, and the Olympic movement in which India was taking a lively interest. As is so often the case, there was a natural tendency for the same people to be involved in the initial stages, and I found myself a member of the new Olympic Committee, of the infant Cricket Association, and Hon. Secretary of the newly-formed All-India Lawn Tennis Association.

These other interests really have no place in hockey reminiscences but the L.T.A. secretaryship did have a direct effect upon my hockey outlook. I was due for long leave in England in 1924 and accepted, with some reluctance, the post of manager to India's tennis team for the Olympic Games in Paris and subsequently of the Davis Cup team. On the Paris trip Sondhi and I became convinced that India must play a full part in future Olympiads.

Hockey organisations, provincial, regional and institutional, were being founded all over India, and it became evident that the time had come to base an Indian Hockey Federation on them. It was also evident that this would be crippled, if not stillborn, without the assistance and full co-operation of the Army Sports Control (later Central) Board which covered the whole of India and was, in fact, the only all-India sports body in being at that time.

At the invitation of the Gwalior Sports Association, five associations and the A.S.C.B. met in Gwalior on November 27, 1925. The meeting was marked by enthusiasm and unanimity in all major respects, and the Indian Hockey Federation was born, with the late Colonel Bruce Turnbull as president. I still possess a printers' proof copy of the first brief rules, and some pencilled notes which mention the possibility of India taking part in Olympic hockey.

There is one rule which merits individual mention here. It is very stern and forthright, deals with payments, expenses, amateur status and professionalism, and leaves no doubt of the fate awaiting the transgressors, individual or collective.

Now, there had been allegations, and one still hears occasional hints that illegal practices amounting to veiled professionalism or "shamateurism" exist in Indian hockey, that some teams or individuals receive excessive expenses, direct or hidden payments, and so forth. Such suggestions must arise in some cases from sheer speculation as to how Indian hockey is maintained at such a consistently high standard. It is sometimes not realised that in India and Pakistan to-day there are approximately 450 million inhabitants, that hockey is a national sport and that it is reasonable to assume that not less than one million play hockey regularly.

There may have been irregularities on isolated occasions during the past forty years; for example, one or two cases of talented players obtaining jobs for which their prowess was a consideration, but that happens in many countries and sports and hardly constitutes professionalism.

During 1925 and 1926, years of intensive development and consolidation, friendly and helpful contact with the International Federation, which had been founded in January 1924, was established. Membership was applied for in 1927 and confirmed in 1928, the year in which hockey played a major role in the Games for the first time. This membership was an essential pre-requisite for India to be able to take part in the 1928 Amsterdam Olympiad.

In 1926 there was an outstanding demonstration of the growing strength of Indian hockey and its organisation, heartening to all who looked forward to India's entry into the international arena. Australia and New Zealand issued a cordial invitation for a representative Indian Army team to make an extensive tour. Four British officers were included in the large and otherwise completely Indian contingent, captained and managed by Captain D. T. Cowan, widely known as "Punch" and one of Scotland's outstanding centre-halves. The trials and subsequent training sessions were held in Lahore, and I had the good fortune to have some exercise with the training squad, to umpire for them and to study at close quarters the developing genius of Dhyan Chand, the idol of India's sportsmen and probably the finest centre-forward the game has yet produced. The tour was one long triumph from every standpoint, and we were fully reinforced in our confidence that since this was a team drawn only from the Indian Army, India had little to fear in the full international field with a team selected from all civil and military sources.

In the same winter of 1926/27, the headquarters of the Indian Hockey Federation, steadily gaining in strength and popularity, were moved from Gwalior to Delhi and, with a view to the future, the first inter-provincial tournament was launched, which brought together almost all the leading players and provided a feast of high standard hockey.

From a purely personal standpoint, that winter was too overcrowded, for it included the pioneering first visit of an M.C.C. team, captained by

Arthur Gilligan, for a very popular cricket tour. They arrived without a manager, and it fell to my lot to act as a kind of universal aunt at several centres in Northern India, and also to do some umpiring. Three years later I became acting-chairman of the Cricket Control Board for nearly a year.

There may have been one or two momentary qualms on financial grounds, but the decision that India should enter for the 1928 Olympics in Amsterdam was unanimous and we started to mobilise. For funds we had to go round cap in hand and, as ever, Sondhi was a tower of strength. Member associations made their own efforts, and some of the Indian princes gave substantial donations. Ultimately, our Olympic trials were held in Calcutta before enormous crowds, with Colonel Ian Burn-Murdoch, who succeeded Bruce Turnbull as president, as sole selector. The skill with which he fulfilled this heavy responsibility from a wealth of talent was amply demonstrated in Amsterdam when India won the Olympic title for the first time. Such was the vindication of all our hopes and beliefs. India had brought new skills and a new conception of the game to the whole world.

My intention of accompanying Bruce Turnbull and Sondhi to Amsterdam was thwarted by other responsibilities which arose, but later there was one delightful compensation when, as acting-president, I received a large, brilliantly designed diploma, signed by the presidents of the International and Dutch Olympic Committees, certifying that India had won the title. It hangs in front of me and in due course will return to India.

Preparations for the 1932 Olympics in Los Angeles began in 1930/31, but I was unable to get too involved as I was to resign my appointment as Editor and Director of the *Civil and Military Gazette* early in 1932. In the end, however, enthusiasm prevailed once again and I made an eleventh hour dash to join the team as umpire. The hockey, with only three teams competing, was most disappointing. India won the final with ease, it was a very hollow victory, by 11–1 over the Japanese who, incidentally and perhaps typically, always had a squad of officials and players taking notes and photographs at our daily practices. To me it was all a most enjoyable adventure for, in addition to umpiring every game played, including the final, I was kept busy umpiring practice games, served on two Olympic juries, played once or twice, and helped to coach the American team and even the girls of the University of California.

There is little mention in my notes and diaries of hockey or indeed any sport in the next thirty months, when I was primarily occupied by the Indian Round Table Conference which was charged with the formulation of a new self-governing constitution. I kept touch, of course, with friends and organisations in India, but references to sport are otherwise confined to umpiring at the Folkestone Hockey Festival, helping the referee at the Wimbledon Championships, being asked by the sports authorities in Moscow whether I would write a hockey handbook for them (I heard nothing further of my guarded agreement), and of seeing the final of the Gaelic Hurley Championship in Dublin. I was fascinated by this game, which demanded great skill, speed and strength, and perhaps could be used as one illustration of the survival of the fittest.

The most important happening, however, of that interim period was my marriage to a charming member of an old Surrey hockey family of the eighties and nineties which had produced two or three distinguished players and could even raise a family team of the same name on special occasions. A sports enthusiast and no mean performer at tennis, badminton and golf, my poor dear wife has been protesting for the past thirty years that she has been dragged all over the world to sports events.

Then came my appointment as Private Secretary to His Highness the Maharaja Gaekwar of Baroda, the veteran doyen of the Indian princes, who ruled for nearly as long as Queen Victoria. It was a wonderful experience, which ended only with his death in 1939.

In 1936 once again good fortune played a part in my life and I was able to accept the International Federation's invitation to umpire in the Berlin Olympiad, including two quarter-finals and a semi-final in which India was not involved. With His Highness the Gaekwar, we normally spent the winter in Baroda, and the spring, summer and early autumn in Europe. Despite his age, His Highness was vitally interested in everything and particularly in new experiences, so when my wife asked him if he would like to see the Olympic Games in Berlin, he agreed at once. We could write a book on that colourful adventure, but suffice it so say we were Herr Hitler's official guests for four days of our stay and met the leading Nazis; that I was in attendance upon His Highness for his private interview with the Nazi leader; that the Gaekwar entertained many leading Olympic officials; and that India beat Germany in the hockey final by 8–1 and so again retained the Olympic title. When we returned to Baroda, His Highness gave orders that multi-purpose playing fields should be provided in the capital, and that some degree and form of physical recreation should be made compulsory in the Baroda College.

During the war years, and for a time afterwards, I spent much of my time on organising and advisory duties in the Indian states, as a temporary member of the Indian Political Service—which was chiefly concerned with states' affairs and administration. This entailed constant touring and I visited over one hundred states.

My final assignment in India was on special duty with the British

Cabinet Mission at the Viceroy's House in Delhi. It was the deliberations and findings of this mission which led to the partition of the India we had known for so long—to most of us a source of profound sadness. The outcome then was a new India and a new country named Pakistan. Needless to say, it also split the hockey resources of that vast subcontinent, and the extent of those resources in turn is demonstrated by the prowess today of both countries. It is, I think fair to say that both suffered, at least temporarily, but that world hockey has subsequently derived some benefit both in rising standards and competitive results.

The 1948 London Olympiad was rapidly drawing near when my wife and I arrived back in England, and we certainly had not settled down when good fortune again played its part in our lives. Through our good friend Kenneth Ingledew, the veteran mainspring of Welsh hockey and then secretary of the new British Hockey Board, came an invitation to George Grimston and myself to be manager and deputy manager respectively of the Great Britain team. Colonel Grimston has been well-known for many years as secretary of Sussex County Cricket Club. A fine hockey player in his time, I had first met him when I umpired the British Army final in 1926. It proved a very happy partnership, for while he ran the team, training schedules, practices and trials, I did the chores as adjutant and quartermaster for food, clothing, equipment and transport, and became everyone's general dogsbody. It was not an easy time, for the war was barely over and nearly everything except enthusiasm was in short supply, but one way or another we managed to overcome all our difficulties. Eventually my own duties were far from confined to team matters and I found myself, as in 1932, a member of the F.I.H.'s Jury de Terrain, of the Technical Bureau, and the organising office which M. Albert Demaurex and my wife ran efficiently in various languages and with much laughter.

The hardest task of all naturally fell to George Grimston as manager and Norman Borrett, the chosen captain, together with the selectors, in building and shaping players from the four home countries into an Olympic team. Only five or six training weekends were possible, one of the happiest and most searching being at Thorpeness, the delightful Suffolk seaside village where we have lived for more than thirty years when home from overseas. Both manager and captain were outstanding players with great experience, and were also astute tacticians. They had in Frank Reynolds one of the finest centre-halves the game has produced—and they did a magnificent job. Probably none of us honestly believed that Britain could beat India, but it was no ordinary achievement to beat Pakistan 2–0 in the semi-final and to lose by only 4–0 to India in a desperately hard final.

Our travels and adventures had still not ended for, a few weeks after the games had finished, we found ourselves in Nigeria where we were to spend five very happy and exhilarating years. My appointment was a new one with the United Africa Company, a dynamic tropical enterprise within the vast Unilever organisation. It involved planning and developing from scratch, and from a sports standpoint Nigeria also followed the pattern of my Indian experience, and there was all the scope that anyone could wish for useful activity. Everyone was keen and helpful, there was a wealth of potential talent and, before long, I was fully involved in sorting out a working pattern.

It was obvious at the outset that there were masses of players, British and Nigerian, but relatively few teams and no organisation to harness, plan and co-ordinate all this material, actual and potential. So the first step was to form the Lagos and District Association, together with a local league, which quickly and steadily grew in numbers, quality of play and umpiring. Next in order came the Nigerian Hockey Federation, affiliation to the F.I.H., and representative trials, and the establishment of regular matches with the Gold Coast (now Ghana). The standard of athletics was very high, and with the 1952 Helsinki Olympiad in view came the formation of our Olympic and British Empire and Commonwealth Games Association, with affiliation to the international bodies of both. Lastly, since a stadium was lacking and very desirable, a National Stadium Board was formed, with delayed but ultimate success.

I had the privilege in the early years of being president or chairman of all these associations, and also of leading the Nigerian team, as Chef de Mission, to the Helsinki Games. Nigerian hockey was not yet of that standard and we had no team there, but I did umpire several matches, including the semi-final between Pakistan and Holland. This

was my twenty-first international, and I decided that it should be my last and the end of a very long and happy innings.

When our stay in Nigeria came to an end, I also decided that the time had really come to retire and take things a little more easily, get down to writing, which was sadly in arrears, and also to broadcasting, of which I had done a great deal—weekly, indeed—when in Lagos.

I was thoroughly enjoying myself in London, broadcasting for the B.B.C. Colonial Service, when I was offered the appointment as Director of Organisation of the Sixth British Empire and Commonwealth Games, due to be held in Cardiff in 1958. This was indeed the opportunity of a lifetime, again organising from scratch, and I needed little persuasion. It involved four and a half years, not of retirement but of unremitting hard work. It was a marvellous experience of which one pleasing outcome was that no less than thirty-five countries sent teams—a Commonwealth record which will not easily be surpassed.

One regret I have is that hockey is not played in these games. Efforts have been made, of course, to secure their inclusion, but no team games are permitted at all in the Empire and Commonwealth Games, firstly because of the cost to overseas countries, and secondly because all nine sports in the full programme must be completed in nine days, and that programme is already overloaded.

Our Cardiff adventures ended in the early summer of 1959 and this time we decided that retirement, or at least semi-retirement, was to be final and irrevocable. So here we are once more in Thorpeness on the Suffolk coast. In the Easter and summer holidays, my wife and I are kept happily busy at the Country Club by masses of young people and their activities. My study is crammed with hockey, Olympic and Empire trophies, books, files and pictures. From the window I can see some youngsters, about the age when I first learned something of the game, chasing about on the hockey ground. I shall be with them again, armed with a venerable stick and a whistle.

It has been my great good fortune to play and umpire in Asia, Africa, Europe and America, and to take some part in the organisation and growth of hockey into a major world game which provides one of the finest examples there can be of final and complete co-ordination between the brain and every part of the body. In my time its popularity and, in a world sense, the standard of play and umpiring have grown almost beyond recognition.

Britain introduced hockey to India and Pakistan, where it has become the national game. In turn, we owe a great deal to both those countries for their skill and tactical techniques which, developed on consistently good grounds and in a climate which permits play practically the whole year, have vitally influenced the world game. Their own standard has not really declined despite partition, but in many other countries it has so improved that margins of victory have tended to become narrower, which means that India and Pakistan cannot afford to rest on their laurels and must aim to play even harder and better.

May these notes and recollections end with the hope and belief that this great and delightful game will continue to go from strength to strength. To that I would add, if it had not already become apparent, that through long years, sport in general, and hockey in particular have brought us much happiness, large numbers of good friends, and an immense amount of pleasure.

46

UMPIRE'S SOLILOQUY

To blow, or not to blow—that is the question:
Whether 'tis nobler in the mind to suffer
The quirks and comments of outspoken men
And still to operate the law of 'vantage
Or sound the blast that brings the move to naught
And with unfettered hit the fault amends
The thought that when the match is o'er
The embattled hordes foregather in the George
And live again the tourney, move by move
Must give no pause; and having paused
To think, perchance to dream; aye, there's the rub!
For umpires are not made as other men,
But suffer from defective sight and brain
And bias 'gainst their fellow men, of whom
They are so jealous as to make a mock
Of sport. The rules of hockey are to them
A closed book to which they pay no heed.
The enemy may hack and wave aloft their sticks
At risk of injury to other players' limbs
And still no penalty imposed: but let
The poor unlucky victim of the umpire's spite
But give offence in venial misdeed
And all the penalties of rule and sanction
Are visited on his unhappy head.
These arbiters in sport should never be allowed
To influence the running of a game,

But forced in sequestration to abide
And blow their whistles in an empty field.
But spite of all the doubts and tribulations
The contest must proceed; the umpire then
Must disregard the personal approach.
And once again, to blow or not to blow
That is the question.

ANON.

47
HOW LONG BEFORE AN AFRICAN CHALLENGE?

BARRY PUTTERGILL

Richmond H.C.

Hockey is enjoyed by Europeans, Asians, Americans, Australasians, and in fact by nearly every race in the world. Yet there is little knowledge of Africans playing the game.

In most of the continent, the African is only just beginning to learn the game, though internationals are played between Ghana and Nigeria in West Africa.

Hockey in Central and East Africa is very much dominated by the European and the Asian, and until recently very few administrators had given serious thought to Africans playing the game. Because of its spectator appeal, the African has shown far greater interest in soccer than in any other "western" game. Even if interested in playing hockey, the majority of Africans can little afford to participate unless subsidised by a club or an organisation.

Since 1958 a considerable number of Africans in both Rhodesian territories have started playing hockey. In that year the African Administration Department of the Salisbury municipality introduced hockey to boys and girls in their welfare and recreational sections. Pitches were prepared and money voted for sticks and equipment. Coaching was carried out by European staff members of the various welfare organisations, and to assist them the department had the rules translated into the two local vernaculars—Shona and Chinyanja.

The start was slow, but within twelve months some hundreds of children in clubs and hostels were familiar with the game and were playing it regularly in Salisbury. No record exists of any fixtures with

European sides—other than those with the European staff of the African Administration Department—mainly due to the department not publicising that hockey was played by Africans in their townships. Neither has there been any noticeable appeal made to European controlling bodies or clubs to compete with African teams or assist with coaching. Closer contact with Europeans in hockey will no doubt come, but in the meantime the game has spread to African welfare organisations in other towns in Southern Rhodesia. A few of the Africans attending the Rhodesia University College have played for the college eleven but, as far as is known, no purely African clubs exist outside those organised by the African Administration Department.

The development of hockey in Northern Rhodesia followed a similar pattern. In 1961 the secretary of the Y.M.C.A. on the Copperbelt approached the Copperbelt District Men's Hockey Board (which is affiliated to the Rhodesia Hockey Association) to arrange games for the Y.M.C.A. All-African team. This was the first indication that Africans were playing hockey on the Copperbelt. Only two multi-racial clubs existed on the Copperbelt at that stage—most other hockey clubs using facilities controlled by large sporting organisations which were still in the process of becoming multi-racial. Whilst no constitutional barrier existed to prevent African teams from affiliating to the Board, the Y.M.C.A. had no facilities.

However, by 1962 most clubs had agreed to the use of their facilities by African teams. Thus when the Y.M.C.A. applied to be incorporated in the hockey league on a purely friendly basis, they were accepted, and whilst not actually affiliated, a programme of friendly matches was arranged for them. This was the first record of any organised hockey between African and European in Rhodesia.

The Y.M.C.A.'s standard was not particularly high, so on behalf of the board, I coached the team at one of the local hockey clubs. It was evident they lacked good coaching at school. The Y.M.C.A. players had little stick-work and ball control, but made up for these deficiencies by sheer enthusiasm and speed.

By 1963 the way was clear for Africans to participate fully in the league—all sporting facilities having become non-racial at this stage.

With the advent of the Y.M.C.A. team it was soon apparent there were other African teams playing hockey on the Copperbelt in welfare organisations operated by the large mining companies, schools, and various town councils.

These organisations operated on a similar basis to those in Southern Rhodesia. Now it remains to be seen whether the African child, given the same background in sport as the Asian and European child, will be enthusiastic enough to form his own club and play hockey when he

WEST GERMANY v. *INDIA at the Lyon International Tournament, September, 1963.*
During a floodlit match a German defender clears somewhat desperately under Indian pressure. The match was drawn 1–1.
(The spectators were all sitting on the other side of the ground.)

THE NETHERLANDS v. *BELGIUM. Amstelveen (Amsterdam), May 1963. The Belgian goalkeeper M. Thill kicks out of the circle. The other Belgian players in the picture are (L–to–R) A. Muschs, W. Delaet and centre-half F. Lorette (behind goalkeeper's arm). Netherlands won 2–0.*

EAST GERMANY v. *POLAND. Magdeburg. 1956. An exciting moment as Gorny, the Polish goalkeeper, prevents Dietze, the East German inside left, from scoring. The result was a 0–0 draw.* (*Photo. Walter Rohrlapper, Leipzig*) becomes an adult. For the present it would seem that hockey is still a Cinderella sport with the African, though the various hockey authorities are now taking a much keener interest in them.

The acceptance of both Kenya and Rhodesia for the 1964 Olympic Hockey Tournament will surely go a long way to make the Africans more hockey-conscious and to consolidate the progress now being made in the Dark Continent.

48

ENGLAND'S LAST GREAT FORWARD—VERA CHAPMAN

JOYCE WHITEHEAD

Between the two world wars hockey in England reached a peak, and players like Marjorie Pollard represented their country for a good many years. Since 1945 hockey has continued to flourish, but the competition from all sources is increasingly challenging, and nowadays few players represent England for any length of time. However, one player who remained at the top of the hockey ladder for a very long time was Miss Vera Chapman.

Vera was the youngest, by five years, of a games-playing family, and grew up in Kingston, Surrey, at a time when pleasures were self-made, and a hockey stick, cricket bat, or tennis racket were part of her everyday life. At the Tiffin Girls' School she was hockey captain, and for sheer fun spent her mid-morning and lunch breaks in the winter with a hockey stick and ball—and there were sown the seeds of her skilful stickwork.

A hockey camp was opened at Ballater during the summer holidays for enthusiasts of sixteen years and over. Vera, then a stripling of some 5 ft. 10 in. tall, was taken along by her eldest sister—though her blue ration book gave away her age. She stayed on, however, and learnt a tremendous amount under the coaching of Miss Doman, of pre-war fame.

In her last year at school, when she was a member of the large Southern Railway Sports Club, Vera made great strides on the hockey ladder, despite the wicked winter of 1947. She was one of the very few schoolgirls to play hockey that season and was promoted from the county second eleven to play for Surrey and South, as left-wing. The country was snowbound but different venues were found for the territorial matches, and Vera had her first chance to play with Mrs Mary Russell Vick as left-inner. The young schoolgirl quickly learnt

Vera Chapman

to admire Mary Russell Vick's great anticipation and ability, and particularly her way of diving on to a centre from the wing and swerving round a back into the circle to shoot. This made Vera feel her role on the left-wing was really worth while.

She went to the I.M. Marsh College of Physical Education in Liverpool in September 1947, and it was there, during the spring half-term holiday, that she received a telegram telling her she had been chosen to play right-wing for England. She travelled alone the length of Wales to play in her first international match in Swansea. Vera was so overcome by the occasion and was concentrating so hard that she ran into and broke a flag post placed perilously near the side line, and rushed on quite oblivious of her path of destruction. Her eyes and thoughts were on the ball, which she was determined to keep on the pitch at all costs.

Apart from a season and a half in 1950 and 1951, when she was in the England reserve team, Vera remained in the England team until she retired after captaining England in 1961—a record for any post-war player. During that time she played right-wing, right-inner and left-inner.

She was very fleet of foot and one of the few post-war players who could swerve at speed and still be in possession of the ball. She seldom played a match without at least one solo run. She would swerve round two defence players and still have the time and control to pause and look before shooting. The roars of applause which greeted these courageous efforts at Wembley Stadium must have disturbed the pigeons in Piccadilly at times!

Nineteen fifty-three was a major year for the International Federation of Women's Hockey Associations Tournament was held at Folkestone. Sixteen nations took part, and Vera played right-inner and her middle sister, Beryl, goalkeeper, for England.

Vera was then a really first-class player. Her stickwork and ball control were beautiful to watch, and the hit-push stroke with which she fed her wing was artistry itself. Her coltishness had gone and she

Mary Russell Vick

had become the finished, graceful, complete forward, unassuming, a maker of goals and a perfect team member.

That season, in one of England's greatest matches, with the score at half-time only 2–1 to England against South Africa and tension mounting, Mrs. Russell Vick and Vera each scored in the second half to give England a 4–1 victory.

Vera was both a devastating goal-scorer and a tremendous worker. In 1958 she played left-inner with Miss Joan Hassall (now Mrs. Wilkinson) at centre-forward. They made a truly formidable pair. At Wembley against Scotland, Vera Chapman was clearly the creator of four of the five goals scored.

After leaving college, Vera taught at a number of schools and colleges, and on at least one occasion had to resign in order to go on tour with the England team. She was a member of the England touring teams to South Africa in 1954; Australia in 1956—where she stayed on after the tour and worked on a sheep station; Germany in 1958, and the Netherlands for the International Federation of Women's Hockey Association's Tournament in 1959.

It was her intense interest in travel and the Church Missionary Society that finally caused her to retire from international hockey in 1961. She decided to train as a missionary, and in 1962 sailed for West Pakistan to work in the Church Missionary Society School at Clarkabad. She has not foresaken hockey completely for while there she has enjoyed playing a little hockey on a hard, dusty, bumpy pitch round two telegraph poles with the boys and masters of the Cathedral School.

49

THE SHY SPORT

ZENON KUROWSKI

President, Polish Hockey Federation

It is taken for granted in Poland that sports that are not very popular receive assistance from the state. Other sports, like football or motor-racing, are watched by thousands of spectators and have large and handsome money intakes. They do not need assistance, and of course they don't get it.

Hockey on grass is the favourite sport of only a few, and I simply cannot imagine its existence without the state's assistance, for there would be no means to pay for anything, and international meetings would be quite out of the question. Before the last war hockey in this country had to be self-sufficient, and a look at the records will show only a very modest number of international meetings compared with the very handsome number since the war.

The reason hockey is not a more popular sport in my opinion is that it does not have sufficient propaganda. Even putting football aside, look at other sports—basketball, handball, netball, ice hockey—all have many different meetings and tournaments such as national, European and even world championships. They fulfil two purposes, making the sports more popular and obtaining revenue for the games.

I appreciate that people go to watch the sports they like or where they know that there is something for the participants to fight for, but I am afraid there is too much conservatism in hockey. We do not make any progress with time; we do very little to popularise the sport and to make the public interested in it.

In my country, by the end of the hockey season, when people know that the first league matches are going to be decisive concerning places in the league, even hockey has thousands of spectators.

50

THRASH THE BALL HARD

FREDDIE SCOTT

Hounslow H.C., Scotland and Great Britain

Most youngsters in India start their hockey at a very early age, and I was only eight when I first picked up a stick. Strangely enough, I was taught by the Irish for I went to an Irish school. Our coaches concentrated on ball control, stick-work, hitting and stopping, the main theme being to improve on our natural ability rather than to drill.

By the time I was fifteen I had played in competitive hockey, and in my last two years at school had taken part in at least a dozen open tournaments against some of the finest senior sides in the country. Though we were only schoolboys, we were quite capable of holding our own and had won at least four of the tournaments. After this sort of early grounding, to start playing senior division hockey was not so awesome, and the transition was quite smooth.

At the ripe age of seventeen I started senior division hockey in the 1950/51 season. I played left-half, and by the end of the season was in the running for a place in the state side. We played a weekly league match and generally one knock-out cup game. The rest of the week we practised ball control, hitting and stopping, and stick-work, talked tactics, analysed our opponents' weaknesses and tried to counter our own. On occasions we travelled to other states and played in their tournaments.

At the end of the 1950/51 season I returned to the United Kingdom, and naturally one of the first things I did was to start playing hockey. It was quite different from Indian hockey, and playing on wet, muddy pitches took a great deal of getting used to. To my eyes, the standard was very low, stick-work was poor, obstruction and awkwardness abundant. The impression I gained was that to get anywhere one had to use an English stick, thrash the ball about and chase like mad.

Having a reasonable amount of stick-work, I found myself a marked man. Our opponents generally became frustrated and lashed out at me; my own side moaned that I held the ball too long; umpires penalised me every time I took the ball on the reverse, and I could not understand what was wrong as I was playing the same type of game that I had been taught in India. By the end of my first season in England, I had vowed that I would never play hockey again, but National Service in the Royal Air Force came to the rescue.

After a season of minor hockey, I found myself playing for the R.A.F. Despite the winter conditions, I really began to enjoy the game again, deriving pleasure from joining up with players like David Roche, Johnny Walker and Neil Nugent, who had played in India. The most enjoyable game up to this time was the Inter-Services match against the Army, and in my opinion, the standard of hockey in the Services was comparable to that of any of the Senior Division sides I had played with and against in India.

By the end of the season I found myself playing for Scotland. The standard of the home international sides' hockey was far below what I had expected and certainly not up to that of any of the India state sides. For this I could only blame the time of the year that hockey is played in Britain, lack of teamwork, and tactical knowledge. Though home internationals are held during March and April and the grounds are firm, most of the players either failed to appreciate this or found it extremely difficult to adjust their type of game. They continued to thrash the ball about and even blasted short passes. This resulted in a distinct gap between halves and forwards; simple triangular movements were lacking and the game did not flow. Of my early international matches, I can quite clearly remember that all we did was run up and down, achieving very little. At the end of my second season in the Scottish team I was in the running for a place in Britain's Olympic side.

After a number of trials I was picked to go to Melbourne in 1956. It was all very strange in comparison with Indian standards and methods; tactical talks were non-existent, but endeavouring to change players' natural styles was in vogue. The fact that trial matches should be played on hard fast grounds similar to those we expected to find in Melbourne was not appreciated; hard hitting, deep through passes and fast running were emphasised, and so that is what we all set about doing.

In Melbourne I met a number of boys representing India and Pakistan with whom I had played in India, and I was shocked to discover how my game had deteriorated in five years of British hockey. I suppose one can blame the winter conditions, lack of facilities and lack of competitive hockey. Our hard-hitting, fast-running style was not suited to the dry, fast conditions, and after about the fourth match the strain began to show. We had trained to play at one pace

Denys Carnill

only, and hence were not capable of controlling the pace of the game in order to give ourselves a breather. The halves were not able to give the forwards the close support they required at the pace we were playing, nor were the insides capable of going back constantly to retrieve. No real attempt at analysing our opponents' strength and weaknesses had been made; consequently the team went on to the field with only limited knowledge. Another disadvantage was that home umpiring was more lenient than the umpiring at Melbourne, and hence we were pulled up for minor infringements which we had come to accept as permissible.

The two outstanding players in our side were Denys Carnill and Neil Forster. Denys played a completely unorthodox game and never really controlled the ball, yet he was able to get away with it—much to the amazement of Indian and Pakistani players. Neil was a success because he played the Indian type of game, shielding the ball and always keeping it on his opponent's left.

Naturally, we learnt a lot of lessons from the tour, and there was quite a song and dance about what should be done during the next four years in preparation for the 1960 Olympics. Very little happened, however, and though our control had improved, for some strange reason the style of play had not been altered by 1960. To make matters worse, of the eight forwards picked for Rome, for some unaccountable reason five were wingers. Our tactical plans were haywire and at times hard to believe. The pattern of our game was similar to that played in Melbourne, and again, after about four matches, the strain began to tell as the link between the halves and the forward line broke down. The weakness was emphasised when we played one of the longest games ever against Kenya in the quarter-finals. We did well though to reach the semi-finals. Harry Cahill was the outstanding goalkeeper and John Neill one of the best backs at the Games.

There is no doubt in my mind that Britain can, in time, be on the same footing as the leading hockey countries of the world. This, however, can happen only if provision is made for more all-weather pitches and the changing of the present season. If it is not possible to change to playing in the summer, even a modification of the present season, from September to December and March to May would be beneficial. It is only by playing on good fast surfaces that one can hope to improve on the basic fundamentals of the game—stopping, hitting, ball control and stick-work. I am well aware that the fundamentals can be improved by individual practice in the summer but this is not enough; match play in good conditions is essential, as only then will one gain confidence and try out more imaginative moves fluidly. From my own experience, I found after my first season in the mud that I had cut out various moves, as they were not possible.

If one compares Indian players with British, it is not difficult to realise that they have more in their bag of tricks. The general standard of coaching at schools should be improved considerably, and boys encouraged to start playing at an earlier age. The general trend at schools is, at present, to produce players lacking in imaginative play. This, I suppose, is due to the blunting of natural ability by stereotyped ideas.

Finally, in the present era of sport, the various associations have got to play their part by putting hockey on a sound financial footing; forward thinking, sound advertising and sponsorship of big matches are a must. What was good enough for us is not going to be good enough for future hockey players.

51

SEVEN A SIDE

JORGE N. PARSONS

President, A.A. Argentina de Hockey

Six a side hockey is played in many parts of the world and is accepted as an exciting and integral part of the hockey scene, but in South America and the West Indies they go one better and play seven a side. Why seven a side is lost in the mists of time; perhaps there were large numbers of Rugby players among the original organisers!

The best known Sevens Tournament is that held by the Argentina Association at Buenos Aires which attracts a splendid gathering of players from all over the Argentine and from neighbouring Uruguay, Brazil and Chile.

The ground where the games are played is an old rowing club, and in the warm, bright sunshine the blue water, yachts, motor-launches and rowing boats help to create a wonderful festival atmosphere. In the centre of the ground a little white-painted booth like a cricket scorebox is perched on stilts from which the organisers control the flow of games from 9 a.m. to evening. Round the pitches in the shade of clumps of trees players and spectators of many different nationalities linger, and there are the inevitable drink, sandwich and hot-dog stands.

The seven a side game is played on pitches seventy metres by forty metres, with the circle reduced to eleven metres. The rules are much the same as those commonly used in six a side—two halves of ten minutes each are played, corners are counted as well as goals, with only the goals counting in normal time. In the event of a tie on goals two extra halves of five minutes each are played, with corners, including those in normal time, counting if goals are still level at the end. Should there still be a tie in both corners and goals at the end of extra time, a final period is started and played to the first goal or corner. Each team is allowed two substitutes for the tournament, but no changes may be made during any game.

The men and women play on separate week-ends, for the tournament attracted no fewer than 163 women's teams and 109 men's teams to Buenos Aires in 1963.

52

PAKISTAN'S "TARZAN"

SULTAN F. HUSAIN

Editor, *Sportimes*, Pakistan

Anwar Ahmad Khan, Pakistan's famous centre-half, is tall dark and handsome—which explains why he came to be known among his school and college friends as "The Indian Tarzan". Like the husky he-man character created by Edgar Rice Burroughs, Anwar's personality stands out on the hockey field. He may not swing on a rope from tree to tree or beat his chest like Tarzan, but he does swing a hockey stick to great advantage.

Anwar is a natural-born hockey player, whose solid ground-work was prepared in the Indian schools of hockey—Aligarh University and Bhopal Wanderers. Spotted early in life, Anwar's talent found a natural expression on Indian fields, where he showed great promise. Migrating to Pakistan soon after partition, Anwar settled down with his family in Karachi, whom he represented in 1952. Within two years he was selected to play for Pakistan, but a broken ankle meant his international debut was delayed.

Anwar's real rise to stardom began in 1956. Playing in the trials held at Lahore to select the Pakistan team for the Olympic Hockey Tournament at Melbourne, Anwar displayed his unmistakable class and won a place in the Olympic team as a centre-half. The selectors' faith and judgment were fully vindicated when he proved an outstanding success at Melbourne.

His unobtrusive positional play, uncanny anticipation, and unlimited stamina made him the ideal pivot round which to revolve both Pakistan's defence and attack. His reach on both flanks was so prodigious that seldom was an adversary allowed to pass him.

Pakistan, who had finished fourth on their two previous appearances in the Olympics, reached the final for the first time and were beaten by India only by a disputed goal. The six-feet-tall Anwar pocketed a silver medal but was determined that next time it should become a gold one. Not surprisingly, he retained his place in the Pakistan team and in the 1958 Asian Championships played a major part in helping Pakistan to draw 0–0 with India. The result was good enough to give Pakistan first place, for they had a better goal average than India. Anwar had won his first "gold" but it was an Olympic champions medal that he cherished most.

A happily married Preventive Officer in the Karachi Customs, he had reached the peak of his career. A shrewd tactician and a seasoned

Anwar Ahmad Khan

warrior, he was a constant source of inspiration to the rest of the team, and for two years Anwar and his Pakistan team-mates practised and perfected. A draw would not be good enough—they needed to beat India at the 1960 Olympics.

The standard at Rome was higher than at Melbourne, and Pakistan had more than one tight match before they eventually reached the final. Once again, as expected, India were their rivals. This time

Pakistan won 1–0 and so became the first international side ever to beat India—and Anwar won his coveted Olympic "gold."

Since he first played in a green shirt, the handsome centre-half has toured with every Pakistan team, visiting Australia, East Africa, S.E. Asia and Europe. He won yet another Asian "gold" in 1962; led the Karachi team to victory in the 1963 National Hockey Championship, and recently toured the continent as the Vice-Captain of the Pakistan team. When skipper Ghulam Rasool was forced to sit out, due to injury, early in the pre-Olympic hockey festival at Lyon, Anwar took over the reins of captaincy and ably led the team.

Anwar has won every honour the game has to offer, and his performances have been so outstandingly consistent that he is now rightly dubbed "the world's best centre-half."

53

STAMPING HOCKEY THROUGH THE POST

ALAN LEONARD

The connection between hockey and postage stamps may not be immediately apparent to the non-philatelist, for one can hardly imagine Britain's Postmaster-General, no matter how enthusiastic he might be about the game, extending to hockey his official "stamp of approval". Ever since Sir Rowland Hill pioneered these "little bits of gummed paper" back in 1840, for pre-payment of postal charges, British stamps have given prominence to the Sovereign's head, though recent designs have struck a more colourful pictorial note.

Postal authorities in other parts of the world take a far wider view of the purposes that can be served by their stamps, treating them as miniature advertising posters, depicting an immense variety of subjects —among which sport has received increasing recognition in recent years. The first sports stamps were the 1896 Olympic series of Greece, but not until the 1948 Olympics did the former trickle of sports designs swell into a veritable flood.

With new issues in an ever-increasing stream now pouring forth from the world's stamp printing presses at an average of some 300 a year, the total number of sports designs will exceed 3,000 when 1964 has seen a record release of Olympic Games commemoratives. Within this vast sporting gallery in miniature, there is plenty of scope for specialisation, and although hockey has achieved only a fraction of the philatelic representation accorded to football, there are enough stamps devoted to the game to make an attractive little collection.

Japan was the first to produce a stamp with hockey as its subject—in 1951, as one of a pair marking the Sixth National Athletic Meeting at Hiroshima in October that year. Printed alternately in different colours in the same sheet, they illustrated putting-the-shot and hockey side by side, the latter with a good picture of a player in action.

Nearer home, the Netherlands—the first European country to beat England at hockey—presented a forceful silhouette of a hockey player on one of their 1956 Olympic Games† series. These stamps were sold at a premium of fifty per cent above their face value for the benefit of the National Olympic Committee.

In the 1956 Olympic final India beat Pakistan 1–0, and an incident from this game made a rather surprising appearance on a stamp from the Dominican Republic in 1958. This was one of the many colourful labels emanating from this source paying tribute to Olympic victors.

This little Caribbean republic derives considerable foreign currency revenue from selling to the philatelic market stamps which go straight into collectors' albums and so never require the performance of any postal service by the issuing authorities. A year later the stamps were re-issued with an overprint related to the International Geophysical Year—a theme far removed from hockey!

Likewise with an eye on philatelic revenue, the Portuguese authorities produced in 1962 a long series of no fewer than forty-eight multicoloured diamond-shaped stamps in sets of six for each of their overseas territories. Each illustrated a different sport, with hockey featured on designs for Macao and Mozambique.

Indonesia put out during the summer of 1962 a total of twenty-four stamps giving postal publicity to the Fourth Asian Games, held at Jakarta. One of these, in handsome large format, printed in green and red, showed three hockey players in action.

Pakistan, Olympic gold medallists in 1960, had good reason to include hockey, along with football, cricket and squash rackets, as one of the subjects of a striking quartet of symbolic sports stamps, issued in August 1962 as publicity for a national sports development programme. The thirteen-paisa denomination in green and black presented an ingenious composition of two hockey sticks, ball, goal-posts, net and diagram of the field lay-out, flanked by the five-ringed Olympic symbol and Olympic gold medal.

The only Commonwealth stamp actually depicting hockey players appeared in Fiji in August 1963, as one of an attractive quartet

† *The Netherlands withdrew at the eleventh hour from the Melbourne Games—Editor.*

publicising the First South Pacific Games held at Suva—an important pioneer regional gathering in which some 600 sportsmen from fourteen territories participated. Hockey enjoys considerable popularity in Fiji, as does Rugby, both games often being played barefoot by the enthusiastic islanders. The one-shilling value covering the postal rate from Fiji to Australia was produced in red-brown, green and black in large upright style allowing the inclusion of the Queen's portrait, the Southern Cross constellation, symbolic palm tree and waves as well as the central picture of two hockey players in action. The models for the stamp have been identified as Adhavji Bhai and M. M. Maharaj, two well-known Fiji hockey players.

The first woman hockey player to appear in the stamp portrait gallery was Kate Tuchella, on one of a series issued in East Germany in September 1963 honouring sportsmen and women who were victims of Hitler's concentration camps. The stamps, sold at a premium of fifty per cent above their face value in aid of a memorial fund, were printed in pairs, with adjoining labels illustrating the sports in which the various martyrs were prominent.

There are two other stamps that deserve mention, as illustrating two of field hockey's forerunners, hurling and ganna. A hurler in action—with upraised stick—was depicted on a neat little Irish stamp, appropriately printed in green at Dublin, and issued in 1934 to honour the jubilee of the Gaelic Athletic Association. More recently, Ethiopia illustrated "Ganna" as one of a series of five unusual sports stamps, attractively printed at Prague in 1962. The official announcement from Addis Ababa described ganna as "Ethiopian hockey", a game played with a wooden ball, not without danger to the players' legs and heads!

The above has been adapted from an article which appeared in Stanley Gibbons monthly magazine.

(*Photo by courtesy of South China Morning Post, Ltd.*)

HONG KONG v. *JAPAN. Women's International. April, 1964. Diana Carter (extreme left) puts Hong Kong 2–1 up in their first ever International. Japan, however, won 4–3.*
L–to–R: Carter, Y. Takada (Japanese goalkeeper), M. Collaco, M. Miki, S. Hewson (with headband) and the Japanese captain, M. Ishida.

LA SELECTION du MAROC v. *CLUB SAN FERNANDO (ARGENTINE). CASABLANCA. March, 1964. San Fernando (striped shirts) attacking during a match in Morocco. The Moroccan players are Perez, M. Vinci, d'Amore and De la Torre.*

BRITAIN IN THE OLYMPICS. G.B. v. Kenya. Quarter final. Olympic Games. Rome 1960. Pritham Singh's shot fails to reach the British goal. Britain won 2–1 after 57 minutes of extra time.
L–to–R: Surjeet Singh (Kenya), Carnill (3), S. Fernandes (behind Carnill), Neill (7), Pritham Singh, Davis, Cahill (goalkeeper), and A. Mendonca (Kenya).

(Photo. Associated Press)

54
ROUND THE WORLD

*A Brief Survey of Hockey all over the World.**

Hockey is played on all five continents and in at least seventy countries. Fifty men's national associations are affiliated to the Fédération Internationale de Hockey (F.I.H.) and twenty-six women's to the International Federation of Women's Hockey Associations (I.F.W.H.A.)

EUROPE

Europe is the cradle of modern hockey and the Hockey Association of England, the first in the world, holds a unique and formidable place in the world structure. As the history of the game shows, modern club hockey was started in 1871, and the Hockey Association was founded in 1886, but it was not until 1899 that an English team left the British Isles to tour—at about the same time as hockey was taking root in South Africa and India.

There followed many tours, both official and private, in an effort to stimulate interest "across the channel."

The game's popularity widened and it was included in the London Olympic Games of 1908. European nations dominated the first two Olympic hockey tournaments and the withdrawal of the sport from the 1924 Olympics precipitated the formation of the F.I.H., the seven founder nations of which were all European countries.

Looking back at this period, the position of the Hockey Association was an invidious one. From the very beginning English hockey has been purely recreational, and the famous 1911 "Declaration of Liver-

* Editor's Notes: (1) Where the information given under one country was largely or completely the work of one man his name is given at the end of the piece concerned. Where no name is given the Editor has collated information from several sources.
(2) The number of women's clubs given in most countries is taken from the International Federation of Women's Hockey Associations' Report on the Towson, Maryland, Conference 1963.

pool'' clearly stated: "So long as the game is played for the sake of the game and all commercial considerations are placed on one side, there is no need for any encouragement such as that given by prizes and cups.'' So Britain had to withdraw their support from the Olympics.

Other European countries, however, decided that competition was the quickest way to progress and so not only did they encourage Olympic participation, but they also instituted club and district competitions.

The European season extends from September to May, the wettest and coldest time of the year, so that the majority of games are played on pitches totally unsuitable for skilful play. Hockey had started as a winter game in England mainly to make use of cricket pitches, and because of that European countries have also played the game at the wrong time of the year ever since. They are at a decided disadvantage when encountering hard pitches in hot climates.

The competition from football in the winter is a major problem for hockey, and lack of great spectator support means that the majority of national associations are not as well off as they would like to be. Few of the Western bloc countries receive state assistance, but all in the Eastern bloc are given a great deal of encouragement, both financial and otherwise. The main problem is to keep the game enjoyable and competitive, even though the price of amateurism is very high.

Austria.—The fiftieth anniversary of the association was celebrated in June 1963 and was marked by an international tournament and a women's match against Switzerland.

Austria has produced many fine players. The late Walter Niederle played many times for his country and was chosen for a continental team to meet England, an honour shared by Ernst Schala, a famous centre-half. Another excellent player was Dr. Wolfgang Klee, now President of the Austrian Association and a Vice-President of the F.I.H.

The Vienna Hockey Stadium, completed in 1955 through the energy and drive of a few real enthusiasts, is a most beautiful and up-to-date ground. The Austrian Association received the famous Leautey Trophy in the same year for its re-organisation after the war.

There are eight men's clubs in Vienna and one in Salzburg, each having two or three teams which compete in three different classes. With only about 500 active players, Austrian hockey is not of a high standard at present. (Emil Hierhold—Secretary Osterreichischer Hockey-Verband.)

Belgium.—After Mr. Pitcairn Knowles and a group of Englishmen introduced hockey to Belgium in 1900, the game was played for several years under Dutch rules.

The Association Belge de Hockey was founded in 1907 and the first international match, against Germany at Brussels in 1910, was won 3–1 though matches against English Hockey Association elevens soon after were lost 13–0 and 19–0. The Racing C.B. was a most prosperous club in the 'thirties—on one occasion ten of its players represented Belgium and the eleventh was captain of the French team!

Nowadays forty clubs and over 4,000 players, mostly situated around Brussels, Antwerp and Ghent, are controlled by the Belgian Federation whose General Secretary, Mr. Rene Frank, is also the General Secretary of the F.I.H.

Since 1945 a club championship has been organised in four divisions, the most successful clubs being Leopold and Rasante.

In 1948 Charles De Keyser, the selector, appointed a professional coach, Georges Vandenbempt, whose tactical knowledge of football was cleverly adapted to hockey. The standard of the national team improved steadily, reaching its peak at the 1958 Munich tournament where it was undefeated and drew 2–2 with India.

In 1958 an Indian coach, Mr Jagadish, was invited to Belgium and better results were expected for the yellow-vested team in the 1960 Rome Olympics. Unfortunately, some of Belgium's greatest players, including Jean Dubois (104 caps) and Roger Goossens (92 caps), were no longer at their best and the hot Italian climate adversely affected the team.

After some hesitation, clubs have recently agreed to release potential international players for extensive training.

There are now twenty-one hockey clubs in Belgium with women's sections. Thirty teams participate in the Belgian women's championships which has been won for ten consecutive years by the Royal Antwerp H.C. Belgium's National Schoolgirls' team of under 18 years have a yearly fixture with their corresponding rivals in Germany and the Netherlands.

Czechoslovakia.—Bandy hockey is one of the oldest sports practised in Czechoslovakia, having been played in the 1890's on grass and ice, with a stick flat on both sides.

The Czech Field H.A. (Ceskeslovenska Sekce Pezemniho Hokejo) was founded in 1908, the oldest clubs being SK Podoli, CKS Karlin, CKS Vysehrad, SK Slavia, DEHG and Hagiber.

The first international match was played in 1922 against Austria, who won 3–1. Two years later Czechoslovakia was one of the founders of the F.I.H., and in 1925 participated in the Geneva tournament with some success.

During the Nazi occupation in World War II all sports activity was restricted, but many new clubs and sports associations were founded, and about 1,600 players were affiliated to the national association.

After the liberation in 1945 many Czech clubs achieved fine successes abroad, and there were encouraging international results against India. In 1948 India won by only 3–2, and in 1955 they were held to a draw. In 1963 an unexpected 1–0 victory was gained over the German Democratic Republic team. TJ Hostivar have won the eight-strong First Men's League three years in succession, and recently won all their matches in Italy and Austria.

Now a days bandy hockey is played in six provinces of the republic. There are fifty-four clubs and 2,300 players.

DENMARK.—Frederik Knudsen, a professor at the Institute of Gymnastics and Sport, returned from a trip to England in 1899 with two dozen sticks and a few hard leather balls. He collected together a number of small boys aged between eight and twelve—one of whom was Henning Holst, destined to become one of Denmark's greatest players—and coached them twice a week until they became proficient. The following year Knudsen introduced the game into his Institute, and by 1904 had founded the Copenhagen H.C. and a rival club, Orient. Other Danes learnt the game from British Navy players, and in 1920 Denmark unofficially finished second in the Antwerp Olympics.

Denmark boasts lawns to rival those in England, but because of its geographical position, does not get the opportunity to play many international matches. The long interruption to the season in winter is another disadvantage, but indoor hockey is becoming more popular.

Denmark has never had more than 17 clubs and in 1964 there were only six clubs with 368 active members (203 men, 93 boys, 45 ladies and 27 girls. Considering the shortage of players, Denmark's international record is remarkable. (Allan Jahnsen, Hon. Sec. D.H.U.)

FINLAND.—There was little hockey played in Finland until the 1952 Olympics, but now there are 150 active players and another hundred associated members, although few women play.

Hockey fields are few and far between, most games being played on sand, but despite the limited numbers, Finland has a league with five or six teams, the best of which are Huevit and Nuijamiehet, who have also been successful in international matches.

The game is played by several well-known ice hockey players, including Taune Timoska, Kauke Korpela, Keijo Kuusela, Unto Viitala and Yrjo Hakala. (Veikke Jerkku, Secretary, S.M.F.L.)

FRANCE.—The game was introduced to France in 1897 by Mr. E. P. Denny in his Anglo-Saxon school, and by 1898 was organised by the Union des Sociétés Françaises de Sports Athlétiques in Paris. At

Easter in 1899 the first English team was entertained, and a series of district and national championships and cup competitions was soon organised. The game spread quickly between the wars, but is played in only six regions—Paris, the North (Lille), Lyon, Bordeaux, Angers and Normandy, and these are so far apart that liaison suffers.

The Fédération Française de Hockey was a founder member of the F.I.H. and has always taken a keen interest in international hockey, playing over twenty matches each against Belgium, England, Netherlands, Spain and Switzerland. The best Olympic performance was fourth in Berlin (1936) and tenth at Rome (1960), one of the Rome players being Philippe Reynaud, captain and centre-half, who played in three Olympics and holds the record number of 81 French caps.

Over the past ten years a great effort has been made to recruit new clubs and there are now over sixty clubs and about 5,000 players (men and women) affiliated. The National Committee of Sport takes a keen interest in hockey and grants suitable aid. (Etienne Glichitch, Sec. F.F.H.)

GERMANY.—Although bandy was played much earlier, devotees of ice hockey introduced field hockey in the spring of 1899. Uhlenhorster Hockey Club (Hamburg) not only represented Germany in the 1908 Olympics in London, but also did a tremendous amount of good by organising Easter festivals to which they invited the best club sides in Europe.

Germany affiliated to the F.I.H. in 1928 and in that year finished third in the Olympics. At the Berlin Games (1936) Germany were beaten 8–1 in the final by India—a game watched by 30,000 spectators.

Since the last war, East and West Germany have had their separate associations and have to play off for a place in the Olympic Games. West Germany won the bronze at Melbourne but disappointed at Rome, finishing seventh.

Hockey is a minor sport in East Germany. There are sixty-one clubs and about 4,450 players (1,600 men, 450 women, 1,900 boys and 500 girls). In contrast, there are about 31,000 players in West Germany (16,000 men, 5,150 women, 6,800 boys and 3,050 girls).

Both East and West stage separate leagues and championships for all grades, both indoors and outdoors, and the sport is annually gaining in popularity.

The 1967 I.F.W.H.A. Conference is to be held at Leverkusen, near Cologne. (West—Martin Suhl. East—Zweck, Gen. Sec. D.D.R.)

GREAT BRITAIN.—England teams won the first two Olympic gold medals in the 1908 and 1920 Games, but Britain then withdrew their support from the Olympic tournaments. The British Hockey Board was instituted by England, Scotland and Wales in 1948 to allow British teams to take part in the London Olympics.

Hockey is one of the few games in Britain where the national associations combine to form a Great Britain team, but the B.H.B. does not control hockey in the British Isles—this is done by each country's own association. The B.H.B. accepts responsibility for the preparation and selection of Britain's Olympic teams, and since its inception Britain has finished second (1948), third (1952), fourth (1956) and fourth (1960). Although not represented on the Board, Irish players are now eligible for selection for Great Britain. There is no Great Britain women's team.

England.—England was the founder nation of the modern game and its original ideals still hold good. There are approximately 700,000 players in the country of which the bulk are schoolgirls, very few of whom continue playing the game. There are 30,000 men and 27,000 women club players.

England has dominated both men's and women's hockey in the United Kingdom and neither national side lost to a foreign side until 1950—then the men were beaten by Holland at Amsterdam, and three years later the women by Australia at the I.F.W.H.A. Conference at Folkestone.

Hockey in England is essentially a participant sport, a game on a Saturday afternoon being the week's effort for most. The season starts in late September, the first part being devoted entirely to club and county hockey, with divisional and international matches taking place in the New Year. It ends with the extremely popular Easter festivals. There is no competitive hockey for women but the men have a home International Championship, and in 1958 an extremely popular County Championship was started.

Little effort is made to publicise the game, and a top-class club match is rarely watched by more than a hundred spectators, and usually by a mere handful. An international will attract about 4,000 with the one exception of the women's annual match at Wembley Stadium which is a "school outing" and is attended by around 60,000.

Women's hockey is very efficiently organised by the All England Women's Hockey Association (founded 1895) which has had a paid secretary for the last fifteen years. The Hockey Association decided to follow suit and Robin Struthers was appointed as paid secretary in October 1963—a great step forward.

Ireland.—The old game of hurling provided the background to Ireland's win in the world's first international match against Wales at

Rhyl in 1895, and in 1908 Ireland were runners-up to England in the first Olympic hockey tournament.

Ireland has, as a rule, ranked second among the four home countries, ahead of Scotland and Wales. It has won the "Triple Crown" ten times and its "golden years" were just before the last war.

The first Schoolboys' International was played in Ireland in 1955 when Ireland met Scotland in Dublin.

The Irish Hockey Union has a country-wide control despite the north-south political barrier, and the system is highly competitive, with league and cup competitions in all four provinces—Leinster, Ulster, Munster and Connaught.

Hockey gets a good deal of commercial sponsorship in Ulster, and also benefits from assistance from the National Council for Physical Recreation. Elsewhere, it is "do-it-yourself", and an Associate Membership scheme was started a few years ago to provide welcome revenue. Although a national ground was opened in Dublin as long ago as 1930, first-class pitches are at a premium.

In spite of the many difficulties, Ireland has produced some truly great players. Between 1935 and 1939 Denis Coulson was considered to be the finest centre-half in the world outside India, and others rated highly were goalkeeper Jack Carroll, T. G. McVeagh, outside-left and captain of those 1937/39 Triple Crown teams, and the present Great Britain goalkeeper, Harry Cahill.

The Irish Ladies' Hockey Union was formed in 1894, the first women's association in the world. Ireland won the first women's international ever played, beating England in 1896. There are about 200 women's teams in Ireland to-day. (Paul MacWeeney.)

Scotland.—The honour of staging the first modern hockey match in Scotland fell to two schools, Fettes and Loretto, in 1891. Prior to this Shinty was played.

The Scottish Hockey Association was constituted in 1901, the fourth men's Hockey association in the world. International matches began in 1902 against Ireland in Belfast, and Scotland played in the 1908 Olympics.

Essentially a Highland country, it is difficult to obtain any naturally flat pieces of land. In addition the climate is wet, the soil is clay, and the grass of a coarse texture, so the type of hockey played depends often on hard hits up field, stick-work being at a premium. But coaching, the change to the Indian stick, and more contact with European countries, is tempering the hard hits with skill and tactical approach.

Travel has always been difficult, even the forty miles between Edinburgh and Glasgow being a problem in mid-winter, with short daylight, icy roads and the vagaries of a quick-changing climate.

There are seventy men's clubs in the country and 135 women's clubs, but in recent years the game has become more popular in schools. Though unofficial competitions had always been held in the various districts, it was not until the mid-fifties that the Scottish Hockey Association gave its official blessing to six a side Tournaments leagues. Now a championship competed for by the six districts is flourishing, and there is a National Scottish Club Cup Competition. (Ernest Wall, Hon. Match Secretary, S.H.A.)

Wales.—The first Welsh club was founded by Stephen Morgan, a former Warwickshire cricketer, at Rhyl in October 1888. This club had the honour of organising the world's first international match, in which Ireland beat Wales 3–0 in 1895.

Mainly because of the incredible fervour for Rugby football, there are still only fifty-six men's and thirty-six women's hockey clubs, and not more than five boys' schools play the game. The national side has to rely on immigrant players or on boys who have been educated in England, but there are signs that this gloomy state of affairs is improving, and both South Wales and North Wales (divided by the mountains) are making efforts to improve their fixtures.

The greatest problems are finding good grounds and improving the stock of home-made players. At present most of the members of the national team play for English clubs.

There is a shortage of money, and at present a football pool just keeps the W.H.A. solvent. International gate receipts do not cover full costs, and clubs do not appreciate being asked to pay increased subscriptions to cover the travelling expenses of players from England. This may sound depressing, but although Wales has never beaten England, the match records with Ireland and Scotland are more evenly balanced, and Pakistan were held to 2–0 in 1963.

In 1964/65 South Wales are to start a men's cup competition, officials realising that this may be the way to stimulate greater enthusiasm. Schoolboy international matches are creating greater interest in schools.

The Welsh women's team, after years of striving, have twice defeated England recently. There are 37 women's clubs and 83 girls' school clubs.

HUNGARY.—The game was first played in Hungary at the beginning of this century. The National Federation, Magyar Gyeplabda Szovetseg, was established in 1924 and in the same year Hungary was one of the founders of the F.I.H.

Hungary took part in the 1936 Olympics but at present there are only seven clubs in the country with about 200 players. The game is not played by women. (Dr. Konorot Gyula, Pres. M.G.S.)

ITALY.—Shortly after the turn of the century hockey was played exclusively by the "nobili" Romans. It did not catch on, and in 1924 the Milan Skating Club had little success when they tried to introduce the game. Not until 1935 was any interest created, when the Swiss, Robert Kurt, taught the rules to a group of Genovese students.

The Italian National Olympic Committee put hockey in the care of the Italian Roller-skating Federation and a tournament took place in 1936 between the teams of Genoa, Milan, Rome and Livorno. A year later Italian championships were commenced, women's teams were formed, and in 1942 a women's championship was started, though there are no women's teams at present.

Italy entered the 1952 Olympics as an experiment, and a period of re-organisation and intense preparation for the improvement of playing standards followed, which included the use of foreign trainers.

Championships and tournaments now take place, and Italy has about 1,500 players. (Enrico Quaranta, Gen. Secretary F.I.H.P.)

THE NETHERLANDS.—Hockey was introduced in 1891 by Mr. W. Mulier, who had seen it played in England. At first, bandy or ice hockey was played, but in 1894 a match took place in Amsterdam on grass. There were six clubs by 1898 and they formed an association, playing according to their own special rules and using an orange ball made of kapok and cord. Holland decided to accept the international rules, as they wished to take part in the 1928 Amsterdam Olympics.

Holland won the silver medal at those Games and subsequently has finished third, third, second and ninth in the Olympics. These results have stimulated interest in the game, which is now second only to soccer as a winter pastime. Although the population is about a fifth of West Germany's, the Netherlands has more players (34,000). Nearly 2,400 teams take part in competitions, and there are 173 clubs affiliated to the Kon. Nederlandsche Hockey Bund, a mixed organisation.

One of the big Dutch advantages is the compactness of the country and the excellent transport facilities.

The Netherlands has an exceptional international record and has produced some first-rate players; Rein de Waal, Ab Tresling, Henk de Looper and Wagener en van Lierop before the war, and more recently Loggere and Bromberg (now the national coach). (H. van den Heide, Secretary, K.N.H.B.)

POLAND.—Hockey was first played in Poland around 1909/11 by the Lechia, Sokol, Macierz, Pogon and Czarni sports clubs, and was revived in 1921 by the Skating Club in Poznan and the Hockey Players Club (Siemianowice), which organised grass hockey sections.

By 1926 the Polski Zwiazek Hokeja na Trawie (P.Z.H.T.), with headquarters in Poznan, was formed, and two years later affiliated to the F.I.H.

The first Polish Hockey Championship was played in 1927, and Lechia (Poznan) have proved to be one of the most successful sides. There are twelve teams in the first league, twenty-four in the inter-leagues, and youth championships are also held.

Poland's first international was against Czechoslovakia in 1929 (lost 4–0), but only one other match was played before the war. Since 1946, however, Poland has won thirty-nine of the seventy internationals played against twenty-two different countries. In the 1952 Olympics, it was sixth, and at Rome (1960) twelfth, after having to return home without completing all its matches. In the last three years Poland has won the "Mario Zovato" Trophy and the Austrian Fiftieth Anniversary Tournament in Vienna.

The best known Polish player is Ryszard Marzec, a centre-half who has played in fifty-six internationals and has been awarded a badge of "Sport Champion of Merit", the highest sporting distinction in Poland. At one time, three brothers, Alfons, Henryk and Jan Flinik played in the Polish forward line.

The Polish Hockey Federation receives financial assistance from the State. (Jerzy Makow.)

[See "The Shy Sport"—Page 165 (Chap. 49).]

SPAIN.—Hockey in Spain is at present going through a period of development, having caught the imagination of young people since Spain finished third in the 1960 Rome Olympics. There are approximately 120 teams and 1,550 players affiliated to the Real Federacion Espanola de hockey, and there are nine women's teams. Catalonia, in particular, and Castille are the regions with the largest number of clubs.

Apart from the players and clubs controlled by the Real Federacion Espanola, others are under the direction of the Frente de Juventudes (Youth Front), which organises school championships, the Sindicato Espanol Universitario (The Students Union), and Educacion y Descenso (Education and Recreation).

The season begins in early October and ends in June or July. Regional and national championships at various levels are held indoors and outdoors. There are twenty-eight fields and twenty-five rinks, most of the fields having earth or cinder surfaces. Only a few are grass which is a major problem. (Miguel Rinon Ramirez.)

SWITZERLAND.—Before the First World War only two clubs, Servette Genf (Geneva) and Hockey-Club Basel (Basle) existed, in opposite corners of the country. With the foundation of the Hockey-Club Zurich, hockey resumed in 1919 and the Swiss Hockey League, with six clubs, was formed. At present the championship comprises fifteen teams in Series A, fourteen in Series B, ten in Series C, thirteen Junior, eleven school and ten ladies' teams, the Stade Lausanne having the outstanding record. The ladies started to play in 1921 and have held a championship since 1924.

Hockey is one of the most active of Swiss sports despite having to be self-supporting. Since 1922, when France won 3–0 in Geneva, Switzerland has played no fewer than 111 internationals against sixteen countries.

In 1931/32 the Leautey Cup was awarded to Switzerland by the F.I.H. to commemorate five internationals won, one drawn and only one lost. (Jacob Schenkmann.)

U.S.S.R.—In August 1957 a hockey tournament was held in Moscow in connection with the Third World Youth Games but Russia did not take part.

At that time there were said to be 1,800 players in Russia, and a year earlier the "Section Hockey de l'U.R.S.S. (Moscow)" had become affiliated to the F.I.H. In 1960, however, the Russians resigned because, "in spite of a great deal of effort" by their federation, hockey had been found "unable to develop". The climate in much of the vast country is completely unsuitable for hockey.

A game called "hockey with a ball", which is currently advertised in the Russian Press, is played at great speed with a hockey ball and sticks on a frozen field the size of a football pitch.

Another similar game called "broomball" is played on ice without skates, Russian-type brooms about eighteen inches long being used instead of sticks. These are not ideal when trying to control a spherical body slightly bigger than a tennis ball!

YUGOSLAVIA.—The first official hockey match in Yugoslavia was played on August 30, 1908, between Concordia of Zagreb and Sismis of Samober. The Federation Yugoslave de Hockey sur gazon was established in Zagreb in 1936 but it was a few years before clubs played teams from other countries, and not until 1951 that Yugoslavia played its first international (lost 1–0 to Austria). Yugoslavia gained its first international victory in 1959, beating Italy 3–0.

The game is played by men only and there are at present forty-five clubs with 1,680 players and 1,298 "helping members." There are senior and junior competitions culminating each year in state and federal championships.

Hockey is one of several sports in Yugoslavia in "relatively rapid evolution." (Ivo Zlatar.)

Besides the European countries already mentioned, Portugal is affiliated to the F.I.H., while Roumania, Sweden and Turkey have all been at one time or another.

ASIA

Although hockey was started in Britain, and the first countries to take up the game outside the British Isles were European, it might now truly be said that the centre of the hockey world is in Asia. There are probably more men playing the game in India and Pakistan alone than in the rest of the world.

The British Services first taught the game in Asia. It admirably suited the Indians with their quick eye, supple wrists, instinctive tactical sense, and their light, lithe bodies and lightning footwork. India won the Olympic title on its first appearance in 1928 and reigned supreme until 1960 when Pakistan took the "gold" at the Rome Olympics.

The peoples of nearly all the Eastern countries are suited to the game and Japan, who first competed in the Olympics in 1932, would undoubtedly have reached a higher standard by now but for the Second World War. Afghanistan (three times), Singapore and Malaya have also competed in the Olympics.

China, the largest populated country in Asia, has not taken to hockey in modern times, though the Republic of China was provisionally affiliated to the F.I.H. when Formosa with 1,000 players applied in 1956. Other Asian countries affiliated to the F.I.H. are Burma, Korea, Indonesia and Nepal (1963), while hockey is also played in Aden, Iran and Thailand.

The only Asian country to take part in an I.F.W.H.A. Conference is India (1953 and 1956), but its women have not shown the same flair as its men for the game.

CEYLON.—Men's hockey is extremely popular in Ceylon and has been competitive since the late twenties. The capital, Colombo, has about thirty teams in its association. Ceylon entered the Asian Championships for the first time in 1962.

The official season is between April and September, though the game is played all the year round. Pitches are grass and of a very high standard. An outstanding Ceylonese player was A. Nylvaganam who played and captained Ceylon more times than any other player.

The game is played by only about seventy-five women (four clubs). (Jair Virasinghe.)

HONG KONG.—Hockey has been played in Hong Kong since before the First World War. A Hockey Association was first formed in 1933, and a league with about twenty-three sides was started in 1934. The game was re-introduced in 1945 and to-day there are twelve men's and five women's clubs with about 350 players in all.

Hong Kong has been very active internationally, and in 1963 sent a touring side abroad for the first time when they played in the Djakarta Asian Games. The colony has recently played its first women's international, losing 3–4 to Japan. (David Metcalf.)

INDIA. (For men's game see "India has lost ground", "My lifetime of sport", "Lesson in India").

Hockey is the only major sport in which Indian women have their own controlling body. Indian girls excel in stickwork and control, but they lack speed, stamina and strength. Seasonal coaching camps are held for both juniors and seniors under the supervision of great players like Dhyan Chand and Rup Singh.

Tremendous progress has been made in the last four years. In 1959 twelve States were affiliated to the A.I.W.H.A. and the figure in 1963 was 19. Senior and Junior Nationals are held every year and efforts are being made to introduce other All-India Women's and Girls' Tournaments.

JAPAN.—An Irish hockey player, the Rev. Canon William Grey, took his hockey stick to Japan with him in the early 1900's and the first club was formed at Keio University, where he taught.

The game spread very quickly and the Dai Nippon Hockey Kyokwai (Japanese Hockey Union) was founded in 1923. Within three years there were fifty clubs in the country, playing mostly on grounds surfaced with ashes rolled out hard and smooth after every match. The Emperor Tenno Heika while still the Kootaishi (Crown Prince) played the game.

Hockey is to-day a "front-line" sport at universities, and great efforts have been made to raise Japan's standard to compare with the best. National tournaments are held for men, women, boys and girls, and the national team has competed in many major international tournaments. Japan now has 147 clubs and some 20,000 men players.

MALAYSIA.—The British introduced Hockey in Malaya in 1892, but the game was mainly confined to Europeans until the 1920s when the first Asian clubs were formed. It was decided at that time to play hockey from October to February — the wet season!

Malaya played her first international in 1932, losing 7–0 to India, and two years later sent a touring team to Hong Kong and Macao.

The Malayan Hockey Council was formed in 1948 to control hockey in the Federation and Singapore, and league hockey, which is to-day an important feature of Malayan hockey, was introduced. A year later quadrangular state matches were started.

The International Olympic Committee ruled that Malaya and Singapore could not compete as one in the Olympics in 1954 and both affiliated separately to the F.I.H. This state of affairs continued until the merger of Singapore, Sarawak and Sabah politically with Malaya in August 1963, when the Malaysian Hockey Federation was formed. (Dr. A. Durairatnam, Vice-President M.H.F.)

PAKISTAN.—(See Chapter 41.)

AFRICA

At Beni-Hasan in the Nile valley near Minia on a wall of Tomb No. 16* is a clear drawing of two (hockey) players bullying. The drawing was made 4,000 years ago.

In modern times the game was introduced into Africa by the British regiments that remained behind after the Boer War at the turn of the century. As Colonialism increased so more and more contacts were made in other parts of Africa, and with the recent trend towards independence, national pride has given hockey a new impetus, and it is making a brave challenge to football and rugby for the leisure time of the continent's multi-racial groups.

Egypt, now part of the United Arab Republic, was the first country in Africa to affiliate to the F.I.H. in 1947, but it is interesting to note that the Transvaal had affiliated to the Hockey Association (England) in 1908, as had British East Africa two years later and Cape Town in 1912. These are still the strongest centres in African hockey, but elsewhere steady progress is being made.

The greatest drawbacks to progress are the great distances to be travelled to establish contact, and the financial burden common to all Hockey Associations. But if internal contact is not easy, visits from India, Pakistan, England, and in North Africa from other European countries, are creating tremendous interest.

The Africans themselves have not as yet taken kindly to hockey, though Ghana and Nigeria meet annually in internationals now. Kenya was the first African nation to compete in the Olympic Games, and their fine results stimulated a great deal of interest in East Africa. Kenya,

* *Editors Note: More likely to be Tomb No. 17 ("QHETY").*

Tanganyika, Uganda and Zanzibar now meet in an international tournament for the Rahim Jivraj Cup.

Until 1964 Kenya was the only African country to be represented at the Olympics, but the development of the game on the continent is clearly emphasised by the fact that Kenya, Rhodesia and the United Arab Republic were all chosen to take part in the Tokyo Games in 1964.

The women's game has not developed to nearly such an extent, though the South African women's team is one of the best in the world.

GHANA.—Due to the limiting factors of distance and finance, Ghana's only international rivals have been Nigeria, and in the series Ghana has won eight of the twelve games played, mostly by the only goal. A new cup for this annual match has been named the Nkrumah-Azikiwe Cup.

Club hockey in Ghana is competitive and very stimulating. In 1963 the finalists of the Accra Region knock-out competition had to play four games before "Olympics" finally defeated "British Council" 1–0.

On National Founder's Day, the soccer competition was preceded by a hockey knock-out competition which undoubtedly helped to create interest in the game in Ghana. (Ohene Djan—Director of Ghana Sports.)

KENYA.—Hockey is a comparatively young game in Kenya, but the weather is ideal. Pitches on the coast are of grass and up-country of fast murram, an excellent surface for producing stick players.

The game was introduced to the country in 1920 and there are now over 4,000 players belonging to 100 clubs. It is played predominantly by Asians, but over the years Europeans have taken a healthy interest, and it is becoming more popular with the Africans, especially in the districts where sports officers are making intensive efforts in the schools.

The Kenya Hockey Union is based in Nairobi, where forty clubs are affiliated to five associations—the Goan Sports, the Asian Sports, the European H.A., the Muslim Sports and the Police Sports. It also features prominently in other major towns.

The game is played competitively with several knock-out tournaments and a league in Nairobi. The premier club tournament is the M. R. D'Souza Gold Cup, organised by the Goan Sports Association. This also attracts teams from the neighbouring countries, and is regarded as the unofficial East Africa Club Championship.

Kenya has won the East Africa International Championship since its inception in 1959, and its rise at international level has been remarkable. All the top players are keen enough to train three days a week under the national coach throughout the season, which lasts from September to April.

Both India and Pakistan use Kenya as a practice and training ground before they embark on major world tournaments, which may account for the phenomenal rise in skill among Kenya's best players. Alu Mendonca was considered by many to be the best left-winger in the world a few years ago.

Kenya went to the Melbourne Olympics in 1956, finishing tenth, and they improved to seventh place at Rome four years later.

In their 1964 tour of India, Kenya were the first team to beat India twice on their home ground.

The Kenya Women's H.A. was founded in 1958 and is multi-racial. Its present membership is 14 European and 6 Asian clubs, schools and colleges, and three African schools, with a total of 400 players. (Jasmer Singh.)

Morocco.—Hockey was first introduced in 1925 and clubs were formed in 1930 in Casablanca and Rabat.

After independence in 1956, a national federation was formed although there were only 250 players in the country, and it affiliated to the F.I.H. Morocco has played regular internationals though with no successes to date. The national side has played in Leipzig, Lisbon, Madrid and Naples, and a selected eleven took part in the Privateers Tournament in New York.

To-day there are seven clubs and only 200 players. The season is from 15th September to 15th May, and the highlight is the League Championship. Matches are all played on hard football pitches. (M. Caparros, Prem. V-Pres. F.R.M.H.)

Nigeria.—Hockey is popular in Nigeria among both the Nigerians and the Europeans. Charles Newham was responsible, in the 1940's, for organising first a Lagos and District Association and later the Nigerian Hockey Federation which affiliated to the F.I.H. in 1950.

The few pitches available are grass, with an odd one or two made of laterite. The season starts in April or May and ends in October with the annual international match with Ghana, which is played alternately in each country.

In the early 1960's Nigeria had the services of an Indian coach, but the game still has a long way to go before further international matches will be possible.

There is limited support in some girls schools and women do not play a lot, although a ladies club was formed in Lagos in 1963. (Jack Farnsworth.)

Rhodesia.—Hockey is multi-racial in Rhodesia and is flourishing with no fewer than ninety-six men's teams. It started at the beginning of the century and was played in the larger centres of Salisbury, Bulawayo and Gwelo.

UNICORNS (*Great Britain Olympic potentials*) v. SPAIN. *Folkestone Festival. Easter 1964.* (*Photo. Anthony Hallas*)
A tense moment as the Spanish goalkeeper Carlos del Coso saves. The English players L–to–R are: Jones, Corby, Hindle, Christensen, and Veit.

(Photo. Fotos Biarnes (Tarrasa

EIGHT NATIONS TOURNAMENT FINAL. Barcelona. 1964. Spain v. *Belgium. The Belgian goalkeeper saves from Spanish centre-forward, Francisco Amat. Spain won the final 2–1 after two periods of extra time.*
L–to–R: Francisco Amat, Jaime Amat, Jorge Vidal, Mercel Thill.

POLAND v. *UNITED ARAB REPUBLIC. Stadion Poznan. 1959. The U.A.R. goalkeeper about to clear as Poland (in white) attack. Poland won 4–1.*

The Rhodesian Hockey Association, which now comprises seven boards, was formed in 1924 as the controlling body for both men's and women's hockey, but the women formed their own association in 1937. Rhodesia was a founder member of the South African Hockey Union in 1925 and remained affiliated until 1961, when it was found necessary to break away and affiliate direct to the F.I.H. The decision was not taken lightly, for participation in all but four of the South African Inter-Provincial Tournaments had cemented close ties.

The inter-board competitions and tournaments, which also serve as national trials, have been largely responsible for progress in Rhodesia. Club hockey is controlled in each centre by the respective boards, which arrange fixtures mainly on a league basis, and inter-club festivals are held from time to time.

Most government high schools and senior schools now include hockey as a regular part of their sports curriculum, and a schoolboy side was sent to South Africa in 1960.

Since affiliation to the F.I.H. in 1961 the senior international side has played two games against Kenya at Bulawayo and Salisbury, winning one and losing one, and has also met South Africa.

The common problem of finance is a limiting factor in Rhodesia's international aspirations, a problem that is likely to increase. Selection for the 1964 Olympics at Tokyo, however, should stimulate interest even further. (Basil Napier.) (See also Chapter 47.)

South Africa.—It was probably at Newlands, Cape Town, in 1899, that Mr V. A. van der Byl arranged the first matches in South Africa. After the Boer War, between 1904 and 1906, rapid progress was made in the Free State and Transvaal, where Sunday play was possible. The rules of the English Hockey Association were observed, the amateur status being zealously guarded, although the game was run almost exclusively on the league system without cup or prize competitions.

It was not until 1924 that the South African Hockey Union was established. There is now no finer sporting event in South Africa than the Inter-Provincial Tournament, first pioneered in 1926, and played in a different centre each year.

In 1938 South Africa visited Kenya and Uganda. The visit was an unqualified success, and only the war prevented South Africa from entering international hockey circles.

In 1946 the now famous "Reunion" Inter-Provincial Tournament at the "old" Wanderers Club in Johannesburg signalled a tremendous revival in hockey.

Success against touring sides stimulated South Africa to tour Europe in 1957 with marked success, and the F.I.H. awarded the Leautey Cup to the S.A.H.U. that year. Since then a feature of South African hockey has been the international tours of schools and university sides to and from South Africa.

Grounds in South Africa are generally good quality grass, but in some centres hard courts are used, most having to be shared with the ladies.

Women's hockey (215 clubs, 448 teams) has a large following among girls of all races, and South African women players are considered among the most brilliant in the world. (Bill Malherbe.)

TANGANYIKA.—Tanganyikans have not yet taken to hockey, the 500 to 800 players being mainly immigrants. The Tanganyika Hockey Association was formed in 1957 in Dar-es-Salaam and affiliated to the F.I.H. in 1959. The best players come from Arusha and Moshi and, to a lesser extent, Tanga. Tanganyika has a few ladies' teams but at present they do not have an association.

Pitches are the greatest problem, being grass but in very short supply.

UGANDA.—The Uganda Women's H.A. was formed in 1961 and consists of eight clubs and four schools at present. A knock-out tournament is held in February and then there is a break until July when the new season starts with a seven-a-side tournament, which is followed by the League programme. A Uganda women's team plays Kenya twice a year.

Women's Hockey in Uganda is multi-racial and African school players show promise.

UNITED ARAB REPUBLIC.—A game called "Hoksha" was played in villages in Egypt between farmers. It was similar to hockey but played with the branches of palm trees, the balls being made of palm leaves.

Modern hockey was introduced in Egypt in 1908 by the English regiments stationed there. A tournament was promoted by the Cairo Hockey League, with headquarters at the Turf Club, Cairo, the two leading teams being Khedival Sporting Club and the Ministry of Education staff. The game was revived in 1919 and was soon introduced into the secondary schools in the Charkieh and Canal Zones.

Club hockey was restarted by the National Sporting Club in Cairo in 1936, and six years later the Federation was established. This was accepted as a member of the F.I.H. in 1947, the first member nation from the African continent. Since then tournaments and local competitions have taken place between clubs and zones. There are now twenty-two first-class clubs, ten second-class clubs, fourteen junior clubs and six ladies' clubs with approximately 1,100 men and 150 women players. The game is played on some of the finest and most beautiful grass pitches in the world, and also on murram.

The U.A.R. started playing regular internationals in 1955, and have visited Spain, Poland, Germany, India, Indonesia and Italy in an effort to bring better hockey to the republic. This has been a success, for its team was accepted for the 1964 Olympics. (M. Rafaat, Sec. A.H.F.)

AMERICA

America is the weakest hockey-playing continent in the world, though the game is played in a surprising number of its countries.

The United States affiliated to the International Federation in 1930, and have since been joined in the Federation by Argentina (1948), Cuba (1955), Canada (1960) and Netherlands Antilles (1960). Sao Paulo (Brazil) and Santiago (Chile) are adherent members, and the Pan-American Field Hockey Federation is a "Recognised Continental Group" of the F.I.H.

When the Olympics were held at Los Angeles in 1932 the United States was one of three hockey teams that competed, and it has since been to three Olympiads. The U.S.A. was beaten for the American continent place at the 1964 Tokyo Olympics by Canada, who makes its Olympic debut in Japan. The only other country from the American continent to compete in the Olympics is Argentina (1948.)

The United States, who had 160 women's clubs in 1959, has taken part in all seven I.F.W.H.A. tournaments held so far, and staged the 1936 (Philadelphia) and 1963 (Maryland) Conferences. It has been joined at I.F.W.H.A. tournaments since 1956 by Canada (1956–59–63), Argentina (1959–63), Jamaica (1963) and Trinidad (1963).

Inter-colonial tournaments have been staged in the West Indies since 1956 for women and 1957 for men. British Guiana, Jamaica and Trinidad compete against each other annually, and a Barbados team joined the men's competition in 1961.

The game is also played in Bermuda and Venezuela.

There is no doubt that visits from overseas national or club sides would be a tremendous tonic to hockey in South America and the Caribbean.

ARGENTINA.—Hockey has been played in the Argentine for over fifty years, having been introduced by Britons who came to the country to build railways, help with the industrialisation of meat, and set up offices for international companies. The National Association was founded in 1908, and at the end of 1963 there were forty affiliated clubs and 1,200 men and 1,800 women players.

The game is played mainly in Buenos Aires and to a lesser extent in the other main centres. There are leagues and, since 1955, some indoor hockey.

Argentina first took part in international competition when it played in the 1948 Olympics in London. It finished runners-up in its group to India, having beaten Spain and drawn with Austria. The national team went into hard training for the 1952 Olympics, but was refused permission to go to Helsinki by the government in power. At this time it was not possible to import sticks or balls.

Argentina staged a Sesquicentennial Tournament in 1960, with Chile and Brazil, which it won. (Jorge Parsons, President A.A.A.H.)

(See also Chapters 22 and 51.)

British Guiana.—British Guiana is economically a poor country, and to the masses the game has naturally been restricted by lack of opportunity. The only recognised clubs are situated in the capital, Georgetown. There are eight men's teams, who play mostly friendlies, though there are league, cup and seven-a-side competitions. Games are played between 4.45 and 6.15 p.m., when players have left work and the heat is not too great.

The pitches are most suitable for the game, being hard and very fast. The primary field is the famous Bourda, where Test cricket is played.

The British Guiana Board of Control was founded in 1945. Up to the end of 1963 the national side had won half its matches against Barbados, Jamaica and Trinidad. Practice sessions are held by the national coach on Sundays.

There are five clubs affiliated to the women's association. They also play league, knock-out and seven-a-side competitions. Owing to the country's economic setback in 1963, the women's association was forced to abandon its proposed visit to the I.F.W.H.A. Conference that year. (H. A. Shepherd, Secretary B.G.M.H.B.C.)

Canada.—(See Chapter 44.)

Jamaica.—Hockey in Jamaica started nearly forty years ago. From 1935 until 1963 the men's and women's games were controlled by the Jamaican Hockey Association, but the game has developed to such an extent that separate governing bodies have been formed.

Hockey is played throughout the year, except for a brief break over the Christmas and New Year holidays, despite an average temperature of eighty degrees. There is great lack of playing fields, and during the dry season the grass pitches become very dusty and uneven, which makes ball control extremely difficult.

The game is not a popular one in Jamaica. There are only about 120 women players, though interest seems to be growing in the schools.

Women play in seven different competitions, including a league. The national women's team took part in the international tournament in the U.S.A. in 1963 and although they failed to win a game, learnt many valuable lessons. (Hazel Samuel, Secretary J.W.H.A.)

Netherlands Antilles.—There were six clubs before the Second World War but only one sports club, Asiento (Shell), remained afterwards. In June 1961, Asiento, Royal Dutch Navy and the Curaçao H.C. formed the Netherlands Antillean Association.

There are about sixty men, twenty ladies and sixty junior players. The season runs from September to the end of July and matches are played on very hard pitches. The association visits the Caracas Sport Club in Venezuela annually and has also twice visited America. These visits have been reciprocated. (A. J. P. Kusters, Chairman N.A.H.A.)

Trinidad and Tobago.—Trinidad staged the first women's and men's Inter-Colonial Tournament in the West Indies and have dominated both competitions ever since.

Hockey is played on week-days after work, between January and August. There are some 350 women players in the women's association and roughly a hundred girls playing in the schools. Women play in league and knock-out competitions and in a six-a-side tournament which is to be replaced by a seven-a-side one shortly.

Trinidad took part in the 1963 conference of the I.F.W.H.A., winning two of their six matches.

Major difficulties are lack of playing fields and lack of funds, but both the men's and women's sections have drawn increased crowds, since many of the popular football clubs are now playing the game. (Mrs Irma de Lima, Secretary T.T.W.H.A.)

United States.—Hockey has never gained a very strong foothold in the United States because of the tremendous amount of competition from other sports, but there are nearly 200 women's clubs.

The game was introduced in Connecticut by a former Welsh player and teacher, Louise Robert, in 1926. With her husband, Henry Kirk Greer, she founded the U.S. Field Hockey Association, and it is mainly through their efforts that the game has developed. Their son, John, a former U.S. player, is now secretary of the association.

The Privateers Club is the best known American club. It was formed in 1956 for the purpose of providing U.S. players with constant opportunities to play international games of the highest standard. It is quite definitely the most travelled hockey side in the world, and it stages an annual festival which attracts teams from far and wide.

(See Chapter 25.)

AUSTRALASIA

Hockey has a firm footing in both Australia and New Zealand and is also played in Papua, New Guinea and Fiji. The season extends from April to September and there is a limited amount of summer hockey in both Australia and New Zealand. The climate is ideal and the grounds dry, except in New Zealand.

Australia and New Zealand affiliated to the F.I.H. in 1938, and both played in the Olympic Games for the first time at Melbourne in 1956, when Australia finished fifth and New Zealand sixth, positions that were reversed four years later. Not surprisingly these two countries play the majority of their international matches against each other, and the honours have been shared.

AUSTRALIA.—Irish goldminers played hurley in Australia before 1880, but the game lost favour when the British introduced hockey just before the turn of the century. For once it was not the British Army that made the introduction but the Royal Navy, who probably played in South Australia—the first state to form a hockey association (1900).

The Australian Hockey Association was formed in 1906, and nowadays each of the six states is a member, and the Northern Territory and Papuan Association are associate members. Queensland and Western Australia have been the most successful state sides in the Australian championships.

The year 1956 was a very significant one for Australian hockey, for as a result of the Olympic Games at Melbourne and the I.F.W.H.A.'s Sixth Conference in Sydney, the game received a tremendous boost. There are now nearly three times as many male players (30,000) and a great number more women's clubs (261).

A great Australian disadvantage is the tremendous distances between the main hockey centres. West Australians have to travel around 6,000 miles and spend over £100 each to compete in a tournament in Brisbane.

Perhaps the best known character in Australian hockey is Charles Morley, who still plays first-grade hockey in Melbourne though "knocking on fifty". He is secretary of the Australian H.A., and is manager/coach to the Australian Olympic team. A keen tactician, he introduced the three backs and no goalkeeper game in Australia.

The most famous hockey family in Australia are the Pearces. All five brothers, who learnt their hockey in India, have represented Australia in the Olympics. An Australian, Jim MacDowell (Victoria), has umpired two Olympic finals—in 1956 and 1960.

NEW ZEALAND.—Hockey was first played in New Zealand in the towns of Tinwald, Kaipoi and Christchurch, in the closing years of the last century. One of the prime movers in the start of the game was the Rev H. Mathias. Hockey gradually spread over the Dominion, and in the year 1902 the New Zealand Hockey Association was formed, with headquarters in Christchurch, where it has since remained.

Possibly the two best players New Zealand has produced have both been goalkeepers, Gerald Fletcher (Waikato), who played for New Zealand from 1926 to 1929, and Bill Schaeffer, who first played for New Zealand in 1956 at the Melbourne Olympic Games and is still a great goalkeeper. Another fine player was former captain and centre-half, Eddie McLeod, who played for New Zealand from 1922 to 1935, and of recent years has been New Zealand's sole selector and coach.

Probably New Zealand's most dynamic coach in the past was the late Sir Sidney Holland who, before he entered politics and became Prime Minister of New Zealand, was a leading hockey player, umpire, coach and administrator. He was the manager and coach of the 1932 New Zealand team that toured Australia, and it was largely owing to his drive and ability as a coach that New Zealand won the Test match on this tour by a record 7–0.

The New Zealand H.A. recently appointed three coaches, Bruce Turner, Ivan Armstrong and Phil Bygrave, who all represented New Zealand as players at Olympic Games.

The present chairman of the N.Z.H.A. is Mr. J. Gordon Leggat, a leading barrister, who represented New Zealand with distinction at cricket.

Up to the end of 1963 New Zealand has played sixty-seven hockey international matches, winning twenty-nine, drawing ten and losing twenty-eight.

New Zealand has about 5,000 men, 7,000 women and 10,000 boy players. (W. Havilah Down, M.B.E.)

APPENDIX I

COMPLETE RESULTS OF OLYMPIC GAMES TOURNAMENTS (1908-1960)

1908 LONDON

Preliminary Round		*Semi-Finals*		*Final*	
England	10	England	6	**England**	**8**
France	0	Scotland	1	**Ireland**	**1**
Scotland	4	Ireland	3		
Germany	0	Wales	1		

FINAL TEAMS

England: H. T. Wood (West Bromwich); H. Scott-Freeman (Staines), L. C. Baillon (Northampton); J. Y. Robinson (Oxford University), E. W. Page (Wolverhampton), A. H. Noble (Alderley Edge); P. M. Rees (Barnes), G. Logan (Hampstead), S. H. Shoveller (Hampstead), R. G. Pridmore (Coventry and N.W.), E. H. Green (Staines).

Ireland: E. P. C. Holmes (Cliftonville); J. Peterson (Palmerston), W. F. Peterson (Palmerston); W. E. Graham (Palmerston), W. I. V. Campbell (Dublin University), H. L. Murphy; C. F. Power, R. C. G. Gregg (all of Three Rock Rovers), E. P. Allman-Smith (Dublin Univ.), F. L. Robinson (Malone), R. L. Kennedy (Banbridge).

Umpires: G. H. Morton (England) and M. Baker (England).

1920 ANTWERP

(League basis)

Belgium	3	France	2	
Denmark	9	France	1	
England	12	Belgium	1	
England	6	Denmark	1	
Denmark	5	Belgium	2	
England	v	France		(France withdrew—England given win)

	Ranking	*P*	*W*	*D*	*L*	*F*	*A*
1.	England	3	3	0	0	18	2
2.	Denmark	3	2	0	1	14	9
3.	Belgium	3	1	0	2	6	19
4.	France	3	0	0	3	3	12

England team: C. S. Atkin, J. H. Bennett, C. H. Campbell, H. D. R. Cooke, E. B. Crockford, R. W. Crummack, H. E. Haslam, A. F. Leighton, C. S. W. Marcon, J. C. W. McBryan, G. F. McGrath, S. H. Shoveller, W. F. Smith, C. T. A. Wilkinson.

Denmark team: H. Bjerrum, E. Blach, Sv Blach, Due, Eigenbrod, Faber, H. J. Hansen, Herlak, H. Holst, E. Hursted, H. Hjaer, P. Koefoed, Metz, C. Pantmann-Hansen, Andr. Rasmussen.

1928 AMSTERDAM

Group winners qualify for final:

	Group A				*Group B*		
India	6	Austria	0	Holland	5	France	0
India	5	Denmark	0	Holland	2	Germany	1
India	6	Switzerland	0	Germany	2	France	0
Belgium	1	Denmark	0	Germany	5	Spain	1
Denmark	2	Switzerland	1	France	2	Spain	1
India	9	Belgium	0	Holland	1	Spain	1
Denmark	3	Austria	1				
Belgium	4	Austria	0				
Switzerland	1	Austria	0				
Belgium	3	Switzerland	0				

India	8 pts.	Holland	5 pts.
Belgium	6 pts.	Germany	4 pts.
Denmark	4 pts.	France	2 pts.
Switzerland	2 pts.	Spain	1 pt.
Austria	0 pts.		

3rd Place: Germany 3 Belgium 0

Final: India 3 Holland 0

India: R. J. Allen; M. E. Rocque, L. C. Hammond; R. A. Norris, B. E. Penniger, S. M. Yusuf; M. A. Gateley, G. E. Marthins, D. Chand, F. S. Seaman, W. J. Goodsir-Cullen.

Holland: A. J. L. Katte; A. W. Tresling, R. B. J. de Waal; J. W. Brand, E. P. J. Duson, J. G. Ankerman; H. P. Visser 't Hooft, R. Van der Veen, P. Van de Rovaert, G. J. A. Jannink, A. J. Kop.

Umpires: W. Simon (Germany) and R. Liegeois (Belgium).

Ranking

1. India
2. Holland
3. Germany
4. Belgium

1932 LOS ANGELES

India	11	Japan	1
Japan	9	United States	2
India	24	United States	1

Teams: India *v.* Japan.

India: R. J. Allen; C. Tapsell, L. C. Hammond; Masud Minhas, B. E. Penniger, Lal Shah Bokhari; R. J. Carr, Gurmit Singh, D. Chand, Rup Singh, M. Jaffer.

Japan: Hamada; Sohda, S. Kobayashiu; K. Kobayashiu, Sakai, Nakamura; Kon, Nagata, Kenishi, Usami, Inochora.

Umpires: C. E. Newham (Great Britain) and T. M. Spence (Great Britain).

Ranking

1. India
2. Japan
3. United States

1936 BERLIN

Winners of Group A and B into semi-finals with first two from Group C:

Group A				*Group B*				*Group C*			
India	9	Japan	0	Germany	4	Afghanistan	1	Holland	3	France	1
India	7	United States	0	Germany	6	Denmark	0	Holland	2	Belgium	2
Japan	5	United States	1	Afghanistan	6	Denmark	6	France	2	Belgium	2
India	4	Hungary	0					Holland	4	Switzerland	1
Japan	3	Hungary	1					France	1	Switzerland	0
Hungary	3	United States	1					Switzerland	2	Belgium	1

India	6 pts.	Germany	4 pts.	Holland	5 pts.
Japan	4 pts.	Afghanistan	1 pt.	France	3 pts.
Hungary	2 pts.	Denmark	1 pt.	Belgium	2 pts.
United States	0 pts.			Switzerland	2 pts.

Semi-Finals:	India	10	France	0
	Germany	3	Holland	0
3rd Place:	Holland	4	France	3
Final:	**India**	**8**	**Germany**	1

India: R. J. Allen; C. Tapsell, Md. Hussain; B. M. Nimal, W. Cullen, J. Gallibardy; Shahabuddin, Dara Shah, Dhyan Chand, Rup Singh, M. Jaffer.

Germany: Drose; Kemmer, Zander; Gerdes, Keller, Schmalix; Huffmann, Hamel, Weiss, Sherbart, Messner.

Umpires: R. Liegeois (Belgium) and T. J. Van 't Lam (Netherlands)

Classification Matches				*Ranking*
Switzerland	5	Denmark	1	1. India
Afghanistan	4	Belgium	1	2. Germany
Japan	4	Denmark	1	3. Holland
Hungary	1	Belgium	0	4. France
Afghanistan	3	United States	0	

1948 LONDON

Winners of Groups A and B qualify for semi-finals with first two from Group C.

Group A				*Group B*				*Group C*			
India	8	Austria	0	Great Britain	0	Switzerland	0	Netherlands	4	Belgium	1
Argentina	3	Spain	2	Afghanistan	2	United States	0	France	2	Denmark	2
India	9	Argentina	1	Afghanistan	1	Switzerland	1	Netherlands	4	Denmark	1
Spain	1	Austria	1	Gt. Britain	11	United States	0	Pakistan	2	Belgium	1
Austria	1	Argentina	1	Gt. Britain	8	Afghanistan	0	Netherlands	2	France	1
India	2	Spain	0	Switzerland	3	United States	1	Pakistan	9	Denmark	0
								Pakistan	3	France	1
								Pakistan	6	Netherlands	1
								Belgium	2	France	1
								Belgium	2	Denmark	1

				Pakistan	8 pts.
India	6 pts.	Great Britain	5 pts.	Netherlands	6 pts.
Argentina	3 pts.	Switzerland	4 pts.	Belgium	4 pts.
Austria	2 pts.	Afghanistan	3 pts.	France	1 pt.
Spain	1 pt.	United States	0 pts.	Denmark	1 pt.

Semi-Finals:	India	2	Netherlands	1
	Great Britain	2	Pakistan	0
3rd Place:	Netherlands	4	Pakistan	1
	(after draw 1–1)			

Final: India 4 Great Britain 0

India: L. H. K. Pinto; R. S. Gentle, T. Singh; Maxie Vaz, A. C. Kumar, K. C. Datt; L. Fernandes, P. A. Jansen, Balbir Singh, K. D. Singh, Kishan Lal.

Great Britain: D. L. S. Brodie; G. B. Sime, W. L. C. Lindsay; M. M. Walford, F. O. Reynolds, F. R. Lindsay; J. M. Peake, W. N. White, R. E. Adlard, M. F. Borrett, W. S. Griffiths.

Umpires: R. Lombaert (Belgium) and H. Rogge (Netherlands).

Ranking

1. India
2. Great Britain
3. Netherlands
4. Pakistan

1952 HELSINKI

1st Round		*2nd Round*		*Semi-Finals*		*Final*	
		India	4	India	3		
Austria	2	Austria	0			**India**	**6**
Switzerland	1						
		Great Britain	1	Great Britain	1		
Belgium	6	Belgium	0				
Finland	0						
		Netherlands	1	Netherlands	1		
Germany	7	Germany	0			**Netherlands**	**1**
Poland	2						
France	5	France	0	Pakistan	0		
Italy	0	Pakistan	6				

3rd Place: Great Britain 2 Pakistan 1

Final Teams

India: R. Francis; Dharam Singh, R. S. Gentle; L. W. Claudius, K. Datt, G. Perumal; R. Lal, Kunwar Singh (Babu), Balbir Dosanjh, Udham Singh, M. Rajagopaz.

Netherlands: L. Mulder; J. J. Drivjer, H. J. J. Derckx; E. H. Tiel, H. P. Loggere, J. T. Ancion; L. H. Wery, R. T. Esser, J. H. Kruize, A. C. D. Boerstra, W. van Heel.

Umpires: A. Allen (Gt. Britain) and M. G. Cowlishaw (Gt. Britain).

Consolation Tournament

Germany	7	Germany	2		
Finland	0			Germany	4
Austria	2	Austria	1		
Italy	0				
Poland	1	Poland	1		
Belgium (after replay)	0			Poland	0
Switzerland	2				
France	1	Switzerland	0		

Ranking

1. India
2. Netherlands
3. Great Britain
4. Pakistan
5. Germany
6. Poland

1956 MELBOURNE

Winners of Pool A and B into semi-finals with first two from Pool C:

Pool A				*Pool B*				*Pool C*			
Singapore	6	United States	1	Gt. Britain	2	Malaya	2	Pakistan	2	Belgium	0
India	14	Afghanistan	0	Australia	2	Kenya	0	Germany	5	New Zealand	4
India	16	United States	0	Gt. Britain	1	Kenya	1	Pakistan	5	New Zealand	1
Singapore	5	Afghanistan	0	Australia	3	Malaya	2	Germany	0	Belgium	0
India	6	Singapore	0	Kenya	1	Malaya	1	Germany	0	Pakistan	0
Afghanistan	5	United States	1	Gt. Britain	2	Australia	1	New Zealand	3	Belgium	0

India	6 pts.	Great Britain	4 pts.	Pakistan	5 pts.
Singapore	4 pts.	Australia	4 pts.	Germany	4 pts.
Afghanistan	2 pts.	Malaya	2 pts.	New Zealand	2 pts.
U.S.A.	0 pts.	Kenya	2 pts.	Belgium	1 pt.

Pool B play-off: Great Britain 1 Australia 0

Semi-Finals: India 1 Germany 0
Pakistan 3 Great Britain 2

3rd Place: Germany 3 Great Britain 1

Final: India 1 Pakistan 0

India: S. Laxman; A. Bakshish, R. S. Gentle; L. W. Claudius, Amir Kumar, P. G. Perumaz; R. Lal, Gurdev Singh, Balbir Singh, Udham Singh, R. S. Bhola.

Pakistan: H. Zakir; A. Munir, M. H. Atif; Rasool Ghulam, Anwar Ahmad, H. Mussarat; N. Alam, A. Hamid, R. Habib, A. Nasir, U. Moti.

Umpires: M. G. Cowlishaw (Great Britain) and J. MacDowell (Australia).

Classification Tournament

Pool I				*Pool II*			
New Zealand	13	Singapore	0	Kenya	3	United States	0
Australia	2	Belgium	2	Malaya	4	Afghanistan	0
Australia	1	New Zealand	0	Kenya	9	Afghanistan	0
Belgium	5	Singapore	0	Malaya	3	United States	0
Australia	5	Singapore	0	Afghanistan	1	United States	1
New Zealand	3	Belgium	2	Malaya	3	Kenya	2

Australia	5 pts.	Malaya	6 pts.
New Zealand	4 pts.	Kenya	4 pts.
Belgium	3 pts.	Afghanistan	1 pt.
Singapore	0 pts.	United States	1 pt.

Ranking

1. India
2. Pakistan
3. Germany
4. Great Britain
5. Australia
6. New Zealand
7. Belgium
8. Singapore
9. Malaya
10. Kenya
11. Afghanistan
12. United States

1960 ROME

First two in each Pool qualify for Quarter-finals.

Pool A

India	10	Denmark	0
Netherlands	1	New Zealand	1
India	4	Netherlands	1
New Zealand	4	Denmark	1
India	3	New Zealand	0
Netherlands	4	Denmark	2

India	6 pts.
New Zealand	3 pts.
Netherlands	3 pts.
Denmark	0 pts.

Play-off for second place,
New Zealand 2 Netherlands 1

Pool B

Pakistan	3	Australia	0
Poland	2	Japan	1
Pakistan	8	Poland	0
Australia	8	Japan	1
Pakistan	10	Japan	0
Australia	1	Poland	1

Pakistan	6 pts.
Australia	3 pts.
Poland	3 pts.
Japan	0 pts.

Play-off for second place,
Australia 2 Poland 0

Pool C

Kenya	1	Germany	0
France	2	Italy	0
Germany	5	France	0
Kenya	7	Italy	0
Germany	5	Italy	0
France	0	Kenya	0

Kenya	5 pts.
Germany	4 pts.
France	3 pts.
Italy	0 pts.

Pool D

Spain	0	Great Britain	0
Belgium	4	Switzerland	2
Belgium	1	Great Britain	1
Spain	5	Switzerland	1
Great Britain	3	Switzerland	0
Spain	3	Belgium	1

Spain	5 pts.
Great Britain	4 pts.
Belgium	3 pts.
Switzerland	0 pts.

Quarter Finals:	India	1	Australia	0	(after extra time)
	Great Britain	2	Kenya	1	(after extra time)
	Pakistan	2	Germany	1	
	Spain	1	New Zealand	0	(after extra time)

Semi-Finals:	Pakistan	1	Spain	0
	India	1	Great Britain	0
3rd Place:	Spain	2	Great Britain	1

Final: Pakistan 1 India 0

Pakistan: A. Rashid; B. Ahmad, R. H. Atif; G. Rasool, Anwar Ahmad, A. Habib; N. Alam, A. Hamid, A. Waheed, A. Nasir, U. Moti.

India: S. Laxman; Prith. Paz Singh, L. Sharma; L. W. Claudius, J. Antic, M. Lal; Joginder Singh, V. J. Peter, Jaswant Singh, Udham Singh, R. S. Bhola.

Umpires: J. MacDowell (Australia) and A. Massart (Belgium).

Classification Matches

For Places 5–8

New Zealand	1	Germany	0
Australia	1	Kenya	1
(abandoned after	120 mins.)		
Australia	2	Kenya	1
New Zealand	1	Australia	0
Germany	–	Kenya	–

For Places 9–12

France	1	Belgium	0
Netherlands	2	France	0
Netherlands	2	Belgium	1
Poland withdrew			

For Places 13–16

Italy	1	Switzerland	1
Japan	5	Switzerland	1
Italy	2	Japan	1
Denmark withdrew			

Ranking

1. Pakistan
2. India
3. Spain
4. Great Britain
5. New Zealand
6. Australia
7. Germany
8. Kenya
9. Netherlands
10. France
11. Belgium
12. Poland
13. Italy
14. Japan
15. Switzerland
16. Denmark

APPENDIX II

INTERNATIONAL RESULTS (MEN)

The following summary of international men's results is the first ever compiled in the world. Each hockey-playing country was invited to submit its own list.

Immediately after each country's name is the month the list was submitted. Where later results have been received, summaries have been amended and indicated in the tables by letter (a).

The lists for India, Japan and Malaya have been compiled from others received and are therefore not complete.

Lists do not always cross-check, though the editor has made amendments where it was possible to verify results.

ARGENTINE
(to Dec. 1963)

	P	*W*	*D*	*L*	*F*	*A*
Austria	1	0	1	0	1	1
Brazil	2	2	0	0	8	0
Chile	2	1	1	0	3	1
India	1	0	0	1	1	9
Spain	1	1	0	0	3	2
United States	2	2	0	0	2	0
Total	9	6	2	1	18	13

* * *

AUSTRALIA
(April 1964)

	P	*W*	*D*	*L*	*F*	*A*
Belgium	2	1	1	0	4	3
Germany (West) ..	1	0	0	1	0	3
Great Britain	2	0	0	2	1	3
India	2	0	0	2	0	4
Indonesia	1	1	0	0	15	0
Japan	2	2	0	0	10	1
Kenya	3	2	1	0	5	2
Malaya..	2	1	1	0	4	3
Netherlands	1	1	0	0	3	1
New Zealand	23	10	3	10	38	49
Pakistan	1	0	0	1	0	3
Poland	2	1	1	0	3	1
Singapore	1	1	0	0	5	0
United Arab Republic	1	1	0	0	6	0
Total	44	21	7	16	94	73

AUSTRIA
(December 1963)

	P	W	D	L	F	A
Argentina	1	0	1	0	1	1
Czechoslovakia ..	6	3	2	1	10	6
Denmark	2	0	0	2	2	4
Finland	1	1	0	0	1	0
France	4	1	1	2	8	8 (a)
Germany (East) ..	5	0	3	2	0	2
Germany (West) ..	8	0	1	7	6	36
Hungary	2	0	0	2	0	2
Italy	10	8	1	1	17	3 (a)
India	3	0	0	3	0	13
Japan	1	0	0	1	0	2
Netherlands	3	0	0	3	0	6
Poland	6	1	0	5	3	14
South Africa	1	0	0	1	0	5
Spain	5	0	1	4	0	10 (a)
Switzerland	4	1	2	1	5	6
United Arab Republic	2	2	0	0	4	1
Yugoslavia	4	3	1	0	10	2
Total	68	20	13	35	67	121

* * *

BARBADOS
(April 1964)

(Inter-Colonial Tournament Matches)

	P	W	D	L	F	A
British Guiana.. ..	2	0	0	2	0	10
Jamaica	2	0	0	2	1	5
Trinidad	2	0	2	0	1	1
Total	6	0	2	4	2	16

BELGIUM
(May, 1964)

	P	*W*	*D*	*L*	*F*	*A*
Afghanistan	1	0	0	1	1	4
Australia	2	0	1	1	3	4
Austria	5	5	0	0	12	3
Denmark	6	5	0	1	11	8
England	7	1	1	5	9	30
Finland	1	1	0	0	6	0
France	48	25	9	14	91	72
Germany (West) ..	23	2	5	16	18	54
Great Britain	5	4	1	0	8	2
Hungary	2	1	0	1	6	1
India	9	0	1	8	8	47
Indonesia	1	1	0	0	3	1
Ireland	2	0	1	1	3	4
Italy	4	4	0	0	15	2
Japan	2	0	0	2	0	3
Malaya..	1	0	0	1	0	2
Netherlands	55	12	7	36	53	107
New Zealand	3	1	0	2	3	6
Pakistan	7	0	1	6	6	26
Poland	3	1	0	2	3	4
Scotland	2	1	0	1	3	2
Singapore	2	2	0	0	8	2
South Africa	4	4	0	0	12	4
Spain	16	6	4	6	28	21
Switzerland	18	13	2	3	42	13
United Arab Republic	1	1	0	0	5	2
United States	1	1	0	0	4	0
Wales	2	2	0	0	5	1
Total	233	93	33	107	366	425

* * *

BRAZIL
(December 1963)

	P	*W*	*D*	*L*	*F*	*A*
Argentine	2	0	0	2	0	8
Chile	2	0	0	2	0	6
Total	4	0	0	4	0	14

* * *

BRITISH GUIANA
(April 1964)
(Inter-Colonial Tournament Matches)

	P	*W*	*D*	*L*	*F*	*A*
Barbados	2	2	0	0	10	0
Jamaica	6	2	2	2	10	10
Trinidad	6	3	1	2	6	4
Total	14	7	3	4	26	14

CANADA
(April 1964)

	P	W	D	L	F	A
France	1	0	0	1	1	2
India	1	0	0	1	0	3
Italy	1	0	1	0	1	1
Japan	1	0	0	1	0	1
Netherlands	1	0	0	1	0	2
United States	2	1	1	0	3	1
Total	7	1	2	4	5	10

* * *

CZECHOSLOVAKIA (C.S.S.R.)
(July 1964)

	P	W	D	L	F	A
Afghanistan	1	0	1	0	2	2
Austria	14	5	2	7	12	19
Belgium	1	0	1	0	1	1
Finland	2	2	0	0	12	1
France	2	0	0	2	1	3
Germany (East) ..	7	2	1	4	7	11
Hungary	5	3	1	1	8	5
India	2	0	0	2	2	6
Italy	1	1	0	0	2	0
Japan	1	0	0	1	0	2
Poland	8	4	1	3	18	13
Switzerland	1	1	0	0	1	0
United Arab Republic	2	0	1	1	0	1
Yugoslavia	4	4	0	0	8	1
Total	51	22	8	21	74	65

DENMARK
(Dec. 1963)

	P	W	D	L	F	A
Afghanistan	1	0	1	0	6	6
Austria	3	3	0	0	6	3
Belgium	6	1	0	5	8	11
England	5	0	0	5	3	28
Finland	2	2	0	0	5	0
France	6	1	4	1	19	13
Germany (West) ..	8	0	0	8	7	41
Great Britain	1	0	0	1	0	2
India	3	0	0	3	1	19
Ireland	1	0	0	1	1	1
Japan	2	0	1	1	2	5
Netherlands	7	0	1	6	10	24
New Zealand	1	0	0	1	1	4
Pakistan	1	0	0	1	0	9
Poland	3	0	0	3	3	6
Spain	2	0	1	1	1	4
Switzerland	4	2	1	1	7	8
Wales	1	0	1	0	4	4
Total	57	9	11	37	84	188

* * *

ENGLAND
(September 1964)

	P	W	D	L	F	A
Belgium	7	5	1	1	30	9
Denmark	2	2	0	0	11	1
France	24	23	1	0	161	15†
Germany (West) ..	4	1	2	1	12	7
Ireland	59	39	9	11	168	82†
Kenya	1	1	0	0	6	4
Netherlands	10	4	1	5	19	19
Poland	1	0	1	0	1	1
Scotland	51	40	8	3	190	47†
South Africa	5	1	3	1	9	9
Wales	55	54	1	0	286	46
Total	219	170	27	22	893	240

†Including Olympics result

FRANCE
(March 1964)

	P	*W*	*D*	*L*	*F*	*A*
Afghanistan	1	1	0	0	2	1
Austria	5	2	2	1	10	10 (a)
Belgium	50	15	9	26	76	94
Canada	1	1	0	0	2	1
Czechoslovakia . .	1	1	0	0	2	1
Denmark	6	1	4	1	13	19
England	25	0	1	24	16	164
Finland	1	1	0	0	4	0
Germany (West) . .	18	0	2	16	16	65
Great Britain	3	0	0	3	0	14
India	3	0	0	3	0	15
Ireland	1	0	0	1	1	4
Italy	9	6	1	2	19	4 (a)
Japan	2	0	1	1	1	2
Kenya	1	0	1	0	0	0
Netherlands	22	3	1	18	20	71
Pakistan	5	0	1	4	7	24
Poland	3	0	1	2	0	3
Scotland	2	1	0	1	4	5
South Africa	3	0	1	2	4	9 (a)
Spain	27	6	3	18	25	46 (a)
Switzerland	26	11	7	8	44	39
United Arab Republic	1	0	1	0	1	1
Wales	1	1	0	0	4	3
Total	217	50	36	131	271	595

* * *

GERMANY (EAST)—D.D.R.
(1953 to February 1964)

	P	*W*	*D*	*L*	*F*	*A*
Austria	5	2	3	0	2	0
Czechoslovakia . .	5	3	0	2	8	5
Egypt	3	3	0	0	5	2
Finland	4	4	0	0	12	2
Hungary	1	1	0	0	7	0
India	4	0	0	4	2	20 (a)
Japan	1	0	1	0	2	2
Morocco	4	4	0	0	20	2
Poland	10	3	2	5	6	12
United Arab Republic	2	2	0	0	4	0 (a)
Total	39	22	6	11	68	45

GERMANY (WEST)
(December 1963)

	P	*W*	*D*	*L*	*F*	*A*
Afghanistan	1	1	0	0	4	1
Australia	1	1	0	0	3	0
Austria	8	7	1	0	36	6
Belgium	23	16	5	2	54	18 (a)
Denmark	8	8	0	0	41	7
England	5	1	2	2	10	20 (a)
Finland	1	1	0	0	7	0
France	18	16	2	0	65	16
Great Britain	7	5	0	2	18	12
Hungary	7	4	2	1	12	2
India	8	0	4	4	4	19
Indonesia	1	1	0	0	10	0
Italy	1	1	0	0	5	0
Japan	4	3	0	1	7	2
Kenya	1	0	0	1	0	1
Malaya..	1	1	0	0	4	1
Netherlands	32	17	8	7	71	36 (a)
New Zealand	3	1	1	1	6	6
Pakistan	8	1	2	5	9	24
Poland	5	4	0	1	21	7
Scotland	2	1	0	1	2	5
Spain	8	7	0	1	28	9
Switzerland	13	12	1	0	49	14
United Arab Republic	2	2	0	0	11	1 (a)
United States	1	1	0	0	7	0
Total	169	112	28	29	484	207

* * *

GHANA
(1952–1963)

	P	*W*	*D*	*L*	*F*	*A*
Nigeria..	12	8	1	3	12	7

o

GREAT BRITAIN
(1948 to July 1964)

	P	W	D	L	F	A
Afghanistan	1	1	0	0	9	0
Australia	2	2	0	0	3	1
Belgium	7	1	2	4	5	10
Ceylon	2	2	0	0	3	0
Denmark	1	1	0	0	2	0
France	3	3	0	0	14	0
Germany (West) ..	5	1	0	4	8	14
India	12	0	2	10	7	42
Japan	1	0	0	1	0	2 (a)
Kenya	2	1	1	0	3	2
Malaya..	1	0	1	0	2	2
Netherlands	7	3	1	3	14	16
Pakistan	4	2	0	2	6	7
Spain	5	2	2	1	8	5
Switzerland	4	3	1	0	9	0
United States	2	2	0	0	18	1
Total	59	24	10	25	110	101

* * *

HONG KONG
(April 1964)

	P	W	D	L	F	A
India	2	0	0	2	1	26
Japan	1	0	1	0	1	1
Macao	23	6	9	8	30	35
Malaya..	1	0	0	1	0	4
New Zealand	1	0	0	1	2	3
Pakistan	1	0	0	1	0	7
South Korea	1	1	0	0	2	0
Total	30	7	10	13	36	76

* * *

HUNGARY
(December 1963)

	P	W	D	L	F	A
Austria	11	5	3	3	14	13
Belgium	2	1	0	1	1	6
Czechoslovakia	5	1	1	3	5	8
Germany (East) ..	1	0	0	1	0	7
Germany (West) ..	6	1	2	3	2	10
India	1	0	0	1	0	4
Japan	1	0	0	1	1	3
Poland	3	1	0	2	6	10
Switzerland	4	2	0	2	7	7
United States	1	1	0	0	3	1
Total	35	12	6	17	39	69

INDIA*

	P	*W*	*D*	*L*	*F*	*A*
Argentine	1	1	0	0	9	1
Australia	2	2	0	0	4	0
Austria	3	3	0	0	13	0
Belgium	9	8	1	0	47	8
Canada	1	1	0	0	3	0
Czechoslovakia ..	2	2	0	0	6	2
Denmark	3	3	0	0	19	1
France	3	3	0	0	15	0
Germany (East) ..	4	4	0	0	20	2
Germany (West) ..	8	4	4	0	19	4
Great Britain	12	10	2	0	42	7
Hong Kong	2	2	0	0	26	1
Hungary	1	1	0	0	4	0
Italy	3	3	0	0	21	0
Japan	5	5	0	0	11	1
			(1964 Series only)			
Kenya	18	11	4	3	31	16
Netherlands	16	14	2	0	64	12
New Zealand	14	11	1	2	49	20
Pakistan	4	1	1	2	1	3
Poland	4	4	0	0	12	5
Singapore	4	4	0	0	14	1
Spain	3	3	0	0	7	0
Switzerland	1	1	0	0	6	0
Tanganyika	1	1	0	0	1	0
United Arab Republic	3	3	0	0	13	0

*Incomplete list

* * *

IRELAND
(September 1964)

	P	*W*	*D*	*L*	*F*	*A*
Belgium	2	1	1	0	4	3
England	59	11	9	39	82	168 †
France	1	1	0	0	4	1
Netherlands	5	0	0	5	7	16
Scotland	51	38	5	8	163	54
South Africa	1	0	0	1	1	6
Spain	2	2	0	0	4	2
Wales	59	49	6	4	227	50 †
Total	180	102	21	57	492	300

†Including Olympics match

ITALY
(May 1964)

	P	*W*	*D*	*L*	*F*	*A*
Austria	7	2	1	4	5	10
Belgium	4	0	0	4	1	15
Canada	1	0	1	0	1	1
Czechoslovakia ..	1	0	0	1	0	2
France	9	1	2	6	3	19
Germany	2	0	0	2	0	7
India	3	0	0	3	0	21
Japan	2	1	0	1	3	4
Kenya	1	0	0	1	0	7
Morocco	1	1	0	0	3	0
Netherlands	2	0	0	2	0	10
Pakistan	1	0	0	1	0	2
Poland	2	0	0	2	0	5
Spain	8	1	0	7	5	24
Switzerland	5	2	2	1	6	5
United Arab Republic	2	0	0	2	0	4
Yugoslavia	4	2	1	1	4	4
Total	55	10	7	38	31	140

* * *

JAMAICA
(April 1964)

(Inter-Colonial Tournament matches)

	P	*W*	*D*	*L*	*F*	*A*
Barbados	2	2	0	0	5	1
British Guiana.. ..	6	2	2	2	10	10
Trinidad	6	1	2	3	2	6
Total	14	5	4	5	17	17

JAPAN*

	P	W	D	L	F	A
Australia	2	0	0	2	1	10
Austria	1	1	0	0	2	0
Belgium	2	2	0	0	3	0
Canada	1	1	0	0	1	0
Czechoslovakia ..	1	1	0	0	2	0
Denmark	2	1	1	0	5	2
France	2	1	1	0	2	1
Germany (East) ..	1	0	1	0	2	2
Germany (West) ..	4	1	0	3	2	7
Hong Kong	1	0	1	0	1	1
Hungary	1	1	0	0	3	1
India	5	0	0	5	1	11
			(1964 series only)			
Italy	2	1	0	1	3	4
Netherlands	4	0	0	4	6	13
New Zealand	4	0	1	3	3	9
Pakistan	7	0	1	6	10	27
Poland	2	0	1	1	2	3
Singapore	1	0	1	0	1	1
Switzerland	1	1	0	0	5	1
United Arab Republic	1	1	0	0	2	1

*Incomplete list

* * *

KENYA
(December 1963)

	P	W	D	L	F	A
Afghanistan	1	1	0	0	9	0
Australia	3	0	1	2	2	5
England	1	0	0	1	4	6
France	1	0	1	0	0	0
Germany (West) ..	1	1	0	0	1	0
Great Britain	2	0	1	1	2	3
India	18	3	4	11	16	31 (a)
Italy	1	1	0	0	7	0
Malaya..	2	0	1	1	3	4
Pakistan	12	2	2	8	9	23
Rhodesia	5	4	0	1	17	8
South Africa	2	1	1	0	3	0
Tanganyika	4	2	2	0	15	2
Uganda	5	4	1	0	10	1
United States	1	1	0	0	3	0
Zanzibar	4	4	0	0	28	0
Total	63	24	14	25	129	83

MALAYA*

	P	W	D	L	F	A
Australia	2	0	1	1	3	4
Belgium	1	1	0	0	2	0
Germany (West) ..	1	0	0	1	1	4
Great Britain	1	0	1	0	2	2
Hong Kong	1	1	0	0	4	0
Kenya	2	1	1	0	4	3
New Zealand	3	1	1	1	7	6
Pakistan	4	0	1	3	1	14
Singapore	20	14	3	3	53	17
United Arab Republic	1	1	0	0	5	1

*Incomplete list

* * *

MOROCCO
(April 1964)

	P	W	D	L	F	A
Germany (East) ..	4	0	0	4	2	20
Italy	1	0	0	1	0	3
Portugal	1	0	0	1	0	2
Spain	4	0	0	4	0	22
United Arab Republic	1	0	0	1	0	4
Yugoslavia	1	0	0	1	0	4
Total	12	0	0	12	2	55

* * *

THE NETHERLANDS
(February 1964)

	P	W	D	L	F	A	
Australia	1	0	0	1	1	3	
Austria	3	3	0	0	6	0	
Belgium	55	36	7	12	106	52	(a)
Canada	1	1	0	0	2	0	
Denmark	7	6	1	0	24	10	
England	12	6	2	4	23	21	
France	22	18	1	3	71	20	
Germany (West) ..	32	7	8	17	36	71	(a)
Great Britain	7	3	1	3	16	14	
India	16	0	2	14	12	64	
Ireland	5	5	0	0	16	7	(a)
Italy	3	3	0	0	12	0	
Japan	4	4	0	0	13	6	
Malacca	1	1	0	0	2	0	
New Zealand	3	0	2	1	3	4	
Pakistan	11	4	3	4	16	18	
Poland	1	1	0	0	4	2	
Scotland	6	6	0	0	26	1	
South Africa	2	2	0	0	7	2	(a)
Spain	9	5	4	0	18	8	
Switzerland	11	11	0	0	44	6	
United Arab Republic	1	1	0	0	4	0	
Wales	9	8	1	0	33	3	(a)
Total	222	131	32	59	494	312	

NEW ZEALAND
(December 1963)

	P	W	D	L	F	A
Australia	23	10	3	10	49	38
Belgium	3	2	0	1	6	3
Burma	1	1	0	0	4	0
Ceylon	1	1	0	0	3	0
Denmark	1	1	0	0	4	1
Germany (West) ..	3	1	1	1	6	6
Hong Kong	1	1	0	0	3	2
India	14	2	1	11	20	49
Indonesia	2	1	0	1	7	2
Japan	4	3	1	0	9	3
Malaya..	3	1	1	1	6	7
Netherlands	3	1	2	0	4	3
Pakistan	5	0	1	4	4	17
Singapore	2	1	0	1	13	1
Spain	1	0	0	1	0	1
United Arab Republic	1	1	0	0	7	0
Total	68	27	10	31	145	133

* * *

PAKISTAN
(July 1964)

	P	W	D	L	F	A
Australia	1	1	0	0	3	0
Belgium	5	5	0	0	13	1
Ceylon	4	4	0	0	29	2
Denmark	1	1	0	0	9	0
France	3	2	1	0	10	2
Germany (West) ..	8	5	2	1	24	9
Great Britain	4	2	0	2	7	6
India	4	2	1	1	3	1
Indonesia	1	1	0	0	8	0
Japan	7	6	1	0	27	1
Kenya	12	8	2	2	23	9
Korea (South).. ..	1	1	0	0	8	0
Malaya..	4	3	1	0	14	1
Netherlands	10	3	3	4	16	15
New Zealand	4	3	1	0	15	3
Poland	1	1	0	0	8	0
Singapore	2	2	0	0	6	0
Spain	3	2	1	0	4	1
Switzerland	1	1	0	0	3	0
Tanganyika	1	1	0	0	4	0
Uganda	2	1	1	0	6	2
United Arab Republic	1	1	0	0	5	1
United States	1	1	0	0	7	0
Wales	1	1	0	0	2	0
Zanzibar	1	1	0	0	5	0
Total	83	59	14	10	259	54

POLAND
(July 1964)

	P	W	D	L	F	A
Australia	2	0	1	1	1	3
Austria	6	5	0	1	13	3
Belgium	4	2	0	2	7	7
Czechoslovakia ..	7	3	1	3	12	15
Denmark	3	3	0	0	6	3
England	1	0	1	0	1	1
Finland	2	2	0	0	12	0
France	4	3	1	0	5	0
Germany (East) ..	12	7	2	3	16	7
Germany (West) ..	5	1	0	4	7	21
Great Britain	1	0	0	1	1	2
Hungary	3	2	0	1	10	6
India	4	0	0	4	5	12
Italy	2	2	0	0	5	0
Japan	2	1	1	0	3	2
Netherlands	1	0	0	1	2	4
Pakistan	1	0	0	1	0	8
Roumania	2	2	0	0	4	1
Spain	4	3	1	0	6	3
Switzerland	1	1	0	0	1	0
United Arab Republic	3	2	1	0	6	1
U.S.S.R.	2	1	1	0	2	1
Total	72	40	10	22	125	100

* * *

RHODESIA
(December 1963)

	P	W	D	L	F	A
Kenya	2	1	0	1	5	4
South Africa	4	2	0	2	8	8
Total	6	3	0	3	13	12

* * *

SCOTLAND
(July 1964)

	P	W	D	L	F	A
Belgium	2	1	0	1	2	3
England	51	3	8	40	47	196 †
France	2	1	0	1	5	4
Germany	2	1	0	1	5	2 †
Ireland	51	8	5	38	54	163
Netherlands	6	0	0	6	1	26
South Africa	1	0	1	0	2	2
Wales	50	28	7	15	108	86
Total	165	42	21	102	224	482

†Including Olympics result

SINGAPORE
(1954–1963)

	P	W	D	L	F	A
Afghanistan	1	1	0	0	5	0
Australia	1	0	0	1	0	5
Belgium	2	0	0	2	2	8
Ceylon	3	2	0	1	5	1
Great Britain	1	0	1	0	1	1
India	4	0	0	4	1	14
Indonesia	7	7	0	0	26	7
Japan	1	0	1	0	1	1
Korea	2	1	0	1	5	7
Macao	1	1	0	0	1	0
Malaya	20	3	3	14	17	52
New Zealand	2	1	0	1	1	13
Pakistan	10	0	0	10	8	62
United States	1	1	0	0	6	1
Total	56	17	5	34	79	173

* * *

SOUTH AFRICA
(May 1964)

	P	W	D	L	F	A
Austria	1	1	0	0	5	0
Belgium	4	0	0	4	4	12
England	5	1	3	1	9	9
Finland	1	1	0	0	2	0
France	3	2	1	0	9	4
Ireland	1	1	0	0	6	1
Kenya	2	0	1	1	0	3
Netherlands	2	0	0	2	2	7
Rhodesia	4	2	0	2	8	8
Scotland	1	0	1	0	2	2
Spain	1	0	0	1	0	1
Switzerland	1	1	0	0	2	1
Wales	1	0	1	0	0	0
Total	27	9	7	11	49	46

SPAIN
(May 1964)

	P	W	D	L	F	A
Argentina	1	0	0	1	2	3
Austria	6	5	1	0	13	1
Belgium	16	6	4	6	20	27
Denmark	2	1	1	0	4	1
Finland	1	1	0	0	7	0
France	27	18	3	6	46	25
Germany	8	1	0	7	9	28
Great Britain	5	1	2	2	5	9
India	3	0	0	3	0	7
Ireland	2	0	0	2	2	4
Italy	10	9	0	1	30	7
Morocco	4	4	0	0	22	0
Netherlands	9	0	4	5	8	18
New Zealand	1	1	0	0	1	0
Pakistan	3	0	1	2	1	4
Poland	4	0	1	3	3	6
Portugal	3	3	0	0	9	3
Saar	2	2	0	0	5	1
South Africa	1	1	0	0	1	0
Switzerland	9	4	2	3	17	12
United Arab Republic	2	1	1	0	3	1
United States	1	1	0	0	8	0
Yugoslavia	1	0	1	0	2	2
Total	121	59	21	41	218	159

* * *

SWITZERLAND
(December 1963)

	P	W	D	L	F	A	
Afghanistan	2	1	1	0	4	2	
Austria	10	4	3	3	12	14	
Belgium	18	3	2	13	13	42	(a)
Denmark	4	1	1	2	8	7	
France	26	8	7	11	38	43	
Germany (West) ..	13	0	1	12	14	49	
Great Britain	4	0	1	3	0	9	
Hungary	4	2	0	2	7	7	
India	1	0	0	1	0	6	
Italy	7	2	3	2	8	7	
Japan	1	0	0	1	1	5	
Netherlands	11	0	0	11	6	44	
Pakistan	1	0	0	1	0	3	
Poland	1	0	0	1	0	1	
South Africa	1	0	0	1	1	2	(a)
Spain	9	3	2	4	12	17	
United States	1	1	0	0	3	1	
Total	114	25	21	68	127	259	

TANGANYIKA
(December 1963)

	P	*W*	*D*	*L*	*F*	*A*
India	1	0	0	1	0	1
Kenya	4	0	2	2	2	15
Pakistan	1	0	0	1	0	4
Uganda	4	2	2	0	6	4
Zanzibar	4	3	1	0	14	1
Total	14	5	5	4	22	25

* * *

TRINIDAD
(April 1964)
(Inter-Colonial Tournament Matches)

	P	*W*	*D*	*L*	*F*	*A*
British Guiana.. ..	6	2	1	3	4	6
Jamaica	6	3	2	1	6	2
Barbados	2	0	2	0	1	1
Total	14	5	5	4	11	9

* * *

UNITED ARAB REPUBLIC
(not including Egypt)
(1955–April 1964)

	P	*W*	*D*	*L*	*F*	*A*
Afghanistan	1	1	0	0	3	1
Australia	1	0	0	1	0	6
Austria	1	0	0	1	1	2
Belgium	1	0	0	1	2	5
Czechoslovakia ..	2	1	1	0	1	0
Finland	1	1	0	0	1	0
France	1	0	1	0	1	1
Germany (East) ..	3	0	0	3	0	5
Germany (West) ..	2	0	0	2	1	11
India	3	0	0	3	0	13
Indonesia	3	1	2	0	2	1
Italy	2	2	0	0	4	0
Japan	1	0	0	1	1	2
Malaya..	1	0	0	1	1	5
Morocco	1	1	0	0	4	0
Netherlands	1	0	0	1	0	4
New Zealand	1	0	0	1	0	7
Pakistan	1	0	0	1	1	5
Poland	2	0	0	2	1	6
Spain	2	0	1	1	1	3
Yugoslavia	1	1	0	0	2	0
Total	32	8	5	19	27	77

WALES
(July 1964)

	P	W	D	L	F	A
Belgium	2	0	0	2	1	5
Denmark	1	0	1	0	4	4
England	55	0	1	54	46	286
France	1	0	0	1	3	4
Ireland	59	4	6	49	50	227 †
Netherlands	9	0	1	8	3	33
Pakistan	1	0	0	1	0	2
Scotland	50	15	7	28	86	108
South Africa	1	0	1	0	0	0
Total	179	19	17	143	193	669

†Including Olympics result

* * *

YUGOSLAVIA
(December 1963)

	P	W	D	L	F	A
Austria	4	0	1	3	2	10
Czechoslovakia	4	0	0	4	1	8
Germany (West)	2	0	0	2	2	9
Italy	4	1	1	2	4	4
Morocco	1	1	0	0	4	0
Spain	1	0	1	0	2	2
United Arab Republic	2	0	1	1	0	2
Total	18	2	4	12	15	35

APPENDIX III

INTERNATIONAL FEDERATION OF WOMEN'S HOCKEY ASSOCIATION
TOURNAMENT MATCH RESULTS

COPENHAGEN 1933

	Denmark	England	Germany (Magdeburg)	Holland (Black Tulips)	Ireland	Scotland	United States	Wales
Denmark ..		0–10			2–2	3–5		
England ..	10–0			8–1		4–1		
Germany (Magdeburg) ..				1–1		5–5	1–5	
Holland (Black Tulips) ..		1–8	1–1					0–5
Ireland	2–2						1–3	5–4
Scotland ..	5–3	1–4	5–5					
United States ..			5–1		3–1			2–1
Wales				5–0	4–5		1–2	

PHILADELPHIA 1936

	Australia	England	Ireland	Scotland	South Africa	United States	Wales	Etceteras
Australia ..		3–6	5–4	5–4	3–9	4–5	7–2	
England ..	6–3		10–1		2–1	5–4	8–0	10–0
Ireland	4–5	1–10		3–3	2–3	1–4	4–2	4–0
Scotland ..	4–5		3–3		2–3	2–1	3–1	4–1
South Africa ..	9–3	1–2		3–2		2–6	1–1	9–0
United States ..	5–4	4–5	4–1	1–2	6–2			7–0
Wales	2–7	0–8	2–4	1–3	1–1			2–3

SOUTH AFRICA 1950

	England	Ireland	Scotland	South Africa	United States	International Wanderers
England			4–0	2–1		6–0
Ireland				2–2	0–1	5–0
Scotland	0–4			0–1	1–2	
South Africa	1–2	2–2	1–0			
United States		1–0	2–1			3–2

FOLKESTONE 1953

	Australia	Austria	Belgium	Denmark	England	France	Germany	India	Ireland	Netherlands	New Zealand	Scotland	South Africa	Switzerland	United States	Wales
Australia ..		6–1		9–1	2–1		1–0						0–5			7–1
Austria ..	1–6		0–2			0–3				0–3		0–2				1–2
Belgium ..		2–0		3–0				3–1					1–3	1–1		1–4
Denmark ..	1–9		0–3			0–1			0–6						0–5	2–1
England ..	1–2						8–0				7–1		4–1	14–0	2–1	
France ..		3–0		1–0				1–4			0–6	0–6			0–3	
Germany ..	0–1				0–8				2–3		1–2	2–0		1–0		
India ..			1–3			4–1			1–7	0–9		1–6		4–1		
Ireland ..				6–0			3–2	7–1		4–1	2–1			5–0		
Netherlands ..		3–0						9–0	1–4			2–2		5–0	1–0	
New Zealand					1–7	6–0	2–1		1–2						2–0	3–0
Scotland ..		2–0				6–0	0–2	6–1		2–2			1–4			
South Africa ..	5–0		3–1		1–4							4–1			4–0	8–0
Switzerland ..			1–1		0–14		0–1	1–4	0–5	0–5						
United States				5–0	1–2	3–0				0–1	0–2		0–4			
Wales ..	1–7	2–1	4–1	1–2							0–3		0–8			

SYDNEY 1956

	Australia	Canada	England	India	Ireland	Netherlands	New Zealand	Scotland	South Africa	United States
Australia		2–0	1–3		8–1	1–0		0–0	0–1	
Canada	0–2		0–2		0–3	3–0	2–4	1–1		
England	3–1	2–0		18–0			3–1		0–1	9–0
India			0–18		0–4	1–2	0–2	1–1		2–4
Ireland	1–8	3–0		4–0		0–2	0–2			1–0
Netherlands	0–1	0–3		2–1	2–0				0–1	1–2
New Zealand ..		4–2	1–3	2–0	2–0			2–0	1–2	
Scotland	0–0	1–1		1–1			0–2		0–3	1–2
South Africa ..	1–0		1–0			1–0	2–1	3–0		4–2
United States ..			0–9	4–2	0–1	2–1		2–1	2–4	

AMSTERDAM 1959

	Argentina	Australia	Belgium	Canada	England	France	Germany	Ireland	Netherlands	New Zealand	Scotland	South Africa	Switzerland	United States	Wales
Argentina					0–2		0–4			0–2	0–2		1–0	1–6	
Australia				5–0	2–3			4–1	4–2		2–0	2–0			
Belgium						3–0	0–2	2–1		0–1		0–1			1–2
Canada		0–5				1–0		0–4	0–1		2–3		2–0		
England	2–0	3–2					3–0					4–0	8–0	4–1	
France			0–3	0–1						0–3		0–2	2–0		1–1
Germany	4–0		2–0		0–3			2–1					3–0	0–1	
Ireland		1–4	1–2	4–0			1–2		0–2		2–0				
Netherlands		2–4		1–0				2–0			1–0			3–1	1–0
New Zealand	2–0		1–0			3–0					1–3	1–2			0–3
Scotland	2–0	0–2		3–2				0–2	0–1	3–1					
South Africa		0–2	1–0		0–4	2–0				2–1					2–2
Switzerland	0–1			0–2	0–8	0–2	0–3							0–8	
United States	6–1				1–4		1–0		1–3				8–0		0–0
Wales			2–1			1–1			0–1	3–0		2–2		0–0	

GOUCHER COLLEGE, MARYLAND 1963

	Argentina	Australia	Canada	England	France	Germany	Ireland	Jamaica	Netherlands	New Zealand	Scotland	South Africa	Switzerland	Trinidad	United States	Wales	International Wanderers
Argentina					0–0		0–3							1–1		1–4	0–3
Australia			3–0	0–3		2–1	4–0				1–0						
Canada		0–3			2–2				0–3							0–4	0–0
England		3–0							2–1	2–3		1–1		7–0	0–0		
France	0–0		2–2					1–1		1–3				0–2			
Germany		1–2					2–0					0–2			0–0	1–0	
Ireland	3–0	0–4				0–2				0–3		0–4					
Jamaica					1–1				0–2		0–4		1–0		1–6		1–0
Netherlands			3–0	1–2				2–0			2–0	0–2			3–2		
New Zealand				3–2	3–1		3–0				2–0		6–0			3–0	
Scotland		0–1						4–0	0–2	0–2		0–1	7–0				
South Africa				1–1		2–0	4–0		2–0		1–0				0–1		
Switzerland								0–1		0–6	0–7			0–4			
Trinidad	1–1			0–7	2–0								4–0			0–3	0–7
United States				0–0		0–0		6–1	2–3			1–0					
Wales	4–1		4–0			0–1				0–3				3–0			1–2